307.109417

Waterford City & County Libraries
WITHDRAWN

SENSE
OF PLACE

Waterford City & County Libraries
WITHDRAWN

D1612072

SENSE
OF PLACE
A HISTORY OF
IRISH PLANNING
SEÁN O'LEARY

**Waterford City and County
Libraries**

First published 2014

The History Press Ireland
50 City Quay
Dublin 2
Ireland
www.thehistorypress.ie

© Seán O'Leary 2014

The right of Seán O'Leary to be identified as the Author
of this work has been asserted in accordance with the
Copyright, Designs and Patents Act 1988.

All rights reserved. No part of this book may be reprinted
or reproduced or utilised in any form or by any electronic,
mechanical or other means, now known or hereafter invented,
including photocopying and recording, or in any information
storage or retrieval system, without the permission in writing
from the Publishers.

British Library Cataloguing in Publication Data.
A catalogue record for this book is available from the British Library.

ISBN 978 1 84588 823 7

Typesetting and origination by The History Press

Contents

Acknowledgements   9
Introduction   11

1. From Monasteries to Wide and Convenient Streets   21
2. Civics and Rebellion   38
3. Planning and the Free State: A Seductive Occupation   62
4. Local Government (Planning and Development) Act, 1963:
   The October Revolution   78
5. Garden Cities, Ballymun and Bungalow Bliss   114
6. Planning Drift   143
7. Boom and Bust   168
8. Picking up the Pieces   186
9. Places for People or Pension Funds?   205

Notes   214
Selected Bibliography   245
Index   249

Then prove we now with best endeavour,
What from our efforts yet may spring;
He justly is despised who never
Did thought to aid his labours bring.
For this is art's true indication,
When skill is minister to thought;
When types that are the mind's creation
The hand to perfect form has wrought.

Dr Bindon Blood Stoney, Preface to The Theory of Strains, Girders and Similar Structures *(1873) as quoted in the Foreword to* Dublin of the Future: The New Town Plan *(1922)*

Acknowledgements

For those interested in sustainable development, the built environment and where we live today and in the future, 2014 marks a series of important anniversaries. The modern Irish planning system was introduced on 1 October 1964, when the Local Government (Planning and Development) Act, 1963 came into force 'to make provision, in the interests of the common good, for the proper planning and development of cities, towns and other areas'. The year 2014 also marks eighty years since the 1963 legislation's predecessor, the Town and Regional Planning Act, 1934 and seventy years since a 'National Planning Exhibition' was held in an attempt to build support for the discipline and map Ireland's post-war future. It also runs into the fortieth anniversary of the Irish Planning Institute – the Irish professional body for planners, which was founded in 1975.

An initial reaction when I told someone I was writing this history was 'that'll be a short book'. In fact the innovations, issues and compromises set out here show that there is a wide and uniquely Irish planning story to be told. The genesis of the book was a meeting with the publishers who saw that there was a worthwhile tale and I am honoured to have been given the opportunity to tell it. Thank you Ronan, Beth and colleagues.

This book would not have been possible without the patience and encouragement of my employers (the institute), and in particular the support of its immediate past presidents and vice-presidents, Joanna

Kelly, Mary Crowley and Amy Hastings. Other past presidents of the institute – Patrick Shaffrey, Enda Conway, Joan Caffrey and in particular Fergal MacCabe and Philip Jones – patiently gave their guidance and time. Thanks also to my colleagues – Stephen Walsh and Ciarán O'Sullivan, who provided research support and always provided constructive criticism.

Many others require thanks for their help and encouragement, including Mary Hughes, Berna Grist, Antóin, Sandra, Gerard, Pat and most especially Ann and Áine.

I wish to thank Colum O'Riordan and all at the Irish Architectural Archive, Dr Mary Clark and Ellen Murphy at the Dublin City Library and Archive, the National Library of Ireland and Bill Hastings for their help and generosity in ensuring many of the images here could be reproduced to enhance and illustrate the story.

Introducing his 1941 Town Planning Report for Cork Manning Robertson said, 'A town planner is much in the position of an editor compiling a volume'. Robertson's sentiments equally apply to this planner and I am indebted to the people who agreed to speak to me for this book, provided me with documents and material or directed me to pertinent but perhaps obscure details. Of course while the final work is far richer because of these contributions, its contents, accuracy, opinions and omissions are entirely my responsibility.

Finally, my most special thanks go to Lorna, for everything.

Introduction

ORGANISING COMMON SENSE

Planning is chiefly concerned with places – regions, cities, towns, neighbourhoods and rural areas – and how they change and develop over time. In each of these places and at these different scales, the purpose of planning is to reconcile the competing needs of environmental protection, social justice and economic development in the interests of the common good.[1] It affects the quality of life of everyone. Though the results of good planning may be silent, bad planning can be all too obvious.

Though organised place-making dates back further, modern town planning rose from the ashes of failed attempts to clear the slums that proliferated in Europe as a consequence of the phenomenal urban growth experienced at the time of the Industrial Revolution. Following the fall of the Ancient Roman Empire, it was not until the nineteenth century that urban populations reached such a size that they could not be managed solely through private interests. Cramped conditions, overcrowding, poor sanitation and lack of daylight access led to successive crises of public health throughout Ireland, Great Britain and continental Europe.

Despite these noble origins and the obvious social, environmental and economic value of taking an integrated, long-term view about the future of land and places, planning in twenty-first-century Ireland has a bad reputation.

Given the popular image of a post-'Celtic Tiger' landscape haunted by ghost estates, ongoing efforts to address the notoriety of some public housing schemes and the fallout from a planning corruption tribunal that spanned fifteen years, the time is ripe for reflection and analysis on the successes and failures of Irish planning. What can the past tell us about planning in Ireland or, more fundamentally, is there something in our makeup that makes planning unpopular, or indeed impossible?

Manning Robertson (1888–1945) was an Eton- and Oxford-educated Carlow native, who settled in Ireland in the mid-1920s. He was a town planner, architect, writer and the first chairman of the Irish branch of the UK's Town Planning Institute, and his untimely death 'robbed Irish planning of its most prominent practitioner' who recognised that 'Ireland's planning problems were as much sociological as physical'.[2]

In 1941 Robertson wrote, 'Town Planning has suffered a good deal from misapprehensions as to its aim and scope. One hears of it as an engine for demolishing masses of building with a view to replacing them with impossibly grandiose conceptions. In actual fact it aims at nothing more remarkable than seeing to it that a town develops on common sense lines. It enables common sense to be organised'.[3] This echoes Robertson's comments in a 1936 paper to the Architectural Association of Ireland where he said 'town-planning has only one object in view – the application of common sense to the growth of a town and the development of the countryside'. Later Robertson observed 'many people appear to believe that town planning means pulling down buildings: really it is the other way round: it aims rather at preventing buildings from being put up in the wrong place and then being pulled down again'.[4]

This is a history of planning in Ireland that looks at efforts to organise space and place in the country, from monasteries and plantations, and the common sense of Robertson, to today's era of greater complexity.

A country's approach to land-use planning cannot be separated from its culture. According to Professor Michael Bannon, who headed University College Dublin's Department of Regional and Urban Planning from 1994 to 2002, 'the aim, scope and nature of planning varies from country to country and each society must devise a planning system and foster a planning profession relevant to its peculiar requirements'.[5] Planning theorist Nigel Taylor argues that the activity and effects of planning should not be interpreted as if planning was an autonomous activity, operating separately from the rest of society, instead it is necessary to 'situate' planning activity within its wider 'political economic context'.[6]

Rather than just an account of the Irish planning system put in place by legislation, this book seeks to 'situate' planning and tell the wider story of how, when and why planning in Ireland emerged and why it operates the way it does. This publication traces the evolution of land-use planning in Ireland and the social, environmental and economic problems and opportunities that gave rise to it. Its structure is largely chronological. It deliberately does not chronicle every inter- pretation of Irish planning legislation or regulation. This is because it is essential to drill deeper and take stock of the wider rationale and principles of Irish planning, not just the legal, technical and admin- istrative aspects which have spawned dozens of legal texts, fact books, manuals and thousands of legal cases.

Planning's role in balancing environmental considerations, scarce resources and constitutional property rights, with the underlying principle of the common good is explored through a study of the Irish experience of democratic accountability, new towns, one-off rural housing and urban sprawl. It concludes by assessing how well planning's cross cutting consideration for environmental, social and economic issues prepares Ireland for the challenges of climate change and developing the sustainable communities of the future.

A STREAK OF ANARCHY

In 1960 Patrick Lynch – chairman of Aer Lingus and lecturer in economics at University College Dublin – argued that 'planning is unpopular in Ireland, sometimes even among those who might be expected most advantageously to employ it. Such are the unreasoning attitudes towards it that the term is often used as an emotive one, suggestive of voices signalling the road to serfdom, or speaking the foreign accent of social engineers'.[7]

For planner Brendan McGrath 'planning has a precarious status in contemporary society' challenged by a lack of consensus and discourse on the 'common good' and a persistent belief that models from elsewhere cannot apply to Ireland.[8] Theories about Irish attitudes to planning, mainly tied up with religion, colonialism and land, abound.

It has been suggested that in a country which derived its independence from a land-based revolution, and where land interests remain strong, concepts of land management and the redistribution of the windfalls from profits in land are often hard to swallow.[9] Planner and architect Fergal MacCabe argues that 'the famine of the mid-nineteenth century and the subsequent land wars and (until recently) an essentially rural society, produced a deep respect for the unfettered ownership of land and a distrust of the compromises of urban living which informs public attitudes to planning to this day'.[10] Bannon argues that the blood and rupture of the War of Independence, Civil War and partition did not allow for long-term national planning and that in both the Free State (prior to independence) and the partitioned Northern Ireland, power rested with rural politicians who had little interest in solving urban issues.[11] The Irish Rural Dwellers Association (IRDA) has criticised 'the extraordinary amount of power bestowed on individual planners by legislation to play God with the rights of Irish citizens wanting to build a home in the country'.[12]

Historian Erika Hanna notes the remarks of a writer from Northern Ireland who saw a 'streak of anarchy' in the Republic regarding planning laws, characterised by 'a common attitude towards law and authority ... a combination of a disregard for the rules by some, and a resigned acceptance by the others that the rules will not be enforced'.[13]

Frances Ruane, director of the Economic and Social Research Institute in Paul Sweeney's optimistically-titled 2008 book *Ireland's Economic Success: Reasons and Lessons* suggests 'the biggest weakness in our system at this point is our attitude to space and physical planning ... the Irish are enormously good at the economic and social but we don't manage the environmental, by which I mean the spatial, very well'.[14] Ruane attributes this to a 'post colonial' legacy of 'I have my house and my land and I should be able to do whatever I want with them' attitudes combined with low population density and a history of population decline. According to Ruane this means we 'effectively have built a mind-set that does not handle space very well and that it is not surprising that we do not embrace planning principles' in contrast to other more dense and urban European countries.[15]

Reflecting as he retired from an eleven-year period as chairperson of An Bord Pleanála which covered the recent boom and bust, John

O'Connor raised the theory that there is an element of chaos in the Irish character that makes us sceptical of regulation or planning. 'Rules are there to be broken if you can get away with it. This may account for some of our very serious failings over the past decade. It may also explain why the Irish body politic has been reluctant to embrace fully real spatial or land-use planning' O'Connor said, explaining that unlike other countries, even when statutory planning documents are adopted 'a laissez-faire approach often prevails and many vested interests – landowners and developers – see plans as something that can be got round or changed'.[16]

Environmental consultant Peter Sweetman is one of the most vocal critics of Ireland's approach to development and environmental issues and is a regular contributor at An Bord Pleanála oral hearings. According to Sweetman 'the Irish have a phobia against planning – not just the Planning and Development Act – we don't plan anything. We have muddled along with water, we've muddled along with sewage, we've muddled along relevant to roads, we built some roads that were necessary and some that were totally unnecessary'. When asked if there has been any improvement in Irish planning he argues 'it's a fundamental point of Irish projects; they tell us what they are going to do rather than ask you – despite the EU-imposed need for Environmental Impact Assessments. So we still don't know where we are – look at the history of the National Children's Hospital. The whole aquaculture system is off the wall – bananas. Then we have raw sewage discharging into places like Newport'.[17]

An official apathy to planning and planners is repeatedly evident at the highest level. At the height of the 'Celtic Tiger' (the now ubiquitous phrase first used by Kevin Gardiner in a report for Morgan Stanley in 1994 that forecast more than a decade of surging economic growth), then Environment Minister Dick Roche complained of the attitude of planners, urging them 'to show courtesy and consideration' in dealing with the public, and to make themselves available to people building new homes. Roche continued: 'You can walk into St Luke's [Bertie Ahern's constituency office] and have a meeting with the Taoiseach, or you can go to his various constituency clinics … I find it mystifying that planning officials, important as they are, don't have anything like the same level of availability', concluding that in any case 'Planning is not rocket science, it is not even an exact science'.[18]

LANGUAGE AND ETYMOLOGY

In one of the first cornerstone textbooks on planning, 1952's *Principles and Practice of Town and Country Planning*, Lewis Keeble wrote 'planning is a subject in which there is room for endless debate and this creates an extremely difficult problem'.[19] As Bannon writes, 'planning might usefully be viewed as a cabinet, rather than a departmental issue'.[20] The term 'town planning' can be traced to the Australian architect John Sulman who used the phrase in a paper titled *The Laying-Out of Towns* in 1890. It has evolved over the years and has been variously described as town and country planning, town and regional planning, physical planning, spatial planning and simply, planning.

When setting the scope of this publication I drew from Manning Robertson, who discussed what he considered might properly be called 'town planning items'. Clearly planning embraces housing but equally housing development was carried out before town planning. Similarly roads and open spaces existed before town planning legislation but how people travel between work, home and amenities is inseparable from good planning.

Authored by Berna Grist, the 1983 report *Twenty Years of Planning: a Review of the System since 1963* began by discussing the nature of the planning 'system', emphasising that while things like economic policy goal setting, service delivery and building regulations, along with spatial planning might all be considered as part of a national 'planning' system, the physical, or spatial, planning system can be separated from these interrelated systems but this rarely occurs in the public mind. Thus sometimes problems are attributed to 'planning' which can undermine public confidence in professional planners when in reality they can often be the responsibility of other, related disciplines.

Members of the planning profession are graduates of professionally-accredited third-level colleges or universities. Their primary function is to plan: to envision sustainable futures for places and to work in partnership with others in bringing about change in meaningful and effective ways.

Planners work in the public, private and voluntary sectors in a variety of roles. With a wide range of skills, they advise decision-makers (such as national and locally elected democratic bodies), communities, investors, interest groups, business people and the public at large on issues to do with the spatial development, growth, management and conservation of regions, cities, towns, villages, neighbourhoods, local areas and parcels of land everywhere, though others offer planning services while not being trained planners or members of any professional planning institute.

The making, reviewing and varying of the plan is a function reserved for the elected members (i.e. councillors) of the planning authority. It is their duty to adopt the plan with the technical help of their officials (the manager/chief executive, planners, engineers etc.), and following extensive public consultation.

All decisions to grant or refuse planning permission are taken by the relevant planning authority and then, if there is an appeal of the decision, by An Bord Pleanála. After reviewing and integrating information from across local authority departments and considering the results of site visit guidelines, plans and policies, the planner recommends a decision and a written report outlining the reasons is presented to the manager/chief executive of the relevant local authority who reviews it and decides whether permission should be granted or refused. The final decision at this stage of the planning permission process lies with the manager of the local authority. The decision-making process is not an arbitrary system; it follows a step-by-step procedure. It is designed to be transparent, to facilitate agencies and to present the public with the opportunity to voice their opinions and become involved in the process.

Fundamentally, there may be an issue with the term 'planner' itself, which suggests a degree of authoritarianism, certainty and control. When planning for an area it might be assumed that planners have control over a range of factors, including health, transport, etc. that will in fact only be delivered to the timetable of the agency or business that supplies them. In Europe other words are used which may more closely capture the nature of the discipline and its role, such as the French term '*urbaniste*' which implies specialism in the study of our built environment, land use, place-making and the interactions around it.

Clinch, Convery and Walsh quote approvingly George Bernard Shaw's assertion that a profession is a 'conspiracy against the laity' and suggest that professions underline this unconscious conspiracy through jargon and their central idea or '*idée fixe*' to which they retreat when seeking solutions so 'the profession predetermines the decision'.[21]

This risks isolating a profession and discipline from the public and increasing distrust and apathy. This is particularly unforgivable for a field with the common good at its core. In this book jargon is either avoided where possible or clearly explained if unavoidable.

The legal rationale for all planning decisions in Ireland is 'proper planning and sustainable development' with sustainable development accepted as encompassing social, economic, cultural and environmental concerns. This confirms that planning can be a broad church and, as shown above, it is inseparable from the wider political and cultural context.

DEEP ROOTS

Despite these perspectives on antipathy towards planning in Ireland, it has deep roots and has seen many innovations. The Dublin Wide Streets Commissioners, established in 1757, was one of the earliest town planning authorities in Europe and the independent third-party planning appeals system operated by An Bord Pleanála (The Planning Board) is still unique in Europe. The 1934 Irish planning legislation was considered far better than its UK equivalent. Before and after independence Ireland was visited by leading figures in Anglo-American planning with the country 'an essential stopping-off point for many planning advocates, apostles and gurus'.[22] The 'First International Conference on Town Planning' was held in London in 1910 and by the following year Ireland was described as 'a most interesting field for the student of town development'.[23]

Writing on post-colonial Dublin, academic Andrew Kincaid notes that few histories of Ireland mention that leading international figures in town planning were involved in planning in Ireland. While 'historians, politicians, and writers' grappled with issues of social, cultural and economic change at various stages of Ireland's history 'architects and planners both reflected those debates and forged their own answers to them'.[24] Kincaid also questions why the wider body of literature on planning history does not examine Ireland in any great depth or assess why such eminent thinkers wished to do work here.[25] This volume attempts to put this right. Post-partition this work chiefly considers planning in the Republic of Ireland, along with recent cross-border initiatives.

It is essential to discuss the history of planning outside of Dublin as many initiatives came from outside the capital. For example, Waterford had Wide Streets Commissioners and the county saw a failed attempt at a new city, as well as one of Europe's finest examples of a model village in Portlaw. The midlands feature some of the best practice housing schemes of the 1940s in the work of Frank Gibney, while Cork and Limerick led the way in regional planning in Ireland.

PLANNING FOR GROWTH

Perhaps to its detriment, planning has always been inextricably linked with economic development in Ireland. For example, Bartley describes the introduction of the Local Government (Planning and Development) Act, 1963 as part of the desire to create a modernised planning system which was seen as a prerequisite for Irish economic growth and prosperity. Bartley states that while the 1963 legislation explicitly linked planning with development, the former 'was viewed as the processes of innovation and activities designed to increase resources or wealth' while the latter 'was seen as the means of managing the process through the allocation and use of resources'.[26] Introducing the 1963 legislation to the Dáil, Minister for Local Government Neil Blaney gave a detailed statement of its aims and content, including that 'property values must be conserved and where possible enhanced'.[27]

Despite this link, it has not necessarily contributed as much as was anticipated. In his discussion of Ireland's economic growth in the 1960s, historian Diarmaid Ferriter suggests that there was a notable failure to copperfasten the country's economic development through planning. Ferriter traces this to wider disinterest in planning, noting that President Douglas Hyde was advised not to attend the 1942 National Planning Exhibition as it was felt planning was not developed in Ireland and attendance 'might eventually, bring the president into ridicule'.[28] The 1963 Act expected local authorities to become proactive development corporations acquiring and developing land commercially. This did not come to pass. Similarly during the 'Celtic Tiger', commentators suggested that Ireland's boom was despite, not because, of planning. Perhaps this narrow focus on the economics of planning without considering the wider context explains some of the hostility and why broad public support for the discipline and its aims has been hard to maintain.

According to a 1983 study of planning in Ireland, the planning process here never attained the public acceptability its counterparts in Britain or Europe enjoyed, characterised by the 1963 Act which was legislature-led with little reference to public attitudes and with public opinion courted only after its enactment.[29]

CONCLUSION

Writing in 2003 Bartley and Treadwell-Shine identified three phases in Irish public policy since independence and associated trends in planning. The first, from 1922 to 1960, was pre-industrial with a focus on economic isolationism and self-sufficiency with a minimal consideration of planning limited to housing. The second phase, from 1960 to 1986, was one of urbanisation, industrialisation and seeking inward investment with authoritarian, centrally controlled planning. The third phase from 1986 was post-industrial with more entrepreneurial and flexible planning.[30] Post-'Celtic Tiger' Ireland has entered a recovery phase, with planning asked to assist economic growth while addressing the mistakes of the recent past. This might be the most challenging phase for the discipline so far, though as we will see, planning has a deep well of Irish experience and achievement to draw from that extends well before the founding of the Free State.

1

From Monasteries to Wide and Convenient Streets

EARLY IRELAND

In fifth-century Ireland there were no towns or cities, forests and bogs were extensive and the 'numerous un-drained lake and river valleys and lowlands created many watery wildernesses in which the travelling stranger would almost literally be at sea'.[1] There was the ráth, an individual settlement usually inhabited by a farmer with dwelling space enough for his family and animals, and the bigger dún, a dwelling place large enough for the king as well as his noblemen.

With the arrival of Christianity in Ireland from AD 431 came the establishment of monastic settlements through the middle of the island and by the sixth century monasteries were evident in all areas of Ireland. These early-Christian sites had similar layouts, in particular a regular curvilinear plan form, which has been interpreted as an early, widely adopted, model of spatial planning. Where urban centres grew up around ecclesiastical foundations, the lines of the original curved enclosures were often still visible in the property boundaries and street-plan of the modern town or village, such as in Kells, County Meath.[2]

Though the monastic settlements were nucleated settlements, it was the Vikings who created Ireland's first true towns. In the ninth-century Viking settlements at Dublin, Waterford, Wexford, Youghal, Cork, Limerick and Galway developed. The Vikings permanently reoriented

Ireland's economic and cultural centre from the midlands to the east coast. Excavations suggest that building styles and plot layouts were rigidly regulated in Viking Dublin in perhaps Ireland's earliest development control system.[3] After the Anglo-Norman invasion beginning in 1169, stone castles and walls were constructed, while these Viking plot boundaries were often preserved into the eighteenth century. The Normans introduced the town charter that conferred urban autonomy and confirmed the importance of the marketplace and town wall.

THE PLANTATIONS

Plantations began in Munster and western Leinster at the end of the sixteenth century and they had a strong urban element. Some 400 new settlements were established by plantation grantees during the seventeenth century. The success of Richard Boyle in Cork had confirmed the role of towns in plantations, laying out Bandon with a grid-iron layout, with a marketplace at its centre. In 1609 Sir Arthur Chichester, the lord deputy of Ireland from 1605 to 1616, sought a survey of Ulster, meaning the plantation was preceded by what might be considered Ireland's first regional plan. Indeed 'the methods used were very much the same that would be adopted in similar circumstances today' as they appointed a committee and commissioned a survey and report.[4] 'The planners took the view that the lands in Ulster, although containing large areas of forest and bog, were capable of supporting a greatly increased population if the resources of the province were properly exploited, and if the population became settled in towns and villages.'[5]

This resulted in the planning of twenty-five new plantation towns, which were to act as centres of civility and stability. The plantation commissioners were to decide how many houses should initially be erected in each town, laying out their sites, and assigning land for further building.

At Londonderry a grid was favoured, in keeping with the Enlightenment support for rational, orderly town plans. Descartes observed in 1637: 'These ancient cities that were once merely straggling villages and have become in the course of time great cities are commonly quite poorly laid out, compared to those well-ordered towns that an engineer lays out on a vacant plan as it suits his fancy.

And although, upon considering one by one the buildings in the former class of towns, one finds as much art or more than one finds in the buildings of the latter class of towns, still, upon seeing how the buildings are arranged – here a large one, there a small one – and how they make the streets crooked and uneven, one will say that it is chance more than the will of some men using their reason has arranged them thus.'

The Irish plantations, and in particular the plantation of Ulster, saw the establishment of formal new towns designed around a central square or 'diamond' in a style very different to Ireland's medieval towns. Timahoe, in County Kildare, is a good example of where the seventeenth-century triangular green or 'diamond' is preserved.

Part of the legacy of the plantations was a new approach to laying out towns and in Ulster the network of new towns, linked by new roads, was to contribute to its economic strength. It has been noted that this imposed background might have set a persistent apathy to planning amongst some.[6]

WIDE STREETS COMMISSIONERS

As Dublin city developed, streets became crowded. In 1780 Arthur Young described walking the city as 'a most uneasy and disgusting exercise'.[7] Despite this 'certain guiding principles of planning did apply' to Dublin's development, post-1660.[8] Part of this saw the city permitting development on greens and commons which historian Colm Lennon somewhat tartly describes as 'an innovative attitude to urban planning on the part of the municipality'.[9] St Stephen's Green was the medieval commons most radically affected. In 1663 the civic assembly approved leasing parts of the green and the following year, 'the process of letting was under way, plots being divided among the aspirant developers by lot. As well as determining the size of the lots (sixty feet as frontage and from eighty feet to 352 feet in depth) and the rental (from 1d per square foot for the north side to a ½d for the south), the city council stipulated the dimensions and materials of houses that lessees were to build'.

The Commissioners for Making Wide and Convenient Streets and Passages, or as they came to be known, the Wide Streets Commissioners, were responsible for massive changes to Dublin's city centre during the

Map showing the Dublin Wide Streets Commissioners first undertaking, the making
of a wide and convenient way from Essex Bridge to Dublin Castle (present-day
Parliament Street). (Courtesy of Dublin City Library & Archive)

eighteenth and nineteenth centuries. Originally established to alleviate a
traffic bottleneck at Essex Bridge, the commissioners eventually shaped
large portions of Dublin to their own tastes by widening narrow streets,
creating new ones and enhancing their own properties.[10]

In 1755 a wider, reconstructed Essex Bridge crossing the Liffey at
Capel Street was opened. The designer of the bridge, George Semple,
published a map in 1757 which proposed a street leading from the
bridge to a square in front of Dublin Castle and a bill setting up
commissioners to oversee the work received royal assent. The 1757 Act
of Parliament to make 'a wide and convenient way from Essex Bridge
to the Castle of Dublin' (present-day Parliament Street) was the first
of a series of street improvements. The commissioners controlled the
planning of Dublin until 1851.

The commissioners set about their work quickly. In May 1758
notices appeared in the *Dublin Journal, Dublin Gazette* and the *Universal
Advertiser*, requesting landowners and residents affected by the new
street to voice their concerns to the clerk of the commissioners,
Mr Howard.[11] Success has many parents and architectural historian
Maurice Craig recounts that both Semple and George Edmond
Howard, the bridge's contractor, both claimed credit for the idea of a
new street, though in fact the first suggestion can be traced to 1751.[12]

MacCabe describes the Dublin Wide Streets Commissioners as 'Europe's first official Town Planning Authority'.[13] Gough has persuasively argued that the Wide Streets Commissioners were 'an early modern planning authority' with 'an excellent grasp of civic design and town planning matters'. The Age of Enlightenment was rippling across planning in Europe and Ireland was to the fore. Following the Lisbon earthquake of 1755, work had begun on re-planning that city with plans also being made for the New Town in Edinburgh.

The 1757 and subsequent acts empowered the commissioners to improve the city by widening streets where they saw necessary. Having opened up Parliament Street in 1762, the commissioners widened Dame Street, then Sackville Street. The commissioners included John Beresford, Revenue Commissioner, Luke Gardiner (grandson of the earlier Luke who was owner of Sackville Street, Dorset Street, Parnell Street and Square (then Rutland Street and Square) and Mountjoy Square), Frederick Trench and Samuel Hayes who studied developments in London and Europe evolving them into a unique approach.

The commissioners had the authority to acquire property by compulsory purchase, demolish it, lay down new streets and set lots along them that were released to builders for development. They had the authority to determine and regulate the façades of buildings erected along its new streets, decide on the heights of buildings, the number of houses in a terrace, the materials to be employed and the number and siting of windows. The commissioners could order rebuilding where necessary and actively resisted encroachments on the building line.

The commissioners' compulsory purchase powers saw valuation juries recommend valuations to the commissioners. Gough describes the process as 'an attorney's paradise' somewhat similar to today, given that the process could take up to thirteen months.[14] Premises were sometimes acquired that were not required for street widening but which were incompatible with the commissioners' vision for the new street.

Leases for plots along the newly-widened streets were regularly publicly auctioned and construction was on the architectural elevations stipulated by the commissioners, with some uses (such as 'offensive or noisy trades') or projecting signs often not permitted. The commissioners took enforcement proceedings against offending buildings, demanding that a carpenter on Dame street alter his windows in line with the plan laid down for example, while in 1801 the Sun Insurance Company was not permitted to widen their doors to admit their fire engines.[15] As funding became an issue, controls were relaxed.

In 1765 Wide Streets Commissioners were created in Cork and in 1784 in Waterford. Funded partially by court fines, the Waterford Commissioners were appointed to improve the city as 'the streets, lanes and passages of the city of Waterford and the suburbs thereof are too narrow, by means whereof the health of the inhabitants is greatly injured and the trade of the said city is greatly obstructed'.

In Waterford the mayor or sheriffs were given powers to remove all encroachments and nuisances, including stairs, window shutters and sheds, which impeded the streets and lanes of the city and the commissioners laid out the Mall. The mayor also had the power to direct owners to move signs, 'spouts and gutters' and certain activities were prohibited close to the thosel.

In Cork, their primary job was to widen the medieval laneways and thereby eradicate some of the health problems stemming from them. Cork's commissioners had powers to create public water fountains to address the undesirable situation where there was only one public fountain in the city. There are no early records of the Cork Wide Streets Commissioners' proceedings (It is likely that these were destroyed in the County and City Courthouse fire of 1891 and the burning of the City Hall in 1921) but the commissioners have been credited with the laying out of Great George's Street (now Washington Street), South Terrace, Dunbar Street and the widening of others.[16] Historian Antóin O'Callaghan notes the similarities between the situation in Dublin and Cork at the time with expansion eastwards in both cities leading to the creation of a new city centre and with a new main street.[17] O'Callaghan notes that in Cork the Corporation and commissioners were largely the same people with a significant Freemason influence, describing the close interaction of commissioners, Masonic lodges and Corporation at the opening of the first St Patrick's Bridge in 1789.[18] In Cork the commissioners seem to have had a philanthropic role, petitioning the Lord Lieutenant in 1822 to release funds for a quay between St Patrick's Bridge and North Gate Bridge for a scheme recommended by the committee for the relief of the poor to provide employment.[19] The relief committee also provided loans to the Cork Wide Streets Commissioners for various public works, including the extension of Penrose's Quay by around 700 feet.

There was a wide interest in planning in the period. In 1789 the Cork Society of Arts and Sciences, an organisation that occasionally proposed new streets, received a map ('A survey of the city and suburbs of Cork') which they had commissioned for town planning purposes. It included a list of references to intended improvements, including the opening of new streets and broadening streets.[20]

Much of the development of Limerick after 1750 is associated with Edmund Sexton Pery, a parliamentarian and a businessman who pioneered the city's Georgian architecture, laying out Newtown Pery. In these projects, his influence in parliament was a major factor as it enabled him to obtain large sums of public money for the improvement of Limerick and therefore of his own property around the city. Blocks were leased and built upon by individuals over a long period of time and the area did not assume its final shape until the 1820s and 1830s, when the last streets, such as Hartstonge Street, Catherine Place and The Crescent, were built.[21]

The Dublin Wide Streets Commissioners themselves were a group of upper-class landowners who were typically members of parliament. Many of the early commissioners were patrons of fine architects and were amateur architects. The initial twenty-one commissioners included Arthur Hill, commissioner of revenue and later chancellor of the exchequer; Thomas Adderley of the Barrack Board, Philip Tisdall, later attorney general and John Ponsonby, speaker of the House of Commons and the Lord Mayor of the day.[22] Many of the initial commissioners 'believed in minimal interference from England'[23] though they had support from the Dublin Castle executive ('as it was in their interest to have a decent approach to its own place of business') and the Chief Secretary William Eden (with one of the commissioners ensuring Eden Quay was named for the Chief Secretary at his request for a street named after him).[24]

Gough writes that 'unlike a modern planning authority the commissioners had no massive development plan but they did have a plan and vision of how they wanted the city to develop'. This was co-ordinated by 'what can only be described as planning policy meetings'.[25] The commissioners looked overseas to cities such as London, Paris and Philadelphia for inspiration. Gough traces a French influence in Dublin's planning in the late eighteenth century, including its quays and building layouts.[26]

Commissioners included early proponents of new towns in Ireland, including Thomas Adderley, Anthony Foster, William Burton

Conyngham and Beresford. Adderley and Foster had laid out their own planned weaving villages at Innishannon in Cork and Collon in Louth respectively while Conyngham planned a new island settlement off Donegal called Rutland with streets named after fellow commissioners.

Beresford, along with some other commissioners, sponsored the proposed development of a new town called New Geneva, designed by James Gandon, in Waterford. This was to accommodate a colony of disaffected Genevese exiles (including many intellectuals, craftsmen and watchmakers) after a failed rebellion against the French and Swiss Alliance, on 11,000 acres near Passage East. An invitation to immigrate to England following the rebellion had come from George III but the Genevese themselves, fearing the jealousy of English watchmakers, pressed that their colony should be in Ireland, not England. The Duke of Leinster offered them 2,000 acres for their colony near Athy and accommodation for 100 in Leinster Lodge until their houses were built, but the Waterford site and a £50,000 grant for the building of the town was arranged by the Viceroy Lord Temple with a view to the Protestant settlers calming nationalist feelings in the region, though the Genevese saw their role differently.[27] The colony was initially to have fifty houses, a bakery, inn, tannery and paper factory. There were plans for a big square dominated by a university. An Irish enthusiast, Mr Cuffe, laid the foundation stone for the projected city in 1784 but six weeks later the plan was abandoned. The Genevans attributed its failure to a change of Viceroy with the Duke of Rutland less enthusiastic than his predecessor. It was then proposed to colonise the site with American loyalists following the War of Independence,[28] but the site became the Geneva Barracks and prison and was featured in the ballad *The Croppy Boy*. If completed the project would have radically altered the shape of the south of the country.[29]

As the members of the commissioners changed through the decades, so did the legislative power given to them. The initial act enabling the commissioners to create Parliament Street was expanded in 1759 to allow the commissioners to examine the possibility of developing more than one street. Their finances were boosted with another act in 1782, enabling them to receive a sum of one shilling per ton of coal imported into the country.[30] In August 1792 the jurisdiction of the commissioners was expanded to half a mile beyond the North and South Circular Roads, thereby increasing the amount of development the commissioners could implement. Additionally, it was advertised

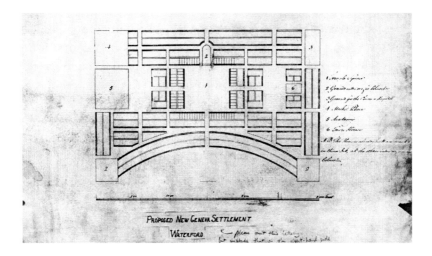

Ink and wash drawing (after James Gandon) of the proposed layout of New Geneva, a new town near Passage East intended for a colony of disaffected Genevese exiles in 1784. (Courtesy of the Irish Architectural Archive)

that anyone who wished to create a new street within the jurisdiction of the commissioners must submit plans to its retained surveyor Thomas Sherrard's private practice office at 60 Capel Street.[31]

Examples of the Commissioners 'planning authority' role abound. Elevations for No. 1 Merrion Square (which was to be the childhood home of Oscar Wilde) showing an extended porch were submitted to the Wide Streets Commissioners in July 1836. They rejected the proposal, ruling that the extension would constitute an encroachment on the pavement. The householder applied for permission again in 1837, pointing out that his neighbours had no objections and approval was granted.

In 1828 property speculator Benjamin Norwood built a wall along a section of Lower Baggott Street to screen stables he had erected, but local residents objected to the commissioners, who ordered Norwood to demolish the stables. Norwood demanded compensation from the commission if he built four houses on the site of the stables in Lower Baggot Street and submitted an elevation in 1832. The Wide Streets Commissioners approved the elevation but declined to vote a subvention as Norwood requested. In the absence of a financial commitment from the commissioners he did not proceed with his plans and in 1834 they successfully brought a court action against him and forced him to demolish the stables.

A development on Cavendish Row was approved by the Wide Streets Commissioners in 1787 that featured an unusual style.

A note by the architect explains 'the style of building proposed here has long been in use on the Continent, and found uncommonly convenient in procuring bed chambers contiguous to shops of the apartments of persons in trade, unconnected with the upper floors'. This refers to the provision of apartments at mezzanine level over ground floor shops with entirely unconnected residential accommodation overhead.

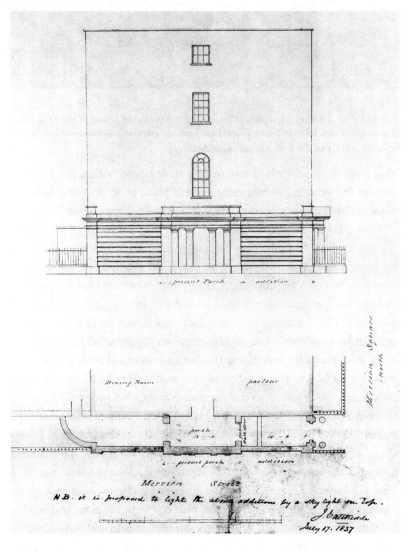

Elevation for No. 1 Merrion Square (which was to become the childhood home of Oscar Wilde) submitted to the Wide Streets Commissioners seeking permission for external alterations. (Courtesy of Dublin City Library & Archive)

In the late eighteenth century, maps of Dublin showed several streets radiating from an elliptical 'Royal Circus' in the north of the city. This was a 'rare and remarkable instance of city plans, indicating some features of street planning not actually in existence' as Luke Gardiner's proposed plaza did not come to fruition.[32]

In the 1790s Henry Ottiwell privately (rather than at auction) acquired a large parcel of land from the commissioners. It was suggested that Ottiwell had a secret partner in the transaction, the son of John Beresford who was both a Revenue Commissioner and a Wide Streets Commissioner. This was investigated and it was suggested that a private sale might secure a better bargain for the public compared to an auction that might be manipulated by a cartel of builders. Ottiwell refused to name his partner and in 1795 a House of Commons committee investigating the deal committed him to prison for a few weeks and concluded that the commissioners had exceeded their powers. In telling Ottiwell's story Gough calls him a 'classic property speculator' who bought the land over the market price and 'inflated the value by lending money to his tenants, who thus could afford the higher prices'. Ottiwell was exposed when the 1798 rebellion and the 1800 Act of Union hit property prices and he was left with expensive land and outstanding loans that his tenants could not afford to repay. This also exposed the commissioners, as Ottiwell had rents arrears of £21,770 17s outstanding to them.[33]

In 1808 the Nelson Pillar committee wrote to the commissioners seeking permission to erect the memorial at the intersection of Henry Street and Sackville Street. In what Gough describes as a show of independence, the commissioners refused permission, citing public inconvenience. The committee subsequently met with the commissioners and when they agreed to reduce the width of the pillar and the shape of its surrounding railing consent was granted.[34]

Gough suggests that the commissioners understood the concepts of betterment – that is that public works can lead to an increase in property values for the private individual, and planning blight, meaning the reduction of economic activity or property values in an area resulting from expected or possible future development or restrictions. To avoid paying for the rising costs of betterment the commissioners had a policy of purchasing all the land they required for a project at the same time rather than buying on a piecemeal basis.[35]

Despite the majority of the commissioners being members of parliament, they did not always receive universal support from the peers.

Lord Carhampton, a member of the Irish House of Lords, was quoted in the *Leinster Journal* in 1798, suggesting that the commissioners did not necessarily serve the wider public well: '... as individuals; he lived amongst them in the habits of closest intimacy, nor were there men in the world with whom he would rather pass the remainder of his life as men of honour and deserved respect, but bound up together, and labelled with the title of Wide Streets Commissioners, he considered them as forming one of the most mischievous volumes extant in any country. Habitually improvident of their own private expenses, it was not very surprising if men became lavish of the public money, when trusted to their expenditure. Thousands upon thousands of the public money had already been squandered by this board, not for the purpose of opening narrow and inconvenient streets obnoxious to the city of Dublin, but with erections of new streets and squares for the accommodation of the rich.'[36]

Researcher Finnian O'Cionnaith sees merit in Carhampton's contention that the commissioners favoured the rich over the poor, noting that it produced a disproportionately high number of maps of the city's 'more affluent and modern neighbourhoods compared to the poorer congested neighbourhoods in the south-west of the city'[37] such as the Liberties.

According to Edel Sheridan-Quantz the commission was a direct result of decades of citizens' petitions (by the upper classes residing in the Gardiner and Fitzwilliam estates rather than the working class) to the Corporation demanding improvements to the core of the city.[38]

In an example of early enforcement or public rights of appeal, the minutes of the Wide Streets Commission record several residents' petitions calling for the commissioners to address undesirable activity. In 1792 a landowner wrote to the commission expressing concern at the inclusion of a narrow laneway in their plans for houses on Lower Sackville Street, feeling the lane would create dirt and become a haven for 'thieves and night walkers'. Similarly the residents of South Great George's Street urged the commission to act on 'waste lots' that had been unfinished from its work on Dame Street and currently being used by one of the city's rubbish disposal men.[39]

In 1830 the *Freeman's Journal* questioned the continued work on 'beautifying our streets, while so many thousands of our fellow creatures are in a state of starvation within the precincts of the city'.[40] Dissatisfaction with taxes to fund the commissioners' work also grew. In 1846 Dublin Corporation member John Reynolds successfully

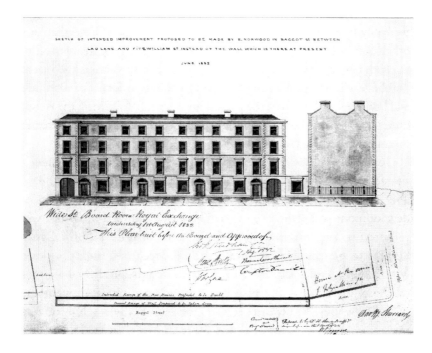

The Wide Streets Commissioners ordered a property speculator to demolish a
screening wall and stables in Lower Baggot Street. He submitted these elevations
for replacement houses, refusing to build them unless he received compensation.
(Courtesy of Dublin City Library & Archive)

called for the Corporation to petition Westminster against a bill to
allow the commissioners to 'impose a rate of one shilling in the pound
to enable them to open an avenue to St Patrick's Cathedral and other
places' as 'probably there was no city in the British empire that was
so completely and entirely overtaxed' as Dublin, many of which were
imposed by non-elected bodies such as the commissioners.[41] Reynolds
also questioned the motivations of the commissioners, noting that
a nearby Catholic church 'at which more persons went to pray in a
week than went to St Patrick's Cathedral in a year' had exceedingly
bad access, but there was no avenue to it proposed. Reynolds also
identified what would today be considered 'mission creep', arguing
that though the commissioners had 'at their backs sixteen acts of
parliament … they were not satisfied … and they had sought for
another act … which contained more powers than were contained in
the whole sixteen acts'.[42]

For Thomas Hall, writing on nineteenth-century urban development
in European capitals, Dublin under the Wide Streets Commissioners

'probably benefited from planning of a more advanced kind than any other capital city in that period'. However, for Hall the dissolution of the Irish parliament led to a weakening of the commissioners and meant Dublin 'entered upon a long period of decline in terms of planning and building',[43] though in the period immediately following the Act of Union the commissioners commissioned two maps of London, seeking inspiration for how Dublin could be improved.[44]

Gough describes an 1802 report by the commissioners neces-sitated by the Act of Union as a review of planning policy to date and blueprint for the future, noting that 'in common with most development plans, the 1802 report was a victim of timing' and was required to accommodate a security zone around Dublin Castle. Similar to planning today the plan had objectors, including one who, having paid a shilling to review the plans, published a series of letters demanding the plan be changed to allow improvements in the Liberties.[45] The 1802 report documents their achievements, including the widening of Dame Street, Lower Sackville, D'Olier and Westmoreland Streets, Lower Abbey Street, Forster Place and the quays east of Carlisle Bridge.

By 1806 the financial restrictions placed upon the commissioners who now needed funding approval from London had begun to bite. This meant that 'simple tasks such as advertisement of works were being curtailed, being viewed by the board as a 'very heavy and unnecessary expense'. From January 1806 the commissioners would 'only advertise in two newspapers, three times a week rather than three newspapers, which had been the practice since the 1750s'.[46] The prestige and influence of the commissioners continued to decline, and by 1818–19 only five of the twenty-five commissioners were MPs in London and few had any expertise in planning.[47]

For Craig the commissioners' work showed 'a very high degree of enlightened planning, and were very well in advance of their time'[48] while being 'the very embodiment of unsentimental utility' demol-ishing all before them 'and that we should feel so sentimental towards them is a typical irony of the historical process'.[49] The main legacy of the Dublin Wide Street Commissioners is how they changed the face of Dublin by redeveloping the city, not by the suburban expansion that was to characterise it in both the early and late twentieth century.[50]

MODEL TOWNS

There have been some key development periods in Irish towns and villages, such as Medieval, Plantation and Georgian, each with its own development characteristics. In the 'Georgian' period baroque planning principles, characterised by uniformity, spaciousness and order, and inspired by developments in Dublin following the Wide Streets Commissioners, were replicated in a number of small towns and villages. These were also informed by a desire to impose order and civility in uncertain times, with landlords leading the development of this style. Birr, Abbeyleix and Strokestown are three examples. For R.F. Foster 'That ascendancy desire to build and to plan deserves some attention: it may indicate an obsession with putting their mark on a landscape only recently won and insecurely held'.[51] This has it limits however. Many 'landlord towns' were built by middlemen and head tenants (such as Castlecomer); their classical shapes were frequently achieved only after a torturous, gradual, metamorphosis, while other 'landlord towns' were simply redesigns of older, successful settlements.[52] Modern Newbridge, for example, developed following the establishment of Cavalry Barracks (1815–1819) on land purchased from three local landlords: Eyre Powell of Great Connell, Ponsonby Moore of Moorefield and William Hannon of Kilbelin. In Ireland there are some examples of a shift from landlords' estate towns to developments where an industrialist was the patron.

Whelan tells the story of the development of New Birmingham, a village on the Tipperary and Kilkenny borders, laid out by the local landlord Vere Hunt, between 1805 and 1815. His diary reveals that the planning of the village was a slow process, where much of Vere Hunt's time was spent lobbying the relevant governmental and local bodies to influence them to locate facilities in his village, including the postmaster general for a post office, the Board of Ordnance for a barracks, the Protestant bishop for a church, the Catholic priest for a chapel, the Grand Jury for roads, the Education Commissioners and the Erasmus Smith Trust for schools. In ways this pattern, where planning can set the principles but relies on others for delivery, can be seen to the present day, despite the attempt to turn planning authorities into development corporations in the 1963 Act.[53]

In the 1820s a model village was developed at Portlaw to house workers at the cotton factory that had been established by David Malcomson on the banks of the River Clodiagh in 1825. In the 1850s and 1860s, under Joseph Malcomson, the village was redesigned using formal planning principles. Portlaw is one of the two major examples of a model industrial village found in Ireland in the nineteenth century, the other being Bessbrook in south Armagh.[54] Its wide streets with uniform house frontages radiated from a central open space known as The Square, which formed the commercial centre of the village. A popular myth is that Malcolmson on sitting down to plan the village laid his hands upon the table, and decided to build in the shape of a hand. Workers' accommodation comprised fifty two-storey houses, and more than 250 single-storey houses on a uniform pattern. The exterior walls were of lime-rendered rubble sandstone, and each house incorporated a distinctive gently curving roof, known as a 'Portlaw roof', a type developed by the Malcomsons to be both efficient and cost effective. The Malcomson venture at Portlaw prospered until the consequences of the American Civil War (1861–1865) pushed the firm into liquidation in 1876, closing the mills and prompting mass emigration from the area. The Mayfield Spinning Company operated on the site until 1904, and after a prolonged period of inactivity, the Irish Tanners Company was established in 1935, closing in 1985.[55]

Though other model or utopian villages were developed, Portlaw is the most significant in terms of its scale and sophistication. It is also the one model development in Ireland which matches the level of achievement of the world-renowned villages found in England, Scotland and North America and it is traditionally held that Portlaw was the inspiration for the Cadbury's village of Bournville, a development thought by some to represent the pinnacle of this form of social and urban planning.[56] The Society of Friends has an unlikely reputation as pioneers of planned developments in Ireland as with Ballitore, County Kildare, developing as a planned Quaker village during the late seventeenth century. Ballitore now has Architectural Conservation Area status to protect and enhance its special character and architectural interest.

CONCLUSION

During the eighteenth century, as home to the Irish parliament and nobility and through the fruits of the Wide Streets Commissioners' labours, Dublin city was developed to the highest standard of architectural design and was considered by many to be one of the most beautiful cities in Europe. The involvement of aristocracy and political figures – such as Lord Edward FitzGerald – in the 1798 rebellion was a source of great alarm to the Crown and was a final nail in the coffin of the Irish parliament, resulting in its dissolution and the passing of the Act of Union in 1800. The resident aristocracy quickly left to be closer to London and with them went much of the demand for luxury items (such as wool, cotton, silk and leather) – the industries which had, up to that point, formed a large part of Dublin's economy. Dublin was unable to establish industry that could compete with major industrial cities like Manchester or Birmingham and, with considerably more unskilled workers than there were jobs for such workers, poverty among that section of society grew dramatically. Despite the work of the Wide Streets Commissioners throughout the nineteenth century, Dublin experienced further decline and decay, becoming a 'deposed capital'.[57] This decline and the resulting housing and public health crisis was to become the next impetus for Irish planning.

2

Civics and
Rebellion

HEALTH AND HOUSING

Unlike other Irish or English cities, the typical nineteenth-century
Dublin working-class family lived in a tenement, something Dublin
shared with Scottish and continental cities.[1] Tenements were characterised by overcrowding with a family (sometimes more than one)
often occupying each room of the former homes of the aristocracy.
These were added to by the sudden appearance of makeshift infill
dwellings to the rear of Georgian terraces and, compounded later,
by the sudden influx of refugees from the famine. However, in many
ways, Dublin's problems were similar to those experienced in Britain,
with poor sanitation resulting in high infant mortality and high rates
of disease, especially in basement or cellar dwellings.

Over the course of the nineteenth century, what were once aristo-
cratic addresses on the north side of the city, such as Henrietta Street
and Dominick Street, became characterised by tenements rather
than the residences of judges, doctors, bishops and professionals.
This reflected a shift towards the south or outer villages, though
tenements were also found in the south of the city. Here, in areas such
as the Coombe, tenements were in traditional working-class houses.
There were few building projects to replace the decaying housing
stock. Low quality, crowded properties were also constructed in

lanes and courtyards to the rear of streets and houses. The provision
of working-class housing by private companies was uncommon,
though the Pim textile firm, Guinness's and Watkins's breweries and
the railway and tram companies did so. From 1890 the Iveagh Trust
was established with a £50,000 donation from Sir Edward Cecil
Guinness, later Lord Iveagh, to provide dwellings for the poorer classes.
The trust's first scheme was the Bellevue Buildings at Thomas Court
in 1891, followed by 335 flats at Kevin Street. These were designed
with windows facing either east or west to ensure all rooms received
the sun at some part of the day.

Despite this in the late nineteenth century and early twentieth
century, Dublin city was widely considered to be the location for
some of the worst slums and housing conditions in Europe. As late
as 1961 some 20,000 families did not have a residence of their own
and 1,425 dwellings demolished by Dublin Corporation between
June 1963 and September 1966 were found to be home to almost
4,200 families. The Myles Wright report of the period notes that in the
Greater Dublin Area (the County and City of Dublin, Meath, Kildare
and Wicklow) 30 per cent of dwellings did not have the benefit of
an indoor toilet and 39 per cent did not have a fixed bath in 1961.
Furthermore, in 1963, four people were killed when two houses
collapsed in Dublin, on Bolton Street and Fenian Street.

Though the housing conditions of Ireland's urban poor was
identified as a major social problem in the early nineteenth century,
it did not begin to be substantially considered until much later.
For historian Frank Cullen, delays in addressing the urban housing
crisis were related to the political emphasis Home Rule and land
reform placed on rural housing.[2] By 1914 Ireland's rural labourers
were amongst the best housed of their class in Western Europe.[3]
Historian Mary E. Daly has observed that the housing problems
of nineteenth-century Dublin derived in the main from the
Corporation's focus on Ireland's right to self-determination rather
than municipal issues,[4] alongside an anti-urban bias in Ireland and
a lack of commitment to dealing with urban problems up until at
least the 1960s, characterised by lower life expectancies in Dublin
compared to Connaught for example.[5] Professor J.J. Lee, however,
argues that any urban rural tensions were trivial and with no 'cultural
chasm between town and country'.[6] It must be noted that in 1914
no fewer than sixteen members of Dublin Corporation were owners

of tenement properties, or small cottages, virtually all of which were found to be in poor repair.[7]

In 1867 the Industrial Tenements Company, formed by a group of businessmen, developed a six block, four-storey scheme called the New Model Dwellings on Meath Street but these quickly became as dangerous as the slums they were intended to replace. A milestone was the establishment of the Dublin Artisans' Dwelling Company (DADC) in 1876 by business and political interests in the city. The subscribers represented most of the elite of the city, including the Earl of Pembroke and the two Guinness brothers. An act the previous year had provided for government loans to such societies on favourable terms. Much of the DADC's activity was on the sites of former slums cleared by the authorities and it, and the Improved Dwellings Company in Cork which developed housing schemes such as Evergreen Buildings, Prosperity Square and Industry Street, remained active into the twentieth century. Initially Dublin Corporation and the DADC worked closely together as the Artisans' and Labourers' Dwellings Improvement Act, 1875 (known as the Cross Act) allowed the former to clear slum sites while the latter developed them, though later the DADC was obliged to provide its own land.

Its first schemes were flats at Upper Buckingham, Echlin and Dominick Streets and latterly one and two-storey houses throughout the city. Plans were drawn up to refurbish existing tenements but this did not occur. In 1880 the DADC began to build cottages near Manor Street. Though the DADC was to provide improved accommodation for the working class, it did not cater for the poorest who could not afford rents, arguing that it was freeing up space in tenements for the poor by accommodating the better-off artisans.[8] Wide squares were a feature of many DADC schemes and the death rate there was below the city average. The DADC had constructed over 3,300 houses by 1914. In echoes of the housing issues that arose in the late twentieth century, the cost of building in Dublin was high, with DADC houses costing more than three times that of a similar house in Belfast.[9] Though a welcome innovation in improving housing conditions in the city, the lack of planning had implications for wider Dublin. Most of their development was on virgin land outside the city centre and F.H.A. Aalen notes that 'the piecemeal and scattered housing schemes of the corporation and the DADC had contributed to the incoherent growth of the city'.[10]

In September 1913 two tenement houses on Dublin's Church Street collapsed, killing seven. An inquiry into The Housing Conditions of the Working Classes in the City of Dublin was established by the Local Government Board for Ireland in response. Its report, published in 1914, showed that just under 30 per cent of Dublin's population lived in slums throughout the city. Over one fifth of tenements had only one toilet for every twenty to forty people and over three-quarters of tenement households lived in single rooms, a trend which continued into the 1960s. The inquiry concluded that over 60,000 people in the city occupied housing which was unfit for human habitation and required rehousing in approximately 14,000 new dwellings.

CIVICS INSTITUTE

For historian Ruth McManus in the period 1910–1915 there was a belief that housing and town planning could be used to build bridges between different interest groups and to inspire a sense of patriotism and citizenship.[11] MacCabe attributes 'the real impetus and interest in town planning' in the period to Lady Aberdeen, wife of the viceroy to Ireland.[12, 13]

Lord Aberdeen first served as Viceroy in Dublin from 1886 and, after a period as Governor General in Canada from 1893 until 1898, the Aberdeens returned to Dublin in 1906 where they remained until February 1915. Lady Aberdeen in particular was dedicated to the causes of social reform, housing improvement and economic development and she continued to visit and to work with Dublin groups throughout the 1920s.[14]

In 1911, on the invitation of Lady Aberdeen and the Women's National Health Association, Scottish planner and theorist Patrick Geddes (1854-1932) brought his Cities and Town Planning Exhibition to Dublin. The exhibition was transferred to Dublin at a cost of £300 and was set up in the Royal Dublin Society, Ballsbridge from 24 May to 7 June. The exhibition returned to the city in August 1911 for the Royal Institute of Public Health Congress, which was taking place in Trinity College.

As a Scot, Lady Aberdeen would have been familiar with Geddes' work and she recognised the potential of his travelling town planning exhibition to help 'stir up public feeling' on Irish housing conditions.

Lord and Lady Aberdeen write in their two-volume reminiscences 'With this end in view [we] invited Professor Geddes to bring his Cities and Towns Exhibition to Dublin, guaranteeing him against loss. He came, not once, but twice, and he and the exhibition made a deep impression upon a small circle of earnest students'.[15] This established Geddes as 'the dominant influence over the nascent Irish planning movement'.[16]

The 'real impetus and interest in town planning' in the early 1900s has been attributed to Lady Aberdeen, wife of the viceroy to Ireland. (Reproduced courtesy of the National Library of Ireland: POOLEIMP 1546A)

Patrick Geddes was a Scottish biologist, sociologist, geographer, philanthropist and pioneer of town planning. His ideas have heavily influenced much of subsequent planning practice, regional economic development and environmental management. In particular, his focus on 'Place – Work – Folk' was a new way of thinking about the relationships between people and their local environments. Geddes also appears to have been responsible for introducing Raymond Unwin to Dublin; both worked together on an examination of Dublin housing estates and Unwin became closely involved in plans for the rebuilding of Rising-damaged Dublin and the Dublin Reconstruction (Emergency Provisions) Act, 1916. Unwin, with Barry Parker, had designed the town of Letchworth in Hertfordshire along Ebenezer Howard's garden city lines, and was author of the influential textbook *Town Planning in Practice.*

In Dublin Geddes presented a lecture ('illustrated by several lamp slides') on the aims of the exhibition and wider town planning. In this introduction Geddes apologised for referring to advances in the field in England, explaining housing in England was of a better standard than that in Ireland or Scotland. In an early recognition of the role of public consultation in planning, Geddes said 'persons of life-long familiarity with the city were the only persons who could keep the promoters from imperfect and rash conclusions'. Thanking Geddes after his lecture, Sir James Dougherty expressed his view that there was a limited interest in planning in Ireland as poverty and population decline made slums the priority, but that planning might be the solution to these problems.[17] Geddes was of the view that derelict sites across the city could be turned into gardens, though some opponents of the idea suggested that they would become targets for vandalism. In 2014 Dublin City Council proposed introducing a levy on 300 vacant sites across the city, with exemptions if they were used as temporary pop up parks or playgrounds with the temporary Granby Park on Dominick Street in the summer of 2013 being an example of this in practice.

Writing to *The Irish Times* on 29 May 1911, R. Caulfield Orpen regretted that the town planning exhibition might be overlooked by the public, partially due to the 'brilliant weather'. Orpen enthused that the points of interest in the exhibition were 'beyond the scope of a letter' but the visitor leaves 'stimulated' by the 'scholarly and practical research conveyed in a delightfully lucid manner'. The total attendance at the exhibition was put at 160,000.[18]

The Lord Lieutenant considered that Geddes's exhibition represented all the features of Irish life and interests.[19] During the exhibition Geddes presented a lecture entitled 'Dublin and City Development', chaired by the Lord Lieutenant who admitted that like a great many other people when he first heard of town planning he had only vague ideas of its practical side but they were lucky that Geddes 'an eloquent apostle' for the movement, was on hand to explain it.[20] In this lecture Geddes linked the exhibition to the development of ancient Rome, Athens and Jerusalem and the Renaissance, before returning to the slums and issues of industrialisation. Geddes also delivered a lecture on 'Ireland and regional development' at the exhibition. Geddes was proud of the impact of the exhibition in Ireland, pointing to the formation of a 'Cities and Town Planning Department' of the National Museum, the creation of the Housing and Town Planning Association of Ireland along with practical improvements.

Geddes remained popular with the elite. In 1914 a tribute to Geddes appeared in *The Irish Times*, sympathising with him on the loss of drawings and exhibits in the sinking of the cargo ship *Clan Grant* by the German cruiser *Emden* off India. This included a call for those with drawings of the cities Geddes had worked on to forward them to the professor.[21] In 1915 a letter appeared in *The Irish Times* from a Mr James Shanks, updating readers with the news that the collection had been replaced in the main. The letter also criticised Alderman Thomas Kelly, chairman of the Corporation's housing committee, for expressing satisfaction at Geddes's loss.[22]

In September 1911 the Housing and Town Planning Association of Ireland (HTPAI) was founded with Lady Aberdeen as president and its membership included the Dublin city architect Charles McCarthy and chief engineering inspector of the Local Government Board, Peter Cowan. This association promoted civic duty and citizenship and garden suburbs (rather than garden cities). It held a conference on housing and town development in October 1912. The association aimed to initiate the process of preparing a plan for Dublin and every other Irish town.

In promoting planning HTPAI focused less on the financing of housing, 'this division of responsibilities was to prove disastrous in practice'.[23] Fraser suggests that as planning did not explicitly focus on the financial problems of housing, 'it was unable to overcome the indifference shown towards urban issues by large sections of the Irish Party's supporters, such as the Catholic Church'.[24]

Lord and Lady Aberdeen and the Housing and Town Planning Association sought to have the 1913 inquiry into housing conditions in the city designated a Vice-Regal Commission, with the aim of securing the appointment of a town planner to the inquiry. This did not occur and instead Lady Aberdeen and the Women's National Health Association brought Geddes to give evidence. In his evidence to the Dublin Housing Inquiry, Geddes warned that 'putting buildings up in a permanent way without town planning is preparing slums for the future'. Geddes and 'his devoted Irish follower, E.A. Aston' put forward the case for proper town planning and garden suburbs, though the final report 'concentrated on the issue of State subsidy and tended to play down town planning claims, save in a minority report appended by one of the inquiry team, J.F. MacCabe'.[25] Fraser called the 1913–1914 Dublin Housing Inquiry a lost chance for advocates of planning.[26]

Following the inquiry Lord and Lady Aberdeen launched two new initiatives, at the apparent suggestion of Geddes. One was the first Civic Exhibition in the UK on the model of one held in Ghent in 1913, the other was a town planning competition.

Writing in 1913 Geddes acknowledged, 'A disadvantage of the Town Planning Movement, as yet, is that people think it merely or mainly suburban, and architectural at best' and argued that it was part of a wider civic movement concerned with working conditions.[27] From 1911 to 1916 Geddes sought to create a broad-based planning movement representative of all groups in society. For Bannon this failed but the embers flickered on through the 1920s and 1930s and the National Planning Exhibition was organised by the National Planning Conference in 1944 at the Mansion House. The Civic Exhibition was developed as a way to advance this agenda, with a Civics Institute founded to campaign further. The Civics Institute held its first annual general meeting on 15 April 1914 and absorbed the Housing and Town Planning Association.

The 1914 Dublin Civic Exhibition had a number of aims, including focusing on town planning as a means of overcoming the social divisions represented during the 1913 lock-out. Another was to suggest planning's role in Ireland's future economic development. Professor of city planning at Harvard John Nolen ('pointedly described as being of Irish-American descent') who was appointed manager of the exhibition warned 'unless there is some hard town-planning done … Dublin will slip back'.[28] Nolen also lectured on 'why planning pays' in Dublin, emphasising a capitalist rationale for planning and demonstrating the desire to harness planning for economic purposes that endured into the 1963 Act and beyond.

Supporting organisations represented on the Civic Exhibition committee included the Housing and Town Planning Association, the Women's National Health Association, the Association of Municipal Authorities of Ireland, the Royal Institute of the Architects of Ireland (RIAI), the Architectural Association of Ireland, the Institute of Civil Engineers of Ireland, the Dublin Chamber of Commerce, the Royal Irish Academy and the Dublin Industrial Development Authority. The Lord Lieutenant was president and the Dublin Lord Mayor one of the treasurers.[29] The committee also had the aim of forming a permanent display in Dublin.

The exhibition opened on 15 July 1914 in the refurbished Linenhall Barracks. Attendance was less than anticipated, attributed to both the outbreak of war and the failure to attract 'Dublin's casual poor, partly because of the entrance charge, and partly because James Larkin called on his supporters to treat the exhibition with contempt'.[30] *The Irish Worker* which Larkin edited, ridiculed 'Lady Microbe's Civic Farce'.[31] Despite this, Geddes and Larkin met to discuss working-class housing issues.[32]

There were photographs, maps and plans from many British cities and most Irish local authorities, as well as American maps. Rooms were provided for refreshments, concerts and lectures, while the King's Inns garden contained outdoor exhibits.[33] It was attended by eighty mayors from all over Ireland and proved financially viable.

According to Fraser, while attendance was made free on the last day 'the working classes responded by making off with much of the furniture and exhibits'.[34] The outbreak of war led to a premature closing of the exhibition and in the last weeks efforts were focussed on organising training for Red Cross workers. A Dublin Civics Summer School run by Geddes was held from 27 July to 15 August 1914.

DUBLIN OF THE FUTURE

In early 1914 Geddes persuaded the viceroy to establish a Dublin town planning competition with a prize of £500 to go to the winning entry. Known as the Marquis of Aberdeen's Competition, it required entrants to consider: Communications, where entrants were asked to reorganise the city's transport system; housing, central and suburban, where they were to provide 14,000 new dwellings in line with the findings of the 1913 inquiry; and metropolitan improvements which were to make better use of the city's river and bay and develop its public buildings. The objective of the competition was to 'elicit plans and reports of a preliminary and suggestive character, and thus to obtain contributions and alternatives which may be of value towards the guidance of the future development of the city in its various directions'.

The planning proposals were to relate to a greater Dublin area, taking in Howth, Glasnevin, Ashtown, Dundrum and Dalkey. The designs, to be completed and submitted before 1 September 1914, were to consist of a written report, containing a summary of the main conclusions, recommendations and estimates, together with drawings mounted on linen and on stretchers at scales of 12 inches or 6 inches to a mile, 25 inches to a mile and street sections at 1 inch to 20 feet.

Eight entrants were received: four from Ireland, two from Liverpool, one from London and one from Illinois. The competition was judged by Patrick Geddes, city architect Charles J. McCarthy and John Nolen in 1916. The winning plans were to enter into the ownership of Dublin Corporation, but a further delay occurred when the physical plans were held up in Liverpool port due to 'inexplicable action' by Customs. Furthermore for a period the only copy of the judges' report resided in the US with Nolen and was unavailable for publication when the winner was announced.[35]

The prize was awarded to Professor Patrick Abercrombie of the Department of Civic Design at the University of Liverpool and Liverpool surveyors Sydney Kelly and Arthur Kelly with the 'magnitude and comprehensiveness of the exhibit, evidencing corresponding thought and labour' and its 'skill and beauty of execution' being cited.

Michael Bannon writes that 'many aspects of the various submissions concur both in respect of the analysis of the existing situation and the resolution of problems' adding that 'so good were some of the entries that one of the adjudicators, John Nolen, regretted that they were legally bound to give the prize of £500 to the outright winner. Indeed, Nolen had earlier expressed the hope that 'some public-spirited gentleman would supplement the Lord Lieutenant's generous prize for plans by at least two more prizes of £200 and £100'.[36]

Geddes had reservations about the applicability of Abercrombie's proposals, and praised the entry by C.S. Ashbee and G.H. Chettle, since 'no other Report expresses a fuller and more comprehensive grasp of civic problems'.[37] It had long been presumed that all competition entries apart from that by Abercrombie had been lost, but two copies of Ashbee and Chettle's entry have emerged, which Bannon has assessed in detail.[38] Ashbee and Chettle's entry included great use of the Dublin canal system, enhanced use of the environment along the canals and an emphasis on the city centre. In awarding the first prize the adjudicators stressed that 'we are not thereby endorsing all, or any, of the particular proposals.' Though as it was the only competition entry published, Abercrombie's entry took on the role of the 'great Dublin plan'.[39]

In November 1916 Raymond Unwin presented a lecture on the competition in which he encouraged the Corporation to debate the suggestions and the winning plan was displayed for the Lord Mayor, while in January the drawings submitted were exhibited at the Chamber of Commerce premises, alongside a 'Civic Week' organised by the Civics Institute where the future planning of Dublin was discussed at events for five successive evenings.

Abercrombie, Kelly and Kelly's winning entry was published as *Dublin of the Future: The New Town Plan* in 1922 given the 'recent change in National circumstances a new epoch has begun, and that the present is a most opportune time to arouse the interest of the Citizens'.[40] The Civics Institute took the view that a well-informed citizenry was essential to shape any reconstruction and the aim of the plan was 'to be educative, and to secure popular support for the general principles of City Planning'.[41]

The published plan included updates, taking into account the destruction of the Easter Rising, War of Independence and Civil War. In its preface the authors acknowledged that it might be considered strange to publish something eight years old but argue that instead of being obsolete, the radical changes and the destruction of Dublin might be a good thing as it allowed new roads and buildings on now ruined sites. There were also some revisions and half of the plans published in the final *Dublin of the Future* were drawn up after the competition. Despite these updates, when published *Dublin of the Future* was 'humbly and respectfully' dedicated to Lord and Lady Aberdeen 'to whose munificence, and personal interest in the welfare

The destruction of the Easter Rising led to the Dublin Reconstruction (Emergency
Provisions) Act, 1916 which sought to regulate the rebuilding of the city centre.
(Reproduced courtesy of the National Library of Ireland: INDH22B)

of the city of Dublin, this scheme of Town Planning for its future is
entirely due' raising questions about the suitability of imperial scale
proposals for a new Free State capital.

They noted that some ideas might be out of date (not least the
use of 'Sackville Street' when it was 'now more felicitously named
O'Connell Street') and some thinking had moved on, for example
the word 'zoning' had come into fashion. Zoning is the legislative
method of controlling land-use by regulating such considerations
as the type of building, for example, commercial or residential,
that may be erected. Issues that relate to appropriate population
densities are also considered within the remit of zoning. Zoning as a
mechanism facilitates orderly development of an area by eliminating
potential conflicts between incompatible land-uses and establishing
an efficient basis for investment in public infrastructure and facilities.
German and Swedish cities applied zoning regulations in the late
nineteenth century to new land being urbanised around the older
city cores as a way of controlling the heights and concentrations of
buildings and avoiding problems of congestion. Though the authors
of *Dublin of the Future* did not use the term, they had considered the
concept.[42]

The authors were also reflective, acknowledging that the competitive origins of the plan meant that some elements might have been too bold. Despite this while Dublin was a noble city it needed 'complete overhauling down to fundamentals' not superficial 'patching' and the plan aimed to encourage this by being provocative.[43] The plan also included some reflections on the nature of plan-making saying 'It can never be said that a Town Plan has been finally and irrevocably prepared: stages are reached, and the scheme then approved, used as guidance until another and revised one is required'.[44]

'The Last Hour of the Night' by Harry Clarke, frontispiece to the 1922 publication *Dublin of the Future: The New Town Plan*, depicting post-revolutionary slum life and the challenges of reconstruction. (Courtesy of Dublin City Library & Archive)

The publication included a frontispiece by stained-glass artist and illustrator Harry Clarke titled 'The Last Hour of the Night'[45] which showed the city's crumbling tenements and key civic buildings (the GPO, Four Courts and Custom House) in flames, stalked by a deathly devil figure and 'although the Dubliners in the image stroll past the destruction, curiously immune to the decay, violence and terror that preoccupy the illustrator, viewers cannot be so cavalier' with Clarke's devil 'implying a modern Gothic complicity in the horrors of post-revolutionary Ireland's slum life'.[46] It is unlikely that a development plan today would include work from a leading contemporary artist, particularly if it were so socially explicit.

The plan encouraged the view that Dublin was a national, not just a local, asset. Abercrombie and colleagues also made recommendations for legislative changes that would facilitate their plans, recommending that Canadian rather than English precedents be followed with the creation of a Town Planning Commission for greater Dublin.

The Abercrombie plan suggested the completion of the crescent around the Custom House by filling in the redundant dock and the removal of the Loop Line Bridge. The plan suggested a new cathedral at the head of Capel Street and behind it a 500-feet-high campanile based on an Irish round tower and crowned with the figure of St Patrick and surrounded by cenotaphs of famous Irishmen. A new national theatre and auditorium was suggested for O'Connell Street and a central 'union' station was also proposed. Though unrealistic in part it was commended for being 'the best one of educating [the] public to what town planning schemes – and drawings – are like'.[47]

Abercrombie and Sydney Kelly were appointed town planning consultants to the city council and their thinking influenced the planning of Dublin into the 1950s. In 1937 Abercrombie was again asked to map out Dublin's future and some of its main elements were to re-emerge in his later sketch development plan. Abercrombie is best known for his Greater London Plan but he regarded his work in Dublin as his 'best piece of constructive regional planning'.

For Bannon 'Perhaps the most important outcome of the competition was the bringing together of the principal planning protagonists of the day and their contrasting philosophies and ideologies as to what constituted the newly-emerging art and science of planning' extending from those who emphasised order, symmetry and elegance

Abercrombie, Kelly and Kelly's new town plan for Dublin set out in *Dublin of the Future*. (Courtesy of Dublin City Library & Archive)

to the City Beautiful Movement which emphasised monumental grandeur, to Ashbee's romantic vision of a pre-industrial society to competitors for whom planning was either an extension of architecture or a matter of transportation engineering.

Writing in *The Irish Times* on the fiftieth anniversary of its publication, Lionel Fleming asked 'what became of the Abercrombie Plan?' For Fleming the plan may have been 'too grandiose' and while it did not anticipate the rise in car use it had the potential to revolutionise Dublin as Hausmann changed Paris.[48]

In 1933 deputy Thomas Kelly told the Dáil 'The major reason I have for my opposition to this town planning is that I am afraid that it is going to do again what it did twenty years ago. The slums still remain with us and now when another determined effort is being made to deal with them, we do not want this well-intentioned idea of town planning to interfere with our work again and we are not going to allow it do so if we can prevent it'. Kelly recounted meeting Geddes and Abercrombie in Edinburgh as part of a delegation from Dublin Corporation. He was not impressed by their work (to the extent that he was not sure he recalled their names correctly) saying 'they had not done anything there' to address overcrowding as 'in the older portion of the city people can easily shake hands with their neighbours across the street for old lang syne's sake'. This did not inspire confidence in him regarding the merits of planning and planning experts. 'Where is the necessity in this City of Dublin for town planning? Are not the streets, generally speaking, amply wide?'[49]

The Civics Institute strongly argued for a scientific, evidence-based approach to planning and did not argue for the implementation of any plan, even Abercrombie's, unless it was founded on a comprehensive survey. A Dublin civic survey was undertaken from 1923 to 1925, prepared by city architect Horace T. O'Rourke and the Dublin Civic Survey Committee for the Civics Institute. It was seen as an essential precursor to any town plan. Across maps and text the survey set out the situation regarding Dublin's housing, geology, traffic and commerce. In findings that could have been used to justify the difficulties connecting Dublin's Luas lines in recent years, the survey explained 'traffic in Dublin travels largely in a semi-circle, for want to a geographical traffic centre, and there is therefore, no opportunity for a direct public transport system from the north side of the city to the south, thus causing a waste of time and further congestion'. In a more mundane echo of the delay in judging and finalising the 1914 competition entries, the publication of the Dublin Civic Survey was delayed as the printers sourced appropriate paper.[50] The civic survey maps were exhibited at Ely House by kind permission of the Knights of Columbanus. The Civics Institute lobbied the government for the preparation of a town plan for Dublin on the back of the survey. However, both the plan and 1925 civic survey were unofficial endeavours and, in the main, were not costed.

A Cork branch of the Housing and Town Planning Association had been set up in February 1913 and three of the association's vice-presidents were Corkmen: the Earl of Bandon, the Lord Mayor and Alderman Beamish.[51]

In 1926 the Cork Town Planning Association (a body set up in 1922, while the Housing and Town Planning Association of Ireland had merged with the Civics Institute by this point) published 'Cork: A Civic Survey' (prepared with Abercrombie and Sydney Kelly as special advisers) which included proposals to zone land and alleviate traffic problems and slum conditions. It also put forward a case for adopting a town plan for Cork and was described as 'the diagnosis of the symptoms for which the town plan is the prescriptive remedy'. The report outlined the 'general lack of order'[52] which hampered the city'. We have schools where there should be warehouses, dwellings where there should be factories, fields where there should be houses, and factories in all sorts of inaccessible and inconvenient places'.[53] In the 1920s Cork Corporation faced criticisms for ineffi-ciency (culminating in its dissolution in 1924 which saw its powers and duties transferred to Philip Monahan, who was appointed City Commissioner and administered civic affairs until 1929 when the Corporation was re-established and Monahan became the first City Manager).

The Cork Town Planning Association came about following calls by D.J. Coakley, principal of the Cork Municipal School of Commerce who was preoccupied with housing conditions in Cork in 1917–1918. One of the lectures which he gave, entitled 'General Principles of Housing and Town Planning', was published as a pamphlet by the Cork County Borough technical instruction committee. This built upon lectures delivered by Abercrombie organised by the Cork Literary and Scientific Society and the Chamber of Commerce. At a conference of the 'principal citizens' of Cork in 1922, the Cork Town Planning Association was formed, with Abercrombie and Sydney Kelly as advisers and Coakley as honorary secretary. It was chaired by Arthur F. Sharman Crawford. Their survey was a forward-looking document that 'established an agenda for planning and development which lasted for some sixty years'.[54] Coakley also suggested a Cork version of the *Dublin of the Future* planning competition.

The survey was presented to Commissioner Monahan with a view to informing a town plan for Cork. Reflecting a regional dimension well ahead of planning theory the civic survey foresaw satellite growth outside the city boundary and the need for closer control of development in the harbour to counteract 'haphazard and unhygienic' residential growth and to co-ordinate industrial development. The civic survey starkly set out the higher mortality rates in areas of the city with the most unsanitary housing, with over 18,000 people in total identified as living in unsatisfactory condi-tions. It recommended rehousing families (one fifth of the city's population) from some of the worst housing to new developments but suggested that due to the compact nature of the city 'there is no need for re-housing to take place at long distances from existing centres of population' unlike an undesirable trend they identified in English towns. It proposed sites for new public buildings as part of a civic centre but praised the city's 'dignified centre' characterised by South Mall, 'the great urban achievement of Cork'.

The Civics Institute's finances often seem to have been precarious. They sold copies of Abercrombie's maps and considered selling *Dublin of the Future* on commission to make money. Abercrombie himself does not appear to have been paid the £100 fee he was due on the publication of *Dublin of the Future* and instead received £50 and the offer of 150 (later reduced to fifty) hard copies of his publication for the balance. Though this may have represented some souring of the relationship (he also wrote to them requesting they return maps they had borrowed) they still sought his advice on the drawing of maps and their presentation of the civic survey. The institute's priorities shifted to running nurseries and childcare. It is notable that its annual reports from 1963 and 1964 do not mention the 1963 planning legislation, for example, and the Civics Institute was wound up in 1986.

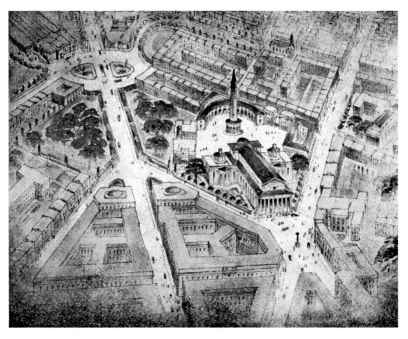

Sketch of the new National Cathedral on Capel Street proposed in *Dublin of the Future*. (Courtesy of Dublin City Library & Archive)

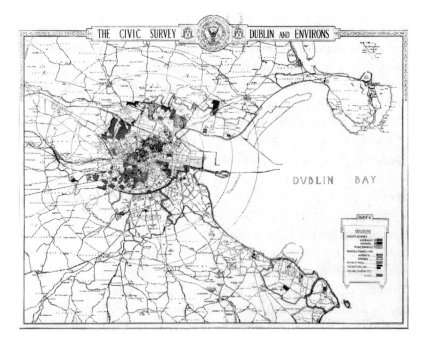

A Dublin civic survey was undertaken from 1923 to 1925 by city architect Horace
T. O'Rourke and the Dublin Civic Survey Committee for the Civics Institute.
Housing developments and tenements were amongst the items mapped and recorded.
(Courtesy of Dublin City Library & Archive)

NATIONALISM AND PLANNING

Andrew Kincaid of the University of Wisconsin has suggested
that modern town planning in Ireland emerged from an imperial
emergency, with planning a 'paternal effort' to show jobs, health and
housing could be addressed by the empire and 'an insurance against
revolution' pacifying unrest.[55] For Kincaid the 'arrival of town planning
in Ireland, complete with new legislation and renewed commitment
to public improvement, was, for its modernising advocates, the latest in
a long line of professional discourses employed in the colonial project
of urban social management'.[56] Kincaid notes the martial language
of Patrick Geddes while addressing the Dublin housing inquiry in
1913 who argued that spatial reform was essential: 'When people are
preparing for war they bring up their resources on every side. You, too,
could be drawing up your plans'.

Geddes (who also worked in India and Palestine) was convinced
that planning might play a role in maintaining the empire, writing

to his son from his planning exhibition in India in 1915 that his 'conservative yet constructive attitude in cities and towns' might 'check the revolutionary spirit by the utopian one'.[57] Geddes met with the Catholic hierarchy and suggested that modern planning could address the situation whereby Dublin had two Protestant cathedrals but no Catholic one. However, Geddes did not ultimately understand the power of nationalism in Ireland and the garden city ideal was too remote from the pressing need to rehouse those in urban tenements.[58] Fraser suggests that Geddes was naïve in trying to remove a political dimension from planning in the period as without appealing to nationalists it was perceived as diversionary constructive unionism. This meant that planning in pre-war Ireland 'failed to establish itself simply because it offered nothing to any of the groups who held power' being viewed as a distraction from the causes of unionism, nationalism or labour.[59]

Geddes and his followers have been accused of using Ireland as a social laboratory, importing British theory and practice, ignoring both Irish pressures and that planning was contentious in Britain itself.[60] For Fraser British planners and officials who sought to plant the seed of planning in pre-First World War Ireland did not understand local conditions, giving the 'pre-war Irish town planning movement a definite air of unreality'.[61]

In 1919 the joint secretaries of the Dublin Corporation housing committee wrote: 'You cannot afford to delay in chasing ideals … You have provided decent dwellings in substitution for kennels not fit to house a dog, whilst others were discussing questions of town planning and garden cities on the basis of wealthy English towns and well-paid English workmen'.[62] Andrew Kincaid argues that town planning was 'a key element of the new social imperialism' and 'a means of defence, a way of keeping their hold on increasingly contested territories'.[63] It has been suggested that British officials enlisted planning and its advocates to pacify the city while also pointing out that the new discipline was attractive to nationalists due to its potential for healthy cities.[64] This has persisted. Critics of the 1963 legislation alleged that it was an imitation of planning acts in Britain (despite there being 'very little parallel' between the two countries) and that it was a 'wrong bill, introduced at the wrong time, in the wrong country and in the wrong circumstances'.[65] In 2011 the Irish Citizens Party manifesto declared, 'Planners were generally trained in England … As the cultures of England and Ireland are fundamentally different, many of the tensions

that exist in planning in Ireland have their origins in the training of
Irish planners according to the English model'.

For nationalists, planning provided an opportunity to set out
their vision for Ireland though that potential was not always grasped.
Abercrombie skilfully engaged in the politics of Ireland of the time –
designing imperial-scale streetscapes while appealing to middle-class
nationalists.[66] Unwin, in a lecture in the meantime, declared that if
better organised Dublin could 'yet again stand foremost among the
metropolitan cities of the world'.[67]

Writing in the Catholic journal *Studies* in 1916 architectural critic
R.M. Butler described the destruction of the city's core after the Easter
Rising as an opportunity to reconstruct a city centre that the nation
could be proud of.[68] For Kincaid 'Town planning, in its potential to
deliver healthy cities, to provide municipal government, and to create
modern citizenship, appealed to the leaders of the fledgling state –
to both their pride and insecurity'[69] while for Larkin and Connolly
suburbs had an anarchistic role, allowing workers an empowered
quality of life far from the slums.[70]

RECONSTRUCTING DUBLIN

The most coherent and successful early town planning laws arose
out of the destruction caused to buildings in Dublin city centre
by the 1916 Rising and the Irish Civil War. Following the Easter
Rising, Sackville Street was reduced to rubble with the extent of
the damage estimated at £2.5 million. The destruction prompted a
debate about the principles of reconstruction. The *Irish Builder* called
for a special board to oversee the rebuilding plans and to give advice
considering that this was a 'unique and unexpected opportunity
for putting into practice the true principles of town planning ... to
give Dublin a piece of architecture worthy of this still beautiful and
historic street'.[71]

A letter from R.M. Butler, editor of the *Irish Builder* and future
professor of architecture at University College Dublin, appeared
in the London *Times* in May 1916 warning that the State must
intervene to ensure the rebuilding was in a 'dignified and suitable
manner' as the Corporation did not have the 'voice or authority to
interfere with design'. Butler called for the reconstitution of a body

such as the Wide Streets Commissioners, 'who did such excellent town-planning work in Dublin' alongside a 'committee of taste' which would capitalise on this 'almost unique' and 'great opportunity' to rebuild a city centre befitting Dublin's status as 'the second city of the Empire'.[72]

In August of that year a further letter from Butler appeared in the *Times* where he again called for a new Wide Streets Commissioners to deal with the reconstruction alongside an advisory 'committee of taste' (comprising architects, businessmen and 'town planning artists'). Butler described the project as 'one of the most important problems of town planning that has arisen in these countries for many years, involving important aesthetic considerations as well as the expenditure of a very large sum of public money' unsuitable for Dublin Corporation.[73]

Alongside the *Irish Builder* the Civics Institute wrote to the government urging the reconstruction of Dublin along planning lines, while traders sought flexibility to rebuild (State funded) based on their experience. In May 1916 *The Irish Times* reported 'the conflicting claims of town planning and of business appear to be quite irreconcilable'.[74]

When the government did indicate its intention to facilitate the restoration of the destroyed areas, the Council of the RIAI emphasised the necessity of imposing restrictions with regard to the design and reconstruction of individual buildings in important thoroughfares such as Sackville Street, since, it pointed out, 'the Municipal Council has no control over the design of new buildings other than as regards their street alignment, sanitary fitness and the fulfilment of certain conditions in regard to construction'.[75]

Powers were sought for the Corporation to control the architecture and design of the rebuilding of the area though there was opposition, as stated by Ronald McNeil MP during the reconstruction bill who doubted that 'any Corporation was a body which was likely to have a very high or enlightened regard for aesthetic interests' and warned that 'it would be deplorable if those who came after us were able to look back and say that, horrible as the rebellion had been, it was infinitely less horrible than the reconstruction which followed'.[76]

Sir Raymond Unwin played a key role in the drafting and enactment of the Dublin Reconstruction (Emergency Provisions) Act, 1916. The legislation was required to mediate the commercial concerns of businesses, the ambition of civic leaders and the nationalist distrust of English planners imposing solutions. For Unwin, in Kincaid's words, 'Dublin proved to be a fruitful site of experimentation for a leading English planner' given that similar mediation skills were required in his later role as England's chief housing officer a decade later.[77]

Under the act the city architect, guided by an expert committee set up by Dublin Corporation which included Raymond Unwin and recommended reconstruction along traditional classical lines, was afforded design control in the rebuilding of the city centre, with the power to examine, modify or reject redevelopment proposals. The Local Government Board was enabled to make loans to cover the cost of rebuilding. Funding difficulties and the shortage of materials ultimately meant that the reconstruction did not meet 'the multitude of aspirations and wishes which had so deeply and enthusiastically been expressed for its reinstatement'.[78]

The rebuilding of Lower Sackville Street was not complete at the outbreak of the Civil War in 1922 and this conflict left the north-eastern site of the street from Cathedral Street to Parnell Square in rubble. The Dublin Reconstruction (Emergency Powers) Act, 1924 empowered the Corporation to acquire destroyed premises and the rebuilding of the east side of Upper Sackville Street was 'more successful in its achieve-ment of unified façades … than was the lower end'.[79]

The destruction of Dublin following the Rising and Civil War (described as 'certain disturbances' in the 1924 Act that followed) did provide some impetus for planning and some control of rebuilding. The Greater Dublin Reconstruction Movement sought to rebuild Dublin as a capital for an energetic new Ireland. The movement differed from Abercrombie's plans in some respects. The loop line bridge would be moved under their proposals with the Custom House becoming the new GPO with the City Hall in the renovated GPO. New stations and a national cathedral were proposed along with a parliamentary complex for the Oireachtas at the Royal Hospital at Kilmainham (a move favoured by President of the Executive Council W.T. Cosgrave). The movement included E.A. Aston, Frank Mears and Lady Aberdeen and their proposals received the general approval of the government but they were criticised by Abercrombie as premature in the absence of a civic survey.

CONCLUSION

The founding of the Free State provided an opportunity to capitalise on the potential of the reconstruction acts, emerging plans and civic surveys. This was reflected in the wide-ranging ambition of the 1927 Dublin Civic Exhibition which included a housing and town planning exhibition in Dawson Street, featuring civic surveys, the Abercrombie plan, exhibits from Europe and the ESB's Ardnacrusha scheme. There were pockets of enthusiasm and much paper plans, but the next step for planning was to secure statutory status.

3

Planning and
the Free State:
A Seductive Occupation

1934 PLANNING ACT

The government's Greater Dublin Commission 1924–1926 promoted an 'orderly and systematised lay-out' of the future development of the region, with a new planning board covering Dublin and parts of counties Louth, Meath and Wicklow. The commission report included a minority report by Dr Oliver St J. Gogarty calling for a town plan to order the low density housing extension which he desired.[1]

Local government legislation following the commission report did not contain any reference to town planning, something condemned by Seán Lemass, when he said, 'If we want to secure that the growth of the city of Dublin will be properly regulated, we must have not merely a town planning authority, but around the city a belt of virgin land on which building has not yet begun and over which any development that takes place can be properly controlled'.[2]

The commission report and subsequent debate undoubtedly added impetus to calls for more formalised planning. On 1 March 1930, on return from a town planning conference in Rome, Minister for Local Government Richard Mulcahy declared that the country 'could not afford to indulge in town-planning undertakings'[3] but just two weeks later he committed himself to a town planning bill.

In 1929 the Seanad proposed a Town Planning and Rural Amenities Bill, prepared by a select committee comprising Senators Barrington, Bigger, Brown, Farren, Gogarty, Sir John Griffith, Johnson, Linehan and Moore. The 1929 bill was introduced at the behest of the Civics Institute and was based on an earlier draft developed by the RIAI in 1923 and updated to reflect 1925 legislation in the United Kingdom. The main provisions of the bill were to enable local authorities to conduct civic surveys and implement town planning schemes, but the bill was set aside in anticipation of the Minister for Local Government's own planning bill.

In 1931 housing and planning legislation was enacted in Northern Ireland. Though repeatedly promised, the Free State's Town and Regional Planning Bill did not emerge until August 1933. Addressing this delay and his hopes for its contents Manning Robertson said, 'we have no reason to suppose that Irish men are less proud of their country, less interested in its future, less observant of its beauty, than men of other nations, and we must hope that the stigma that we alone amongst civilised countries have taken no steps to organise by statute will be removed'.[4]

Many experts were consulted during the preparation of the bill, including Raymond Unwin who was adviser to both the Stormont and Dublin governments. The bill was more elaborate than the English legislation that inspired it. Robertson warned that the bill did not have to restrict its influence to England, citing recent planning legislation in Western Australia. However, the government did not view planning or planning legislation as a priority, saw little public support and was alarmed at the potential for compensation claims under any planning legislation.[5]

The 1934 legislation received a lukewarm reception in the Oireachtas. It allowed each local authority to prepare a planning scheme (the precursor to the development plan of today), which was to govern future development. The provisions of the act were not mandatory and it was up to an individual local authority to decide to become a planning authority. The act did not provide for the content of their planning scheme, allowing individual local authorities decide what would be included in the scheme for their area.

If the minister made an order approving the planning scheme, he was required to lay the order before the Oireachtas and either house could annul the order by resolution. This represented the ethos of the act where the plan was to have force of law and developers were required to ensure they complied with the act rather than the local authority developing a large development control regime.

The local authority could frame policies placing liabilities on landowners and on the local authority, with the onus being put on developers to ensure that they were in compliance with the law. Section 44 of the 1934 Act empowered the local authority to draft provisions in their planning scheme, which suspended regulations, by-laws and statutes. Once the planning authority had resolved to make a planning scheme then there could be no dealing with property without first obtaining the permission of the planning authority. That was provided for in Sections 57 and 58 of the 1934 Act.

The procedure for adopting a planning scheme was significantly more onerous than that for adopting a development plan under the subsequent Local Government (Planning and Development) Act, 1963. When compared with the planning schemes intended by the 1934 Act, the legal effect of the development plan under the 1963 legislation was severely curtailed and relatively uncertain. Indeed, it was not until the early 1990s that it was definitively determined that a local authority was bound by the provisions of its own development plan.[6]

Credit for the 1934 Act seems to have gone to the Institution of Civil Engineers of Ireland and in November 1934 their president, Nicholas O'Dwyer, congratulated the institution on the passing of the bill, although he suggested that the powers of planning authorities could have been more extensive.[7]

The act was of its time. Few people had even heard of town planning, concepts such as ecology were unknown and the countrywide local authority management system did not exist.[8] The memory of the slums was still fresh in the minds of policymakers. Speaking in 1938 Minister for Local Government and Public Health Seán T. O'Kelly said of the 1934 Act: 'The power of limiting the number of houses to the acre is one of the most important powers that a planning scheme confers. It will secure in a planned area that there is no recurrence of the conditions which are associated with slum dwellings. It will also tend to reinforce the efforts that are being made throughout the country to raise the standard of public health. Rates of mortality, especially infantile mortality, are highest in overcrowded areas. Local bodies should, therefore, avail of the powers that town planning confers to ensure that our people may enjoy proper sanitary surroundings both in home and workshop'.[9] Writing in 1985, Michael Gough records a similar memory in Cork, saying 'the fear of disease haunted Cork for a very long period and the outbreak of poliomyelitis in 1958 reinforced this fear once more' colouring housing and planning policy in the city for another twenty-five years.[10]

Apathy was evident from the beginning. Local authorities were invited to make comments on the 1933 bill but all declined. For Robertson public education meant that the provisions of the 1934 Act had to begin slowly, saying, 'the preservation of beauty and architectural character was common sense, because there was no sense in making a country ugly and without character. It was because the public did not realise this that we had to go slowly at first'.[11] The minister understood the need for public support, saying 'progress could not be hoped for unless there was a demand for it in this direction, and a public opinion behind the demand'.[12] A large number of public meetings and lectures on planning issues were held, with Robertson alone covering topics such as 'Our Cities and Towns', 'Town Planning and Slums' and 'The Towns We Live In'.[13]

The Town and Regional Planning (Amendment) Act, 1939 aimed to increase the flexibility of the planning scheme procedure but still few authorities passed the necessary resolution giving themselves planning powers to prepare planning schemes. The 1939 Act provided that certain areas could be designated as 'restricted development provision' within the planning scheme. It would then be possible to prepare and adopt a form of local area plan for that area. Interestingly, while this provision was not contained within the 1963 Act, similar provisions appear in the Planning and Development Act, 2000, as amended.

In his contributions to the debate on the 1938 amendment bill Ernest Benson TD showed an enlightened appreciation of emerging planning issues, regretting the lack of enthusiasm for the potential of the 1934 Act amongst local authorities, arguing that not enough was being done to counteract ribbon development and suggesting that local authorities must do more to allow play space for children. Concerns about ribbon development had been expressed as early as 1935 in a parliamentary question to the Minister for Local Government and Public Health who stated the powers of the 1934 Act were sufficient to deal with the issue.

By 1952 only seventeen of the twenty-seven county councils had adopted the planning acts and by 1963 forty-four county, borough and urban district councils had passed a resolution to make a planning scheme for their planning districts while three counties still had not done so along with twelve urban district councils (including eight from County Cork).[14] This may be somewhat attributed to the complicated planning scheme procedure, limited technical skills and lack of political or public impetus as well as the slow pace of development in the period.[15]

In December 1943 the cabinet committee on post-war planning asked the Department of Local Government if legislation should be passed to make adopting planning schemes under the planning acts compulsory. The department saw no need for such legislation and blamed the Emergency for delays in adopting planning schemes, rather than the powers available.[16]

For some there was considerable potential in the 1934 Act but a lack of will to implement it. Robertson considered the Irish legislation more advanced than that of England at the time as it gave those administering the system 'a freer hand' and he anticipated that aspects of the Irish legislation would be incorporated in UK law in the future. For Robertson the act's silence on requiring an authority to make a planning scheme before a certain date was wise as 'town-planning depended too much upon the self-starting properties of public education and opinion to be amenable to compulsion. A town plan scramble through by someone ignorant of the subject and just good enough to be considered a scheme within the meaning of the act was more a hindrance than a help'.[17]

NATIONAL PLANNING EXHIBITION

In 1942 the Minister for Local Government and Public Health Seán MacEntee drafted proposals for a planning board to 'consider and make recommendations regarding the technical and other problems involved in providing housing accommodation for the people of Dublin City and County'. It was proposed that it would draw up demographic projections and allocate responsibility for housing development, directing housing strategy.[18] The government took a view that housing could not be separated from other aspects of development, suggesting a body with a wider role in the economy, directing factory building and public works.

Wider economic development was not integrated into spatial planning under the Department of Local Government, instead being moved to Seán Lemass's Department of Industry and Commerce.

For Mary Daly the Department of Local Government's lack of interest in any aspect of building except housing was a missed opportunity to realise comprehensive physical planning legislation.[19] It was not until 1946 that a planning section was formed within the Department of Local Government.

In the face of this official indifference, those involved in planning at the time were working to build its reputation and opportunities. In 1934 Dublin city architect Horace T. O'Rourke advised young architects to study planning to avail of employment opportunities arising in the field. Architecture and engineering both frequently saw planning as an extension of their own profession. Both set up groupings to facilitate the study of planning and in 1939 a joint planning board of architects, surveyors and engineers was set up to deal with town planning which proposed founding an Irish town planning school. Ireland's first association of town planners, the Southern Irish Branch of the UK's Town Planning Institute was finally formed in 1941.

Manning Robertson was the leading figure in the effort to establish a broadly based, cross-professional planning movement through a 'National Planning Conference'. The stated aim of the National Planning Conference was 'to present the results of Research, Conferences and Studies of Planning Problems'. Its genesis came in June 1942 when a group comprising forty representatives of engineering, business, health, architecture, unions and rural organisations met to discuss the importance of planning for the post-Emergency era. In the words of Civics Institute chairman Fr J. Canavan who presided, 'the main object is the appointment of a body of men in whom they [the public] would have confidence, to organise an exhibition next year in Dublin, to collect data and plans, and through lectures and conferences, educate the public to the necessity and importance of national planning' while also showing to the government that there was broad-based support for planning.[20]

To achieve its aims the National Planning Conference, with its logo of a crossed hammer and sheaf of wheat in a set square, set about organising a National Planning Exhibition. Interestingly the conference disagreed with the British model of planning focused on local authorities, promoting instead Danish and Swedish models with a strong national plan guiding regional plans and followed by local planning.[21] In an interview with *The Irish Times* at the time Patrick Abercrombie echoed this, saying a Ministry of Planning was required to allow national scale planning.[22]

The organisers wrote to the President and senior ministers, asking that they become the exhibition's patrons. This request was denied on the advice of officials who seemed unimpressed with the organisers warning that the exhibition 'might at some time or other produce results or recommendations which would be very awkward for the government, or else merely fatuous, which might eventually bring the President into ridicule'.[23]

With an office on Lower Abbey Street and then later on Nassau Street the conference sought donations and suggestions from the public. There seems to have been some public confusion about the conference and its aims, however, and a letter from the conference to *The Irish Times* in October 1942 explained that while the government was being kept informed of its work and broadly approved, it was an independent, voluntary effort.

In April 1943 Taoiseach de Valera attended a meeting of the National Planning Conference at the Mansion House, chaired by Senator J.T. McGee. In his speech de Valera put forward his own agenda saying that while the government would consider the findings of the conference, planning 'is a very interesting but a very seductive occupation. It can very easily become little more than daydreaming or building castles in the air, unless you get down to earth, and still have in mind the practical application of your plans'.[24] In keeping with its all-island spirit, other meetings of the conference heard from speakers from Northern Ireland in an attempt to build cross-border collaboration about planning.

The 1944 National Planning Exhibition was intended to 'create an intelligent public interest in the treatment of post-war problems of reconstruction'.[25] The exhibition opened on the afternoon of 25 April 1944 and was attended by Taoiseach de Valera, Finance Minister Seán MacEntee and opposition leaders. Chairman Senator McGee explained that 'the exhibition was only intended to suggest what the conference thought might be done in the way of post-war planning. They had deemed it their duty to bring grist to the government's legislative mill. They could, however, only propose; the decisions had to be taken by the government'.[26]

The National Planning Exhibition ran from noon to 9.30 p.m., with entry set at sixpence for adults and threepence for the under 16s. Shops in the city decorated their windows along a planning theme with cinemas also showing adverts for the exhibition.[27]

The exhibition compared favourably to similar exhibitions in Britain and covered the Round Room and parts of the Supper and

Oak Rooms of the Mansion House. The centrepiece of the exhibition was a huge relief map of Ireland, viewed from a raised platform, which illustrated current developments and future plans including electrification, bogs, fisheries and shipping by way of coloured lights and strips of felt representing roads. The map had been erected by engineering and architecture students. Films displayed by the Irish Film Society included *Young Farmers* and a film on food production called *World of Plenty* described as 'the most ambitious documentary film yet made'. A schools essay competition was also run in conjunction with the exhibition. Attendance at the exhibition was below expectations however, with an average of 900 visitors a day in its first week, half of what was expected.

Associated with the exhibition a number of pamphlets were issued with the motto 'Ireland is ours for the making; let us make it'. A book on town planning in Ireland was published featuring accounts of the system in Northern Ireland and 'Éire'. In a review of the publication the *Ulster Journal of Archaeology* waspishly wrote: 'Éire has inherited from its brilliant Anglo-Irish past some of the best-planned cities in Europe, whereas Northern Ireland has suffered from unregulated industrial and suburban expansion in and around her capital city. But Dublin has her tenements, and Belfast is partly redeemed by the spacious layout of the civic centre'.[28] The exhibition did, however, include members of the Ulster Planning Group.

This effort does not seem to have been appreciated by all. An opposition TD during a debate on a finance bill in June goaded the government: 'Quite recently an effort was made by a group of outsiders calling themselves the National Planning Conference, who showed in a variety of ways their ideas for dealing with the big problems of production and development in agriculture and industry with a view to securing a better future for our people. Deputy MacEntee was very piqued about the matter, and indicated that, so far as the government were concerned, they had no belief in the capacity of people outside the government and outside government departments, to use intelligence and ability in planning a better future for our people.'[29]

Though the National Planning Conference aimed to build broad-based support for planning, scepticism came from many quarters, some unlikely. The inaugural meeting of the Literary and Dramatic Society of St Mary's College Rathmines Union in 1945 heard a paper titled

'This Planning Business', which warned that there was a danger that planners might produce a planned people as well as a planned country as 'once planners got started there was no stopping them'.[30]

Reflecting on the National Planning Exhibition, Myles na gCopaleen remarked in *The Irish Times:* 'The whole country lacks the density of population that would sustain even the fraction of "planning" that is proper to the temperament and economy of this country ... 80 per cent of what has been put before us is blatant imitation...our "planners" have lacked the wit to dish up even some native sort of jargon ... To plan so elaborately the material surround-ings of the few folk one sees around doesn't make much sense ... As well erect traffic lights in a grave-yard'. Na gCopaleen also queried why this new, planned Ireland required the planned-for hospitals if the future was to be as positive as the planners presented.[31]

Former IRA flying column commander George Lennon, who had been attached to the Irish Tourist Board, acted as the National Planning Conference's honorary secretary. Lennon appears to have grown disillu-sioned with the reaction to the conference, writing to *The Irish Times* in January 1945 following the paper's series of articles on post-war recon-struction: 'The National Planning Conference ... have reason to know something about the task you have undertaken, and more especially about popular indifference to issues which are of deep and pressing importance to the lives of this and coming generations of Irish citizens. If you can do anything to suspend the current lethargy, your efforts will merit the gratitude of an indolent public, who are more disposed to indulge in destructive criticism of official activities than to contribute their quotas to constructive thought and action'.[32]

THE 1934 ACT IN PRACTICE

The first resolution to prepare a town planning scheme came from Dún Laoghaire Corporation, who then developed a background study, similar to a civic survey. In 1935 Galway Corporation passed a resolution and prepared a sketch development plan for Galway city which assessed its geology, history, notable buildings, open space and industry and proposed residential development for between 4,000 to 6,000 people between radial routes, setting an optimal size of 80,000 for the city. Galway Corporation were particularly interested in the clearance of unhealthy areas in the city and the use of these sites in any subsequent planning scheme.[33] In 1938 Limerick City Council adopted a resolution to make a planning scheme. In Waterford architect and town planner Frank Gibney (1905–78) prepared a report in 1943 calling for the erection of over 1,000 dwellings, along with a new bridge and docks.

Dublin City Council at its meeting on 6 January 1936, adopted a resolution to prepare a planning scheme for the whole municipal area. Abercrombie, Sydney Kelly and Manning Robertson were retained to prepare a sketch development plan following this resolution. The designs were submitted in October 1939 and published with the Corporation's views in 1941 as the sixty-two-page *Dublin Sketch Development Plan*. Though ambitious, this was a more restrained document than the earlier *Dublin of the Future*, reflecting the realities of the Irish economy.

Despite its restraint in places, the sketch plan still proposed a new cathedral on a site the size of Merrion Square bounded by Lower Ormond Quay, Lower Liffey Street, Capel Street and Upper Abbey Street. It paid particular attention to open space with middle-class housing in the city centre proposed while working-class housing would continue in the suburbs. Stemming the tide of migration from rural areas was considered important and a 4 to 6-mile wide green belt four miles from the city centre, was proposed. This was to limit the city's expansion to a population of 765,300 with a number of centres within the greenbelt (such as Castleknock and Lucan) also allowed expand. The final population of these satellites was to be 61,500. This reflected proposals the Dublin city architect Horace T. O'Rourke had made in 1936.

Proposals were also made, for the first time, for a six-category land-use zoning of the central area and for the density zoning of the entire city.

The Dublin Sketch Development Plan was based on circumferential road routes and historian Erika Hanna has said that from then on 'the tangent route became a point of orthodoxy in Dublin town planning' copperfastened by Karl-Heinz Schaechterle's 1965 traffic report to Dublin Corporation which proposed two ring roads close to the inner city and the Travers Morgan Partnership's 1973 proposals for a motorway along the line of the canals.[34] For Hanna though many of these roads were never completed 'their spectre hung over' the Gardiner Street/Mountjoy Square area 'leading to widespread planning blight' and no investment in case they came to pass.

For Bannon, the *Dublin Sketch Development Plan* was both ideo-
logically driven and politically inept, a criticism that could also be laid
against many of the other advisory plans prepared in the period which
'lifted their ideas from English preoccupations, lacked any financial
realism and paid scant attention to the realities of implementation'.[35]

Niall Cussen, Principal Planning Adviser at the Department of
the Environment, Heritage and Local Government, has noted that
Cork has a long history of planning. One manifestation of this is the
Cork City Library's online archive, which includes a section on the
planning of the city. In 1935 Cork Corporation made a resolution
under the legislation and in 1941 Manning Robertson produced the
Cork Town Planning Report which modestly begins 'The City of
Cork has for long been a pioneer in Town Planning as can be seen
by the spirit of enterprise which converted waterways into fine open
streets'.[36] This Cork sketch development plan provides an insight into
the thinking of planners at the time of the 1930s legislation.

Robertson recommended that Cork urgently adopt a town plan,
acknowledging 'a Town Plan has to steer the difficult course between
the grandiose conception, which may be very nice, but is financially
impossible, and the trivial improvements which leave the real problem
untouched'.[37] Reflecting this, his report was not only ambitious but
also specific, recommending road widths, garden sizes for new housing,
vistas to be protected and a zoning scheme. The report even recommended securing a specific site in the north of the city for a public
abattoir. At a macro level Robertson called for new roads, proposed
airport sites, gave options for car parks, recommended bridges for
demolition, suggested a green belt around the city, improved housing
and called for increased green space and playgrounds.

Robertson was against very large cities and calculated that a green
belt could be identified that would accommodate up to 254,338
inhabitants, though 'it is unlikely that this figure will be reached
during the next hundred years'. This he suggests should be the
permanent maximum population for Cork with a density of 23.1
persons per acre with any additional growth directed to satellites. In the
city centre Robertson set out his preferred option for connecting St
Patrick's Street and Cork City Hall by a new street sweeping past the
GPO and replacing the 'monstrously ugly' Parnell Bridge.

Robertson's desire to 'thin out the population in central areas' is
understandable in the context of the trends at the time but a key

challenge for Cork city's planners today is growing a vibrant city centre population. Some of Robertson's assertions remain sound while others reflect their time. For example, the report acknowledges the restricted budgets of the Emergency era but suggests that if planners' advice had been heeded there would be lower density cities which would be less susceptible to aerial bombing or suicide aeroplane strikes.[38] Reflecting the time, the report also recommends standards for building design which would minimise damage from bombing (perhaps an early precursor of the branch of planning now known as Crime Prevention Through Environmental Design (CPTED) and the growing emphasis on planning for urban resilience in the event of natural or man-made disasters).

GAELIC BRASÍLIAS

From 1910 the growing possibility of Home Rule and the re-emergence of Dublin as the seat of parliament encouraged an interest in developing the city 'on more spacious and orderly lines'.[39] Writing in April 1916, just before the Easter Rising, Patrick Pearse described his vision of Ireland thus: 'In a free Ireland there will be work for all the men and women of the nation. Gracious and rural industries will supplement an improved agriculture. The population will expand in a century to twenty millions, it may even in time go up to thirty million. Towns will be spacious and beautiful ... but since the country will chiefly rely for its wealth on agriculture and rural industry there will be no Glasgows or Pittsburghs.'[40]

For some an essential part of making Pearse's rural idyll a reality in the Free State was to move the capital from the less than spacious Dublin. Speaking in 1923 Ernest Blythe suggested 'the character of the capital will have a very important influence upon the progress and development of the state'.[41]

Gearóid Ó Cuinneagáin founded the fascist movement Ailtirí na hAiséirghe (Architects of the Resurrection) in 1942. Aiséirghe's programme for what it called 'the New Order in the new Ireland' included a wholly new capital city, with Dublin considered vulnerable to *tionchur galldachais* ('alien Influence') and unsuitable as the administrative centre of the 'free, Gaelic and exemplary Christian state' of the future.

Amongst its proposals was the construction of an entirely new monumental capital of an Aiséirghe Ireland 'a kind of Hibernian

Brasília' on the Hill of Tara to replace Dublin.[42] To build a new capital at Tara would be a 'highly visible symbol' and 'break the alien influence exercised by the denizens of Rathmines, Rathgar and the Royal Irish Academy over the Government of Ireland'[43] according to architect Daithí Ó hÁinle in Ailtirí na hAiséirghe's journal.[44] The new city was to feature a new national university, theatre, cathedral and stadium; a massive 'Great National Avenue'; and a 'Garden of Heroes' with a Millennium Spire-like 'Column of the Resurrection' as its centrepiece. The Aiséirghe capital, Ó hÁinle wrote, was to be a showpiece of the national revolution and prove that 'we were in earnest in our intention to create for ourselves a fresh new world in Ireland'.[45]

Waterford sketch plan author Frank Gibney's interest in planning and his vision for Ireland found expression in an ambitious proposal for a national survey (Suirbhéaracht Éireann) and his Framework for an Irish National Plan (1943), which proposed a decentralised, garden city-style Ireland with its capital in Athlone.

For MacCabe these 'fanciful Gaelic Brasílias' were born out of the radical visions of frustrated and isolated young planners and architects in a stagnant economy. All had a common genesis as cultural nationalists and a distaste for the 'ancient capital of Dublin which was seen as the outpost of the former colonial power'.[46]

More notably Gibney was also the proponent of 'one of the few examples of good planning in this period'.[47] Following the Emergency, Bord na Móna (the turf development board) began building villages for the workers who harvested peat or turf. The housing designed by Gibney for Bord na Móna address the public road, and create an organic green at the centre of the development. A good example is Doire Dhraighneach near Rochfortbridge in County Westmeath and Coill Dubh in County Kildare. Of these Coill Dubh, established with 160 houses as an entirely new village in the 1950s to accommodate workers on the Bord na Móna works supplying the Allenwood peat-fired power station, can be considered the most substantial, the most remote and the most ambitious of all the schemes. It was the nearest to a complete village in itself, containing schools and shops. Other facilities such as a church were not originally planned for but developed later.[48] For academic and one-time Minister for Planning Ciarán Cuffe, Gibney's Bord na Móna settlements can be considered an Irish answer to the garden city.

There have been other arguments for a new capital based on spatial and symbolic reasons. In 1989, to counter the lopsided

The 1950s Frank Gibney-designed village of Coill Dubh today. Gibney's villages for Bord na Móna stood as examples of good planning undertaken following the Emergency.

growth of Dublin, University of Edinburgh Professor of Canadian Studies and sometime Cork resident Ged Martin called for the building of a greenfield capital at Sixmilebridge in County Clare, arguing that Dublin would 'choke' under urban sprawl otherwise. In 2002 political activist Paddy McGarvey argued for a new capital in Ballyjamesduff which might be acceptable to Northern Ireland and Republic of Ireland parliamentarians in the event of Irish unification. From the 1960s *Meath Chronicle* columnist Garret Fox suggested moving the capital from Dublin to Galway to remove Dublin's housing problems and guarantee the growth of the west. In 1968 New Zealand native and Florida resident William Edward Patrick O'Donnell submitted proposals to the government for a new administrative capital at Tara which would include the Dáil and a new university and would be funded by the Irish diaspora. O'Donnell reiterated his proposals to the government in 1974. When the government began drafting the National Spatial Strategy in 2000, Galway businessman William A. Thomas proposed to them a new low density 'City of the Sacred Heart' in east Mayo that was to grow to 250,000 people within twenty years.

DROPPING A HOT PLANNING POTATO

There was little departmental expertise or ministerial commitment to planning under the 1934 Act with the aids to planning authorities consisting of a booklet of 'model clauses' and a circular about the siting of petrol stations.[49] Robertson recognised that the fate of the act depended on public support: 'Without a sound public opinion our position will be without hope, since no legislation can instil a cultural attitude of mind, neither can we expect our local authorities to exert adequately any powers of control that may be conferred upon them if they know that the electorate is indifferent or hostile to any restraint exercised for the public good'.[50] Lectures were organised to drum up public and professional support for the act, with Manning Robertson taking to the media outlets to promote planning.

Having adopted the 1934 and 1939 planning acts, a planning authority was expected to prepare its planning scheme 'with all convenient speed' but the complexity of the procedure led to some authorities giving up in their attempts to prepare a scheme. The only scheme prepared was the 1957 draft Dublin planning scheme and that was driven by legal action by a Dublin building company Modern Homes (Ireland) Ltd. In July 1953 the High Court found that Dublin Corporation had not proceeded 'with all convenient speed' in the preparation of a planning scheme and required that the Corporation produce the scheme within two years. Developers claimed that a planning scheme was essential to give them clarity with the RIAI arguing that there was too much indefiniteness about what a plan might or might not do.[51] The 1955 Dublin plan was developed by a special committee of officers from the Corporation drawn from planning, engineering, architecture and health and was based on the Abercrombie sketch plan.

The hot potato of the draft Dublin scheme was then submitted for approval to the Minister and an ill-equipped Department of Local Government, 'where its arrival could hardly have been less welcome'.[52] Some 3,600 objections were made against it and no final decision was ever taken. Ultimately it was decided to repeal the 1930s planning acts, to draft new legislation and to begin all over again, leading to the Local Government (Planning and Development) Act, 1963.

For some the difference between the 1934 and 1963 Acts is not as pronounced as imagined, with many differences administrative rather than fundamental.[53] The 1934 Act included references to betterment (absent from the 1963 legislation) which sought to recover three-quarters of the increase in value brought about by a planning scheme from property owners. This met with opposition from landowners, particularly small property owners, who rejected the concept of control and the failure to put any planning scheme into effect meant the mechanisms were never tested. As we shall see, the absence of any betterment provisions in the 1963 Act deprived local authorities of the funding required to carry out the more positive planning envisaged through acquiring land or initiating development.

The decline in the fortunes of planning from the 1930s to the 1963 Act can be explained by a number of factors, including the lack of flexibility in the 1934 and 1939 Acts, the absence of finance for staff training and government apathy towards planning. Alone amongst the ministers of the Lemass era (Lemass's son Noel was to act as Fianna Fáil spokesman on planning in the 1970s), Lemass and Erskine Childers (who was involved in the Civics Institute) both exhibited an interest in planning. The National Planning Conference demonstrated the potential for a widespread platform for more responsible planning but it was not capitalised upon and it had little political support. So little had been achieved under the 1930s legislation during its more than twenty-five-year existence.

4

Local Government (Planning and Development) Act, 1963: The October Revolution

The idea is now being accepted that proper planning is an economy rather than the reverse. Previously, planning was regarded with considerable suspicion and was regarded more as something for cranks and idealists.

Lionel Booth TD, Second Stage Dáil Debate on Local Government (Planning and Development) Bill, 31 January 1963

The Local Government (Planning and Development) Bill was introduced to the Dáil on 12 July 1962 by the Minister for Local Government, Neil T. Blaney. The second stage commenced on 12 November and the act cleared both houses of the Oireachtas on 31 July 1963. It was signed into law on 7 August 1963 and was to have effect from 1 October 1964, known as the appointed day or 'The October Revolution' by some. Fine Gael expressed concern that while the progress of the bill through the Oireachtas was slow, more time could have been found to debate its contents.

Ireland was changing quickly at that time. Between 1950 and 1960 the number of cars registered in Dublin city and county increased from 28,000 to 50,000 and by 1970 there were 115,000. The First Programme for Economic Expansion in 1958 set ambitious national economic targets and planning was intended to play a role in promoting growth.

While town planning was seen in almost utopian terms in the early part of the century, the impetus for the 1963 Act was far more practical: 'In as much as there was a value system behind the planning act, that set of values was strongly motivated in favour of orderly development through growth and expansion'.[1] The 'renaissance of planning in the 1960s was directly related to the perception that good planning and well-planned and attractive environments were a catalyst to economic and industrial expansion'.[2] Physical planning was seen to have 'an intimate interrelationship' with the move towards economic and social planning.[3] Speaking in 1969 Taoiseach Jack Lynch declared, 'the emphasis in our interest in physical planning is on the positive contribution it can make in the process of national development'.[4]

For Blaney planning would 'pay dividends in economic and social well-being in the years to come' and was particularly important for Ireland for 'the poorer the resources of a country, the greater is the need for careful planning'.[5] According to the Minister, 'Planning has a considerable significance in helping to foster economic development, especially in locations which offer prospects of becoming centres of commercial or industrial growth ... planning for a better physical environment is of national economic importance ... A good environment and prosperity are closely associated'.[6]

PLANNING GONE MAD

On 24 May 1960 the government requested advice from the United Nations (UN) on '... the feasibility of redeveloping cleared central areas with a view to making the process more economic and to reduce the burden on public funds such as by a mixed development of residential, commercial and industrial enterprises. This would involve examination of the possibilities of attracting such enterprises to these areas and of so designing redevelopment projects as to bring about an economic and balanced use of the land.'[7]

The government also sought guidance in particular on the following aspects of urban renewal:

1. Land uses, based on the economic development programme
   for Dublin, indicating locations for different enterprises, such

as public and private housing, shops, office buildings, hotels and light industries.

2. The kinds of investments that should be made to attract businesses and industry, including any facilities that should be provided.
3. A financial plan necessary for the proposed redevelopment.
4. The procedures to be adopted to ensure co-ordination of public and private interests and uses.[8]

The UN approach was to recruit experts who would gather data about countries, provide further training for their personnel and offer advice requested, leading to their appointment of Charles Abrams to Ireland. Between 1953 and his death in 1970 Charles Abrams was an adviser to twenty-one countries through UN assignments, including Bolivia, Pakistan and Ghana. Abrams was a Polish-born urbanist, housing expert, lawyer and academic, known for his good humour and indefatigable appetite for work. His early work was under Mayor LaGuardia, drafting legislation to establish the New York City Housing Authority, the country's first. Abrams' approach was not one of the consultant parachuted in to regurgitate standard solutions without considering local circumstances. According to his biographer, apart from a few general principles, his recommendations were always tailored to local situations.[9]

It quickly became clear that what Dublin Corporation could do in terms of urban renewal was restricted by national legisla-tion and the existing planning laws and Abrams' remit expanded quickly to include a review of planning and development legislation. He interviewed the various parties involved in the summer of 1960 and 'the problems raised weave into a variety of political, economic, and social considerations'.[10] As Abrams' brief became wider it is notable that his primary experience was in urban development in a country that still considered itself as very rural. For Abrams it seemed that the Irish experience of landlordism still conditioned policies relating to land.[11]

Abrams advocated an unashamedly expansionist role for planning in accommodating the needs of both industry and business, especially in the case of Dublin which was 'both of national and municipal concern'.[12]

Abrams made a total of twenty-four recommendations. For him the planning system as established under the 1930s acts was too complex and he called for a more 'realistic approach to master-planning' saying the 'fatal flaws in the current law, are that like Abercrombie's [1922] Plan … it required too much and thereby got too little'.[13]

Abrams suggested that public funding for housing could be cut.[14] Other recommendations covered planning legislation and the objectives thereof, the preparation of an urban renewal programme, the amendment of compulsory purchase legislation, the commissioning of a study on industrial location and the preparation of a scheme for land acquisition for industrial estates, along with a revision of housing schemes so roads were safer for children. There were also specific recommendations relating to Dublin, as well as the preparation of city plans for Dublin, Cork and Limerick. In relation to planning education and research, Abrams called for the 'institution of research in planning, housing, building materials, building cost, city development, and fostering of courses so as to broaden the reservoir of personnel in these areas'.

There was also a recommendation for the 'encouragement of civic organisations to assume public leadership in planning and housing and to improve public relations in planning', indicating that apathy and misunderstanding were issues. The lack of a broad-based support for planning and the 1963 legislation were to prove significant barriers to its successful implementation. Abrams concluded 'what is lacking in the main, is a public awareness of the situation and the essential policies to correct it'.[15]

The Department of Local Government received the report in April 1961 and it was sent to Dublin Corporation for their views, finally being submitted to cabinet in October 1962. In the foreword of his 1961 report he notes approvingly that the Minister had introduced a planning bill in December 1960 which somewhat disrupts the usual narrative that the Abrams' report provoked a move for new legislation. By 1960 it was clear that the 1934 and 1939 planning acts were unworkable and change was needed.

The Abrams report is notable as one of the first instances where the Irish Government looked beyond England for inspiration and best practice in planning. Though motivated by the growth-orientated approach to planning evident in North America, the legislation that followed did not cast its net so widely and was closely modelled on 1947 English legislation.[16]

The government first considered outline proposals for planning legislation on 6 December 1960 when Minister Blaney was given leave to introduce the Local Government (Planning and Development) Bill, 1960 to Dáil Éireann. Though the bill 'to make provision for the orderly and progressive development of cities, towns and other areas, whether urban or rural, and to preserve and improve the amenities thereof' was introduced the following day, no text was circulated 'and it is uncertain whether any then existed'.[17] The bill lapsed when the Dáil was dissolved in September 1961. Blaney expressed frustration that the Attorney General was of the view that drafting the bill could take at least three months. This sense of urgency may explain why the bill followed the English act so closely.

Introducing the bill to the Dáil on 22 November 1962 for its second stage reading (recorded as taking two hours to deliver) Minister for Local Government Neil Blaney outlined his rationale for planning: 'The object of planning is to make our towns, villages and countryside better places in which to live and work, by improving their appearance, their public services and facilities and their opportunities for employment and recreation. This necessitates vigilance and constant effort. A community's needs and expectations are not static: they are growing and changing all the time. It is one of the tasks of planning to secure that current developments make allowance for this growth and for keeping up with changing or improving standards. Thus we must plan not alone for the community's present needs but also for its future needs in the light of prospective growth in demand. The future improvement of a street corner must not be made more costly, or perhaps rendered impracticable, by the shortsighted location of an expensive building. The ever increasing demand for access to the more remote beaches and lake shores must not be frustrated by developments which block the only convenient access routes.'[18]

Blaney acknowledged that the 1934 Act 'has not been devoid of achievement … much undesirable development has been prevented' though the 1934 Act 'had many defects'. The 'procedure for the making of a planning scheme which was too lengthy and too cumbersome' and could not 'readily be adapted to changing circumstances' something the 1939 amendment could not remedy.[19] Blaney believed that the 'greatest obstacle to the use of the 1934 Act as an effective measure to secure proper planning and development is the fact that the powers provided are largely regulatory and only to a limited degree enable planning authorities to undertake or secure positive development. A planning scheme might prevent bad development but it could not secure good development'.[20] This was to be corrected by the new act. Blaney argued that legislation was required to bring Ireland up to date with international standards.[21]

Blaney told the Dáil, 'There is considerable evidence of widespread public interest in the need for a planning code more suited to modern requirements ... consideration was given to the question of amending our present planning acts but no satisfactory solution was found practicable in that direction', hence the bill.[22]

The specific objectives of the bill were outlined as follows:

1. To set up a new and more flexible planning system to be operated by local authorities throughout the country;
2. To enable local authorities to facilitate industrial and commercial developments and to secure the re-development of these parts of built-up areas which have become outmoded, uneconomic or congested;
3. To secure that the amenities of town and countryside are preserved and improved;
4. To relate compensation to property owners to the restrictions imposed on them by individual planning decisions rather than to provisions in planning schemes and to end their liability for betterment charges.[23]

According to Bannon 'In as much as there was a value system behind the planning act, that set of values was strongly motivated in favour of orderly development through growth and expansion'.[24] For Blaney under the legislation, 'Property values must be conserved and where possible enhanced'.[25]

An editorial in *The Irish Times* in July 1962 complained of 'the lamentable weakness of our planning legislation so far' but acknowledged that planning 'of course, is troublesome'. Giving a lukewarm response to the bill, its editorial borrowed from Michael Collins's contention that the Anglo-Irish Treaty gave the freedom to achieve freedom, by saying the bill might not seem to 'provide the complete answer; but it does offer a framework within which local planning can be revolutionised'. Given the time limits for preparing a mandatory plan *The Irish Times* foresaw 'panic ... in town and county halls throughout the country; for it faces councillors and their managers for the first time with the new problem of thinking about the physical appearance of the area which shelters and feeds them'.[26]

As the bill progressed through the Oireachtas *The Irish Times* maintained its cautious tone saying 'the bill can only be welcomed with a rider expressing a hope that the planning authority will in future when fully empowered bat resolutely on the side of the angels' though it regretted that the bill did not do enough to counter anyone 'who neglects their house so that it becomes an eyesore'.[27]

The 1962 planning bill was not warmly welcomed by Blaney's colleagues. The Department of the Taoiseach was concerned that the compensation measures were unduly restrictive, while the Department of Finance was concerned that the compensation provisions would cost the exchequer substantial sums.[28] The bill was intended to apply to State developments such as Garda stations and post offices, though prisons and military construction was exempt. The Departments of Finance and Lands objected to any possible restrictions, with Minister for Lands Michael Moran condemning the bill as 'planning gone mad'.[29] Minister for Social Welfare Kevin Boland was concerned that the bill was balanced in favour of the community over private property owners, warning that the assumption that local authorities can do no wrong was mistaken and citing the 'scandal' of unfinished housing estates that had not been taken in charge by local authorities.[30]

Addressing criticism Minister Blaney said 'other countries in Europe were using planning to advance their economic development and we cannot afford to ignore their example'. For Blaney the government's policy 'of aiming at a progressive improvement in the national economy cannot achieve maximum success unless all sectors of national activity are co-ordinated. In this context a comprehensive system of physical planning is obviously necessary. The direct association between economic planning and physical planning is being increasingly recognised'.[31]

The Second Programme for Economic Expansion (published in 1964) pointed out that the government's proposals for physical planning were designed to ensure that economic and physical planning were properly co-ordinated at both regional and national level. Linking planning with economic development in Ireland was not new. The brochure for the 1914 Civic Exhibition claimed that it would 'show how Dublin can be made a better and more profitable place to do business in'.[32] According to Blaney, 'planning for a better physical environment is of national economic importance. We are trying to attract new industry and encourage expansion of existing industry. Our prospects of success will be enhanced if our towns are clean and bright and our countryside has a pleasant appearance. A good environment and prosperity are closely associated'.[33]

During its passage through the Oireachtas there was some support for the need for the bill, with Senator Gus Healy commending the Minister saying the 'legislation is as important as any that has been passed not alone by his department but by any other department'.[34] Deputy Lionel Booth admitted: 'Previously, planning was regarded with considerable suspicion and was regarded more as something for cranks and idealists. Now it is being accepted as a realistic policy to have wholehearted long-term planning'.[35]

Discussing the bill Senator Carton was concerned about the personal aesthetic preferences of planners dismissing development that might have merit for others: 'town planning is a most inexact science … I am thinking of Bobbie Burns, when people were wondering why he did not line up with Bonny Mary of Argyle … He said: "Nobody can see her with the eyes of Bobbie". He saw her beauty but the others could not. So it may be in town planning; what one person believes is beautiful, others may not'.[36]

For barrister and TD Stephen Barrett the new legislation was 'a new despotism at its zenith, tantamount almost to indecency. The bureaucrat has full and final power as to a man's fundamental rights'.[37] This debate over the interaction between private property rights and planning would not go away.

In the debate on the bill Patrick Hogan TD suggested that the bill would lead to local authority officials becoming 'tinpot planners' and it had a 'dictatorial flavour which I completely deprecate. It was said here today that dictators make the best planners. Certainly, I suppose, they make the most effective planners. One may ask oneself do planners become dictators. I think the answer would be that the tendency is definitely so'.[38] This would not be the only time politicians linked planning with dictators. For Michael Ring TD the 2006 strategic infrastructure legislation was 'evidence that the state is becoming a dictatorship' while in committee debates regarding the 2009 planning bill Fine Gael environment spokesman, and future Minister for the

Environment, Phil Hogan accused the government of presenting a 'uno duce, una voce' approach to planning.[39]

In the Oireachtas there were suggestions that planning experts might overshadow the role of local councillors as elected representatives of the people, a suggestion strongly refuted by Minister Blaney. Deputy Patrick Hogan warned, 'The authority will, in practice, be the county manager and his assistants, working in close conjunction with the higher officials in the Custom House'.[40]

Powerlines were contentious in the Oireachtas with Deputy Robert Briscoe wondering if the ESB could be controlled sufficiently by the legislation given 'that body can do what they like. If we are considering proper planning, which will include the appearance of the city, then there must be an amendment of the electricity supply acts to enable the local authority to decide whether or not wires should run overhead or whether buildings should be constructed in certain areas. All too often these buildings are eyesores'.[41]

Donegal TD and auctioneer Joseph Brennan challenged those who 'are inclined to regard town planning as something which merely restricts one from doing what one wants to do ... planning as envisaged in this bill covers a far wider field than merely restricting persons from doing certain things in relation to building and so forth. It takes power to develop and that is an important aspect of the bill which is possibly overlooked by many people who think of it in terms of the type of legislation which has been in operation in this respect in the past'.[42]

The Irish Town Planning and Country Development Association had reservations regarding the bill, suggesting that it was being misrepresented as allowing 'positive planning' ('whereby the planners themselves develop the town. The classic modern example is Brasília') when instead it focused on 'negative planning' that is, prohibiting development. The association were also concerned that the compensation sections were insufficient and might deter developers.[43] This association was set up in 1962 by a number of professionals including barristers, solicitors, engineers, architects, landowners, surveyors and auctioneers. It aimed to promote planning while 'protecting owners of property from the dangers and disadvantages of unplanned and wrongly planned development or the excessive extension of arbitrary control'.[44]

Writing to The Irish Times on 4 August 1962 a person called J.C. Martin criticised the bill heavily. Dismissing it as a bill 'drawn up by bureaucrats … for them the most important section in the bill is Section 80 which will give rise to a few big jobs and possibly promotion'. The writer concluded that he was sure the Minister 'has never studied this measure and that if he has he must have been completely confused by the jargon'.[45]

Senior local government officials from every local authority attended an 'appreciation course comprising lectures by the President and other leading personalities' of the Irish branch of the Town Planning Institute to explain 'the purpose and methods of planning'. Lecturers at the four-day appreciation course in the Custom House which began on 23 October 1962 included Dublin planning officer Michael O'Brien who told attendees the bill had 'provisions which compare with other countries where the law in relation to planning has been reviewed and changed'.[46] Opening the course Minister Blaney called for 'more colour and imagination' in housing developments and emphasised the role of planning in protecting amenities and tourism. Blaney intended to offer similar information to councillors.[47] John O'Dea, chairman of the Irish Branch of the Town Planning Institute called the bill 'a magna carta for country planning' and a 'revolution for the whole country' but that it was essential to have planners in every county. O'Dea went on to predict that the bill could lead to new towns and a reduction in smaller villages.[48]

All local authorities (except town commissioners) were granted planning powers when the 1963 Act came into force. Creating one central planning authority was not entertained, with Deputy Lionel Booth suggesting 'no one would like a plan imposed on them by the central authority. It is far better that the local authorities, both the elected representatives and the staff, should satisfy themselves on the point and then carry out the necessary work for the preparation of the plans and thereafter accept full responsibility'.[49] However, it was argued at the time that there were too many planning authorities.[50] This has been a recurring criticism. In 2012 the Irish Planning Institute President, Brendan Allen, suggested 'the decision-making arising from too many small planning authorities often results in poor decision-making in a national and regional context and a focus on "localism". I believe that for planning purposes we need larger planning regions with greater power'.[51]

THE 1963 ACT IN PRACTICE

Despite looking to the UN in 1960, the new planning system was similar to the post-war British system under the Town and Country Planning Act, 1947. At the appreciation course the bill was described as 'more advanced than any similar English legislation'. For the *Architects Journal* Ireland had made a late start in planning but this could prove to be 'a great advantage to a country; it is the pioneers who make the worst mistakes, and latecomers learn from them'.[52] Unfortunately as the Irish legislation was being developed British planning was undergoing one of its regular upheavals in an effort to counter accusations that it was undemocratic while also economically irrelevant. This perception arose from reports of problems in the British 'New Towns', which had been spearheaded by unelected, technocratic planners.[53]

While preparing the 1963 bill, department officials drew on professional bodies and local authority officials, in particular the officials of the Dublin and Cork Corporations.

The central principle of the planning system established was that permission was required in respect of the development of land. Development was defined under Section 3 (1) of the 1963 Act as 'the carrying out of any works, on, in or under land or the making of any material change in the use of any structures or other land'. The term 'pre-63' or 'pre-64' development is sometimes used by estate agents and others to refer to development carried out before the 1963 planning act came into operation on 1 October 1964 and which are lawful but do not have planning permission.[54]

The act obliged eighty-seven local authorities to act as planning authorities and prepare a development plan for their area within three years of its commencement. It set down certain items which had to be included in the development plan, but Blaney maintained that the act deliberately allowed for 'considerable variation in the scope of plans made by different planning authorities ... having regard to the wide variation in the size, needs and circumstances of the areas which fall to be planned'.[55]

The development plans, consisting of written statements and supplemented by maps, were required to deal with land-use zoning, traffic and circulation, the renewal of obsolete areas and the preservation and improvement of existing amenities. In non-urban areas the plan should also have regard to provision of services. Development plans were to be reviewed every five years, could be varied and required public participation. Section 22 enabled the minister to co-ordinate the develop plans of two or more planning authorities and to vary any given development plan.

Though based on British acts, the Irish legislation was adapted to reflect the local government structure.[56] In Ireland the 1940 County Management Act introduced the councillor/manager division in local government (called 'Ireland's major invention in the field of government'[57]). This divided local government functions into 'executive' functions carried out by the manager and 'reserved' functions exercised by councillors. In planning, the councillors adopt the development plan and the manager decides whether to grant or refuse applications for planning permissions (this is frequently delegated to a senior official). Lawyer Yvonne Scannell suggests that the ambition of local councillors makes the planning for unpopular developments (such as landfills) almost impossible and suggests that councillors' lack of action on such issues has been facilitated by legislation that then places powers to provide for such facilities in the hands of city and county managers, insulating the elected members from electoral retribution.[58]

Other sections of the act dealt with amenities, compensation and powers of land acquisition. Some of the 'modern' requirements for the act in the minister's view included the need for economic growth, the rise in car ownership and the need to preserve the landscape for tourism. The landscape protection aspects of the legislation were welcome at the time and were seen as far reaching. For one commentator 'the rape of Killarney seems to have made a deep impression on the draughtsmen of this bill' but it was also recognised that turning down development to protect visual amenity was always going to be a difficult balancing act.[59]

The act was virtually silent on architectural conservation, only being mentioned in the Third Schedule Part IV, where 'Preservation of buildings of artistic, architectural or historical interest' was listed. It was not mandatory to take action in this area. Under the 1963 Act the interiors of listed buildings had to be separately designated for protection. This was particularly regrettable in light of events in the run up to the legislation coming into force.

Discussing Dublin, Frank McDonald is scathing of what he considers the 'devious' lack of protection historic buildings were afforded under the 1963 Act, writing 'The new planning act included

demolition in its definition of 'development'. But when Neil Blaney
brought the act into force, he made a series of regulations classifying
various categories of development as 'exempt'. And buried in the
small print of an obscure twenty-two-page statutory instrument was
the following very strange sentence: 'Any alteration consisting of
the plastering or painting of any external part of any building or the
demolition of any building ... shall be exempted development.'[60]

No. 13-30 Fitzwilliam Street Lower prior to demolition. ESB's proposal to break up the
Georgian façade resulted in a popular preservation campaign which has resurfaced as a
new headquarters is proposed. (Courtesy of the Irish Architectural Archive)

No. 13-28 Fitzwilliam Street Lower during demolition, 1965. (Courtesy of the Irish
Architectural Archive)

Plans announced by the ESB in the early 1960s to break up what was Dublin's longest Georgian facade, from Mount Street to Leeson Street by demolishing sixteen Georgian houses on Fitzwilliam Street, resulted in a popular preservation campaign with nearly 1,000 Dubliners attending a protest meeting at the Mansion House in 1962.

In a Dáil debate on the then planning bill, Parliamentary Secretary Joseph Brennan tackled colleagues who disagreed with the ESB's Fitzwilliam Street demolition and sought the intervention of planning. According to Brennan: 'there are cases where commercial interests must transcend any provision of town planning, unless it is completely in conflict with the basic principles of planning as set out in any act or in this bill. If we allow the aesthetic mind to run riot and have its way in the matter of enacting legislation of this type, we shall be going too far in that direction, just as, if we allowed commercial interests to dominate legislation of this type, we should be going too far the other way. Anybody who examines this masterful piece of legislation must agree that it makes ample provision for good middle of the road planning which will meet every situation.'[61]

Dublin Corporation heeded the protests and refused permission for the demolition but it was granted by Minister Blaney the day before the commencement of the new act. The Georgian terrace was lost, replaced by a Stephenson Gibney and Associates designed modern head office. In 2013 controversy re-emerged when the ESB announced their intention to replace the 1960s block, leading some to call for the reinstatement of the Georgian façades while others derided this as pastiche.

The 1963 Act included An Taisce, the National Trust for Ireland, as one of the prescribed bodies (and the only one not publicly funded). The other bodies included Bord Fáilte, the Arts Council and the National Monuments Advisory Council. These were entitled to comment on certain proposed developments.

Founded in 1946 An Taisce was established an as association 'for the protection of places of interest and beauty in Ireland'. Reminiscent of the broad coalition interested in planning prior to the First World War and in the inter-war years, the early organising committee included representatives of bodies as varied as the Irish Youth Hostel Federation and the Royal Society of Antiquaries of Ireland and this grew to include bodies such as the Irish Roadside Trees Association and the Photographic Society of Ireland. From its inception it showed a strong interest in matters that would be considered planning issues, including advertising hoardings and the environmental impact of works carried out by Bord na Móna and the ESB and submissions on the draft scheme for Dublin drawn up under the 1934 Planning Act. According to John O'Loughlin Kennedy, writing in An Taisce's official history 'not infrequently, planning authorities have found it useful to hide behind An Taisce's advice when defending proper planning and development decisions against the ire of pressure groups or disappointed applicants'.[62]

The dismissive attitude of those in government in the 1960s towards Ireland's architectural heritage has been linked to their nationalism, exemplified by Local Government Minister of the time Kevin Boland's dismissal of Georgian Dublin as not part of 'our real national heritage'[63] and his view that conservationists were 'a consortium of belted earls and their ladies and left-wing intellectuals'. To this day suspicion of conservationists and their motives can emerge. Objectors to developments have recalled being jostled and spat at on their way to Bord Pleanála oral hearings.[64] During contested attempts to construct a visitor interpretative centre at the foot of Mullaghmore, within the Burren National Park, a local Fianna Fáil councillor described the members of the anti-Mullaghmore development campaign as 'Blowins, hippies, homosexuals, drug smokers, intellectuals, and non-meat eaters'.[65]

Interpretative centres proposed in both the Burren and the Wicklow National Park in the late 1980s led to objectors bringing legal challenges to the assumption that State authorities such as government departments or the Office of Public Works were exempt from the obligation to apply for planning permission that existed since the 1963 Act came into force (they were still required to consult with the relevant local authority). The Supreme Court found that the obligation to consult did not remove the obligation to apply for permission. This had potentially far-reaching consequences, as no planning permissions had been sought for developments such as schools, hospitals or government offices built by the State, possibly rendering them as unauthorised developments. The 1993 Planning Act regularised the situation of these developments retrospectively but it did not seek to give the State the exemption it presumed it had.[66]

Under the 1963 Act, complete exemption was given to the use of land for agriculture or forestry. In the 1980s issues such as acidification of water associated with afforestation emerged and from 1990 large afforestation projects were made subject to planning permission and environmental assessment, along with large-scale peat extraction and the use of previously uncultivated land for intensive agriculture.[67] Further changes to peat extraction and afforestation were made following European Court of Justice judgements, with some projects coming under the remit of the Department of Agriculture.

IMPLEMENTATION

A year after the act came into force *The Irish Times* reported that planning no longer had to be 'argued in principle. The need for some sort of positive control of our physical environment ... is now widely accepted: and the (still very large) areas of disagreement between rival schools of thought in the matter nowadays concern the "how" of planning rather than the "why" or "whether".[68] The article goes on to debunk a common refrain in Irish discourse that Irish people only like to live in houses in the language of the time saying 'the old diehard question – would you like to rear your family in a flat?' – is about as enlightened and relevant as the one about your daughter 'marrying a negro'. The article anticipated some 'very hastily scrambled and half-baked schemes' amongst the development plans emitting from the act but despite this 'no great system from Christianity downwards, can be judged solely on the record of its black sheep'.

All eighty-seven planning authorities were required to prepare and adopt development plans for their areas on or before October 1967, but 'for a country with a lack of a planning tradition, or adequate technical staff, this was a daunting task'.[69] Preliminary to the preparation of the first development plans, the minister directed planning authorities to prepare provisional plans, with the Department of Local Government preparing an outline of a typical provisional plan and demonstrating its application to County Meath. A series of seminars were held around the country to demonstrate this approach.

Many planning authorities had to establish and staff planning departments, while even Dublin with its long planning tradition, struggled to meet the requirements of the new legislation. Shortly after its commencement the Association of Municipal Authorities of Ireland sought grants for planning authorities to alleviate the cost imposed on them by the act. In May 1964 An Foras Forbartha (The National Institute for Physical Planning and Construction Research) was established to 'undertake research into and provide training in and advance knowledge of the physical planning and development of cities, towns and rural areas'. An Foras Forbartha participated in the preparation of a provisional plan for Galway city, with the plans acting as a 'dress rehearsal for the development plan'.[70]

It was suggested in the press that, overwhelmed with their new range of responsibilities under the act, some under-resourced planning authorities responded with 'a kind of intellectual lock-jaw or fright-paralysis' resulting in 'refusals of a most nebulous kind'.[71]

In the Dáil concerns were expressed to Minister for Local Government Kevin Boland about the 'grave understaffing in the planning department of Dublin Corporation' which might affect its ability to deliver the plan required under the 1963 Act, with Deputy Michael O'Leary saying Dublin's 'planning staff is ludicrous in comparison with the planning staffs in British cities with populations of a similar size. This is an unfair burden'.

Many planning authorities, most notably Dublin Corporation, failed to meet the October 1967 deadline for the completion of what were termed the 'Mark I' development plans. Their draft plan was published in 1967, generated 7,000 objections and was not approved until 1971. The plan for Dublin County, which was prepared with the help of planners from the Department of Local Government and broadly followed the lines of a report by Planning Consultant Myles Wright took effect in 1972.[72]

Richard Stringer provides an overview of the quality of many of these early development plans: 'Most of the first development plans were based on a quick survey yielding minimal information, often using second hand data, which was well on the way to being obsolete. The analysis of the information gathered rarely deserved so fine a name. As a result, the fact-to-policy link often seemed very tenuous indeed. Some allowances must be made for the absence of a national and regional policy, but this weak fact-to-policy link is best seen in the first or policy sections of the development plans, which were often vague, imprecise and sometimes amounted to little more than pious sentiment. On the social and economic side the link was particularly weak. Here the surveys were even more superficial than guesswork. The tactical components of the development plans were usually better than their policy statements. Yet the programme of intensive objectives was rarely more than the set of projects already in the local authority's files, with some amenity items added. There was inadequate allowance for change, for it was not sufficiently realised that we were trying to foresee or to forestall change. Much of the work was subjective and too many topics were left to that great loophole – further study.'[73]

MYLES WRIGHT'S PLAN FOR DUBLIN

As early as 1911 Geddes had emphasised the importance of regional planning and the regional element was specifically noted in the first Irish planning legislation with the 1934 Act entitled a 'town and regional planning act' though the word 'region' was not defined therein. Adjoining local authorities could resolve to create planning regions but no resolutions were passed, meaning a lost opportunity for joined-up thinking. The act enabled the council of an urban area to add to its district the contiguous parts of an adjoining county council area for planning purposes. In 1940 Tralee Urban District Council secured planning control of the adjoining county area, something Dublin Corporation failed to do when it attempted it later.

There had been a rise in regional consciousness in the 1940s linked to the government's designation of eight emergency regions to be controlled by regional commissioners in the event of an invasion.[75] It was suggested that these bodies might undertake surveys and other roles in the absence of an invasion to better link central and local government.

In his 1961 study Abrams had identified the need for 'a plan for regional development and for the resolution of jurisdictional conflicts'.[76] Despite this the 1963 Act lacked a regional dimension and it has been suggested that this was 'so as not to delay the passing of the act whilst this highly delicate and controversial subject was being debated'.[77] A key weakness was that there was no regional context or co-ordination for the development plans emerging from the eighty-seven planning authorities. The only legislative provision for regional planning was the weak reference in Section 22, which allowed the minister to 'require that the development plans of two or more planning authorities to be co-ordinated in respect of matters and in a manner set out by him'.

In 1964, the country was divided into nine regions for planning purposes, and using his powers of co-ordination under the act the minister appointed international planning experts to undertake studies of the Dublin and Limerick regions. The 1968 Buchanan Report was prepared for the remainder of the country.

By 1965 Minister Blaney was insisting that one of his most important tasks was 'to establish a regional planning framework for our social and economic development programmes'[78] but a 1965 White Paper on Regional Policy was never implemented though a national conference on regional planning was held in Dublin that year.

The British planning consultant Myles Wright was appointed to produce a report on the planning and future development of the Dublin region, largely to assist in its regional co-ordination. His task was to address the problem of how the Dublin region (Dublin City and County, together with Drogheda in County Louth and the counties of Kildare, Meath and Wicklow) should best cope with projected population growth. Metropolitan Dublin, extending into the surrounding counties, was predicted to expand by 275,000 by 1985, while the city centre was expected to lose 73,000 residents simultaneously.

The Greater Dublin Commission 1924–1926 had promoted an 'orderly and systematised lay-out' of the future development of the region, through a new planning board covering Dublin and parts of Louth, Meath and Wicklow. The 1934 Town and Regional Planning Act gave Dublin Corporation the possibility of becoming the 'statutory regional planning authority' for Dublin, Meath, Kildare and Wicklow. However, when Dublin Corporation adopted the act they did so only for their county borough area. In 1936 it was proposed that Dún Laoghaire Borough, Dublin Corporation and Dublin County Council create a joint town planning committee but this was deferred and the Local Government (Dublin) Tribunal of 1935–1938 also recommended a unitary council for County Dublin. The Local Government Tribunal also called for a detailed plan and a land requisition policy where the council would proactively acquire land for future planned uses.

Following the 1963 Act a draft development plan for the Dublin city and county area was prepared by a team, advised by Nathaniel Lichfield and Associates and planner Walter Bor (who was involved in developing the overall plan for Milton Keynes).[79] The Draft Dublin Development Plan (1967) aimed to enhance the economic functions of the city core and attempted to plan for the whole metropolitan area (Corporation and County Council). It aimed to give direction to the separate city and county plans and better balance land use and transport. It drew on a preliminary report from Myles Wright to suggest restrained new towns extensions to the west of the city, requiring greater co-ordination of suburbanisation and the need to avoid premature development. The plan was poorly received by the County Council which wished to assert its independence from the Corporation and it remained a 'holding' or 'shadow' plan in lieu of a ministerial decision on Myles Wright's final report.[80]

Wright's final Dublin *Region Advisory Regional Plan & Final Report* was published in 1967. Although never formally adopted 'it stands as a seminal document in terms of planning ideology and praxis in Ireland. It was particularly influential in the decision to develop new towns'[81] and has been described as the most influential report shaping Dublin's development to the end of the twentieth century.[82]

The Wright plan is a landmark in Irish planning for a number of reasons: it was commissioned to advise central government, it was long term up to 1985, and it was an official recognition of the need for regional planning.[83]

Commonly known as Dublin's 'finger plan', Wright proposed the development of four new linear towns to the west of Dublin, each focused upon a number of small existing settlements: Tallaght-Saggart, Clondalkin-Milltown, Lucan-Palmerstown and Blanchardstown-Mulhuddart, with little consideration given to topography. The term 'finger plan' comes from a 1947 plan that has been the main guiding principle of city planning in Copenhagen. The idea of the Danish plan was to concentrate the urban development of greater Copenhagen in the urban 'fingers' created around the railway network. The Dublin model was to be less sustainable.

Wright's new towns would be separated from one another by green wedges and separated from existing built-up areas by green belts but were closer to the city than the trend in the UK at the time. There was little consideration for how these green wedges could be secured against private development. Within the built-up area, open space was to be provided at the rate of 0.2 hectare per 1,000 persons for small informal parks and a similar per capita allocation for play areas within the residential neighbourhoods. Local areas of open space, churches, shops, pubs, clubs and other basic social facilities were to be no more than 0.8 kilometres from any dwelling, while small shops and primary

schools should be no more than 0.4 kilometres away. These neighbourhoods would be low-rise and low density. The plan proposed
accommodating population growth of over 300,000 by 1985 in the
four new towns each with between 60,000 and 100,000 people. Less
than thirty years earlier Abercrombie's sketch plan had suggested that
these villages might reach between 3,000 to 10,000 people. Three of
these towns; Tallaght, Clondalkin-Lucan and Blanchardstown were
developed. Wright underestimated population growth in the region,
assuming a population of 1,200,000 by 1985 but this had already
reached 1,288,000 by 1981. This saw overspill into neighbouring
counties. The private car was a key driver of Wright's plan: 'Ireland
is coming late into the age of a car for most families. There is every
sign that Irishmen, as sturdy individualists and democrats, will wish
to use cars fully … Achievement, step by step, of the best practicable
conditions for greatly increased motor traffic is thus a main aim of
the Advisory Plan, and the prime determinant of where to place new
urban developments.'[84]

Elsewhere Wright argued that there was no evidence that a
suburban rail service could be economically viable in Dublin and
that there was no reason to subsidise rail passenger transport 'on social,
humanitarian or any other grounds'.[85] He also rejected high-density
development, which might support passenger rail and emphasised the
need to balance a sense of openness with the benefits of an urban
location: 'The optimum location in a motor age is one that combines
local spaciousness (at home and work) with regional concentration –
that is, easy access to a wide choice of jobs and employees, customers,
suppliers, and facilities of all kinds'.[86]

Frank McDonald attributes the focus on road development and car
users to engineers who 'were able to get away with this because they
always held the whip hand, tracing their lineage in local government
back to Victorian times. The city planners, by contrast, were mere
parvenus, without the power to impose their will even if they had
a mind to do so. Thus, in any contest between the two professions,
the engineers usually won hands down. Throughout, they also had the
attentive ear of successive city managers who were more than willing
to endorse their road schemes'.[87]

The risks of sprawl in Dublin were evident by the late 1960s with
geographer J.P. Haughton noting 'there is a belt of development
around Dublin which is greater in extent than the whole existing

built-up area of the city' and warning that there was increasing pressure from developers to expand outside the city while dereliction in the city centre grew.[88]

The Wright Plan visualised little or no role or prospects for city centre Dublin, particularly as regards residential use. The Wright Plan made only passing reference to Dublin's architectural qualities and there was no detailed plan for the city centre. Wright hoped that the full range of employment prospects and social facilities would be provided in the new areas. However, this did not happen. The new towns in the UK were developed by special corporations who had power to acquire and distribute land, and to provide, where necessary, all other facilities like shopping, recreational, and other community uses. The Dublin situation was different, as most land remained in private ownership.[89]

Wright suggested that a special agency be created to oversee the physical development of the entire Dublin region in order to guide the implementation of the regional plan. He argued that without such an agency insufficient administrative and technical skill would be available to support the plan, leading to disappointing performance and, consequently, public disillusionment with the planning system. This did not take place and the lack of co-ordination between transport infrastructure, land use, rising traffic and sprawl can be somewhat attributed to this.

Though Wright's plans to accommodate rapid expansion rather than piecemeal development along existing village main streets such as Drumcondra and Stillorgan was well received politically, the report was never adopted formally by the minister. Despite this, certain aspects of its proposals were to shape the subsequent development of the city. Elements were incorporated into the 1972 Dublin County Development Plan. Erika Hanna has described town planners 'enthusiastically' supporting 'a radical remodelling of Dublin's landscape in order to support mass car ownership' in the period and cites a report by Karl-Heinz Schaechterle's *Traffic Investigation Concerning the Future Main Road Network* report of 1965.[90] For Hanna, with their emphasis on family housing and open space, the 'creation of large suburban housing estates as envisaged by Myles Wright' represented a 'physical manifestation of an attempt to create the Christian, family-centred society as inscribed in the constitution'.

Geographers Andrew MacLaran and Michael Punch, assessing the Myles Wright report, concluded: 'Ultimately, the suggested method of physical planning was fairly traditional, involving a blueprint approach orchestrated by a body of "experts" with little direct consideration for the needs or values of the likely end-users, nor indeed with much room for flexibility or informality in form or function of the future urban environment. Wright's prescribed standards for open space and walking distances coincided with those set down by Perry (1929) who, in turn, had been strongly influenced by the work of Unwin and Geddes'.[91]

Addressing the Irish Planning Institute's National Conference in 1991, then deputy leader of the Labour Party Ruairi Quinn noted that 'whether one agrees with the conclusions of Myles Wright, which were disputed at the time, there was a political direction and there was a political purpose'.[92]

Problems with planning for Dublin continued. The Eastern Regional Development Organisation (ERDO) strategy was published in 1985 and was to set out a strategy for the growth of the region to 2011. The future city predicted by ERDO was of a population of 1.5 million in a sprawling metropolis connected by four- and six-lane motorways with little growth of the city centre. Blanchardstown was to grow to 125,000. Contemporary reactions to the ERDO strategy differed. At its publication the strategy was praised as a milestone study prepared by Irish planners without overseas experts. Writing in the winter 1985 edition of the journal Pleanáil, planner Brendan McGrath argued that to success-fully influence development on such a scale over a thirty-year period required a persuasive and coherent argument which was absent in the ERDO strategy. McGrath also criticised the lack of consideration for the traffic impacts of the strategy.[93] In a response to McGrath's comments then Deputy Chief Planner for Dublin Corporation Leo O'Reilly who led the development of the ERDO study dismissed professional criticism of the strategy as coming from the 'cosy' school of planning which was more interested in radical action that reality.[94]

Local government reforms in the 1990s and 2000s find their origins in the establishment of an expert group in 1990 under the chairmanship of Tom Barrington. The key issues with local government identified in the report included a poor level of integration of public services at local/regional level; the lack of a structured regional level and a poorly developed municipal level; along with a central government policy role which was poorly linked with meeting local expectations.[96]

There were two addendums attached to the 1991 Barrington Report on Local Government, one by architect Mary Doyle, who proposed a more defined Metropolitan Region for Dublin incorporating Kildare, Meath and Wicklow, defined by the limits of daily commuter travel. She hoped that a 'Metropolitan Regional Authority would co-ordinate the activities of its various subdivisions in relation to future planning policies for environment, finance, housing, transport and many other relevant bodies and activities'.

LICHFIELD AND LIMERICK

UK planning consultant Nathaniel Lichfield was appointed to undertake a study of the Limerick region (Limerick, Clare and North Tipperary). This region had Ireland's strongest history in regional thinking. In 1959 Shannon Free Airport Company (SFADCo) was established by Lemass. It was later to become Shannon Development. Under Brendan O'Regan, SFADCo acted as Ireland's first regional development agency for the Shannon region. This included planning and development above the county unit, developing strategies to encourage regional growth centres and the region's infrastructure, tourism and economic offering. Bishop of Limerick from 1974 to 1995, Revd Dr Jeremiah Newman was a former Professor of Sociology at St Patrick's College, Maynooth who led the compilation of the Muintir na Tíre-funded Limerick Rural Survey 1958–1964. This can be seen as a successor the civic surveys of the 1920s and 1940s and aimed to influence policymakers and decision-making by analysing trends in Limerick. He also wrote on regional planning, publishing *New Dimensions in Regional Planning: A Case Study of Ireland*, and was the first chairman of An Foras Forbartha's physical planning and development committee.

In 1968 the Mid-West Regional Development Organisation – a voluntary co-ordinating body along the lines proposed by Lichfield was established for the Limerick region. The following year this was extended to the other eight regions and the Regional Development Organisations (RDOs) were to 'co-ordinate the programmes for development in each region'.

BUCHANAN REPORT

With studies underway for the Dublin and Limerick regions, in 1966 the government, with the support of the UN, commissioned the English architects and town planners Colin Buchanan and Partners, in association with Economic Consultants Ltd and An Foras Forbartha, to carry out studies of the remaining seven regions of the country, to 'indicate economic growth potential, identify possible development centres, establish the level of change needed in infrastructure to facilitate growth and make proposals for policy decisions to be taken by the government, including measures to implement such proposals'.[97]

Essentially the team was expected to prepare a strategy for development for the country which would resolve a long-running dispute on the size, number and location of 'development centres' for industrial development and, provide a physical strategy for the achievement of the economic objectives as set out in the Second Programme for Economic Expansion.[98]

The consultants concluded that greater concentration would lead to greater employment. The Buchanan Report advocated the concentration of industrial development within the 'growth centres' of Dublin, Cork, Limerick–Shannon, Athlone, Drogheda, Dundalk, Galway, Sligo and Waterford; and four local growth centres in Castlebar, Cavan, Letterkenny and Tralee. The report was based on the assumption that growth could only be self-sustaining in centres above a critical size and advocated prioritising these centres.

Though internationally acclaimed, the Buchanan Report was shelved 'pending further examination' and new studies requested from the newly-established advisory Regional Development Organisations in each of the nine regions.[99] Reflecting the tensions of building a strong international Dublin as well as balanced regional development alongside a parochial political system, the recommendations were ignored.

Researchers Meredith and van Egeraat note that the backlash to this controversial proposal for a largely rural country led to alternative measures which actively discouraged concentration and promoted dispersion of industrial investment.[100] In 1972 the government accepted the Buchanan target population figures for the nine main growth centres (Dublin, Cork, Limerick-Shannon, Waterford, Dundalk, Galway, Drogheda, Sligo and Athlone) but did not support these with any policy instruments and the industrial policy implemented by the

Industrial Development Authority from the same year on was incompatible with the government's targets.[101, 102]

Former head of Research at the Institute of Public Administration Desmond Roche considered the 1963 Act the most notable innovation of the 1960s but held that with Neil Blaney's departure from the Department of Local Government in 1966 'went much of the verve and force behind the physical planning movement' as his successor 'lacked his fire and determination to transform the planning system into a positive agency for national development … Blaney would certainly have put up a powerful fight against the fate of the Buchanan Report'.[103]

In 1969 the Report of the Public Service Organisation Review Group recommended the establishment of a super ministry of regional development, with an enhanced role for 'Regional Planning and Development' but this too was ignored. A government statement on industrial policy in 1969 ignored the Buchanan Report and advocated dispersing industrial activity as widely as possible. In Northern Ireland the Macrory local government report of the following year proposed a central Ministry of Development in charge of planning, roads, water and sewerage. This was heavily prompted by the Troubles and the Department of the Environment became the sole planning authority for Northern Ireland in 1973. The Planning Act, 2011 transferred planning powers back to local authorities in Northern Ireland in 2015.

It is interesting to contrast the approach in the Republic with that of Northern Ireland where a Regional Physical Development Strategy 1975–1995 was finalised in 1977, which in theory at least distributed growth points across Northern Ireland. It has been described as a strategy of forecasts and projections produced by planners for planners but it showed that viable regional policy could be developed on the island.[104]

MODERN REGIONS

Throughout the 1980s the status of regional planning fell further.[105] Later, in 1991 the Local Government Act empowered the Minister for the Environment to establish regional authorities 'for the purpose of promoting the co-ordination in different areas of the state of the provision of public services'.[106] In 1994 eight regional authorities were established, made up of councillors from the city and county councils in the region. They were required to prepare a non-statutory regional report on the needs of their region and review development plans.

In 1999 the country was divided into two regions to ensure poorer counties could continue to draw down the maximum level of EU funding. This saw the creation of two regional assemblies, the Border, Midland and Western Regional Assembly and the Southern and Eastern Regional Assembly. For Grist, their impact on the planning system has been negligible though they can consider the reviews of development plans conducted by regional authorities.[107]

In 1999 a report was drawn up for the Greater Dublin Area local authorities with the Dublin and Mid-East Regional Authorities and the Department of the Environment to investigate the rapid growth rates in Dublin, Meath, Kildare and Wicklow. The Strategic Planning Guidelines for the Greater Dublin Area (GDA) looked at matters such as economic and development trends and infrastructure as a way of co-ordinating planning across the region. The 2000 Act included a provision for the preparation of regional planning guidelines for every regional authority and gave the GDA guidelines the status of statutory regional planning guidelines. These were to link development plans with the forthcoming National Spatial Strategy.

Ciarán Cuffe has identified the multiplicity of statutory 'regions' for different purposes as a source of confusion and an impediment to joined-up thinking and a regional tier of planning in Ireland. For example, the three regional assemblies under the 2013 Local Government Bill do not align to the three European Parliament constituencies; the Irish river basin districts are different to the waste districts; tourism regions and the Health Service Executive (HSE) regions which all have different boundaries and this compounds the problem.[108]

POSITIVE PLANNING

The 1963 Act was heralded with a great deal of hope and hyperbole. MacLaran and Punch describe an 'optimistic and expansionist spirit of the age'.[109] For Frank McDonald the act was to sweep away 'bureaucratic cobwebs' in a new era of positive planning.[110] The legislation was considered a potential panacea for many ills, with *The Irish Times* reporting that the bill might allow Dublin Corporation to fund the development of amenities at Portmarnock strand which was in the

County Council area though 'used mostly by people from the city'.[111] At the time of the 1963 Act the inclusion of 'development' in its title was seen as addressing the complaint that 'planning was too negative and that its powers were often used by public authorities solely to prevent private enterprises from doing what the authorities themselves were unwilling or unable to do'.[112]

Central to the 'positive planning' objective of the act was Section 77(l)(e) which enabled a planning authority to undertake the development or renewal of obsolete areas, which theoretically permitted them to become involved in development and dealing in land. This emphasis quickly abated. Lacking finance, a risk-taking mentality and organisational nous, local authorities did not become involved in the commercial world of land acquisition and development as Section 77 of the act envisaged.

The government did provide a loan of £3 million to the local authorities of Dublin Corporation and Dublin County Council (£1 million annually from 1966 to 1968) to provide for the creation of a land bank. The facility was mainly taken up by Dublin Corporation to acquire 730 hectares of land, mainly in the new towns for public housing and ancillary uses.[113]

McDonald is critical of the work attempted at the time, calling Dublin Corporation's proposal to redevelop the entire area bounded by O'Connell Street and Capel Street, Parnell Street and the quays as an 'utterly absurd idea … conceived by the English master planner Nathaniel Lichfield and endorsed by the City Council in 1964 at a time when everything seemed possible'.[114] A report on the north Dublin city centre called for the redevelopment of a 35-acre area that would require £35 million to acquire and redevelop. Comprehensive redevelopment, including compulsory purchase orders and demolition was proposed in the face of local concerns. In 1966 the Corporation decided to scale down the redevelopment across a number of phases. According to *Build* magazine 'the Lichfield plan is in a heap … Empty pockets have brought back a sense of realism' but this was after 'a headlong rush by speculators, auctioneers and other professional wide boys to acquire property in the area ahead of the Corporation', according to the magazine.[115]

The abolition of domestic rates then increased local authorities' financial dependence on central funding. This further eroded the potential of 'positive planning' and saw the emphasis shift to development control.[116] Many Industrial Development Authority (IDA) industrial estates, particularly in towns, were, however, acquired and developed in conjunction with the planning authorities.

McGuirk and MacClaran suggest that weaknesses in the current planning system derive from fact that its role is 'essentially permissory. The fact that planning departments lack spending powers severely hampers what can be achieved, as planners have to rely on the private sector and the co-ordination of other local authority spending departments for the execution of plans. This clearly places planning in a position of dependency in relation to private-sector property development and investment interests, requiring development plans to be drawn up in a manner which complements market processes'.[117]

Without adequate powers to implement the development plan or the ability to control the most vital development resource, land, the local authority witnessed the emergence of a scramble for land between large-scale housing developers desperate to acquire large amounts of land zoned for development. Land dealing became a significant and profitable element in the development of new residential areas, with developers of large parcels subdividing their holdings and selling them on to smaller builders. This ensured that any public control or co-ordination of the phasing of development was rendered almost impossible with conditions prevailing within the private market becoming the sole determinant.[118] By the 1980s political disdain for planning and its long-term nature along with the absence of positive planning were regular features of planning debates. Where low-density suburban housing estates grew quickly, local authorities took the blame for a shortfall in services and facilities, which in fact could only have been prevented by integrated regional planning and a coherent national urban and settlement policy.[119]

PLANNERS

The 1963 Act has been described as when planning 'came of age' and became a distinctive discipline in Ireland but when the act came into force in 1964 there was no full- time planning course in the country. Up to that point there was little demand for town planners and few people qualified.

A crash course was organised for interested engineers and architects in the local authorities. County engineers outside of Dublin and

Cork – most of whom knew little or nothing about planning – were allocated the role of providing planning services and a travelling roadshow of senior Department of Local Government officials and UK consultants toured the country to brief and sell planning to the elected members. An Taisce gave a lecture to county managers, county engineers and planning officers on nature conservation in the context of the act at a Town and Country Planning Symposium.

E.H. Doubleday, the Hertfordshire county planning officer, had told the Town Planning Institute's appreciation course in 1962 that from the 'tiny core of highly skilled men' (which was just ten 'whole time and experienced planners' – three in Dublin County Council, five in Dublin city, one in Cork and one in the Department of Local Government) it would be necessary to 'school a new generation of planners; to teach the public representatives and people the nature of, and the vital necessity for, first class physical planning'. Doubleday offered to take eight student planners to Hertfordshire for summer work experience.[120]

The shortage of professional planning expertise had significant consequences. The bulk of time and limited resources was put into service in control and it meant early development plans were of varying quality. In many local authorities planning functions were vested in engineering staff as an interim measure but this became the status quo in places. This was despite Blaney's assertion that 'The importance of planning in local government is such that I think we must look ahead to the time when local authorities or groupings of local authorities will employ qualified planning advisers or the chief professional officers will have planning qualifications. Indeed I envisage that in due course the possession of a qualification in planning will become at least a desirable qualification for the top technical posts'.[121] It was almost a decade after the act that (unimplemented) local government reforms first advocated creating a planning and development officer as head of a planning and development team in each authority which would have formalised recognition of a planner's professional skills and offered a career structure to planners.

In July 1963 the Minister told the Dáil that he was conscious of the need for planning training and research and that 'in order to augment the overall supply of qualified planners I have secured the cooperation of the Dublin Vocational Education Committee – for which I am most grateful – in providing a two-year postgraduate course in planning for suitably qualified architects, engineers and surveyors'.[122] For Blaney planning was a 'necessary, continuous and co-ordinated process directed towards the good of the community. To advise on the principles and measures necessary for the proper co-ordination of development is the function of the planner'.[123] Blaney saw a survey of the existing area as a key part of developing a plan; however, here the minister foresaw a limited need for planners, arguing 'Needless to say, much of the preparatory work for a development plan can be undertaken by persons who are not qualified planners. Extensive use can clearly be made of the professional and administrative skills which are found in every local authority establishment'. This undermined the profession from the outset.[124]

In 1936 Manning Robertson had called for more to be done to ensure planning was seen as a distinct profession in Ireland, saying this required a high-quality town planning course, of a standard equivalent to those in architecture, engineering and surveying and recognised that 'we should have in mind the ultimate formation of a Town Planning Institute of Ireland'. This took almost another forty years.[125]

The first planning school was set up in Bolton Street (Dublin Institute of Technology), offering a Diploma in Town Planning. In 1973 University College Dublin established a diploma which became a Masters in Regional and Urban Planning in 1979, while Queen's University Belfast also offered a planning qualification.

At the time, the Royal Town Planning Institute's Irish Branch, which consisted largely of planners who had passed the Institute's external examinations or had studied in the UK, did not accept the UCD qualification, leading some planners and recent graduates to investigate the establishment of an Irish institute to represent the interests of current and future graduates and the profession as a whole.

Planners working in central government, led by Bernard Muckley and Gerry Walker, came together with a group of local authority planners, the Association of Physical Planners of Ireland set up by Enda Conway, to establish the Irish Planning Institute (IPI) in November 1975 with Patrick Shaffrey as its first president.[126] Further professional planning degree courses were established in DIT in 2001 and in University College Cork in 2006, both of which were quickly accredited by the IPI.

A factor which constrained the 1963 Act was the absence of a professional or career structure for planners in most local authorities. Discussing the eighty-seven planning authorities 'of whom at least 75 per cent had not the population or resources to support a planning team. For many of these, planning was essentially a control function to be exercised by a member of the engineering staff. Bannon said many focused on meeting statutory requirements, nothing more.[127]

According to Frank McDonald most members of the public who viewed the 1967 Draft Dublin Development Plan 'came away thoroughly confused by all the coloured zonings maps that the planners had to put together to meet their statutory obligations under the 1963 planning act' though for McDonald the fact that a draft development plan 'was produced at all was something of a miracle' as 'the new act imposed enormous responsibility on the local authorities yet, when it was being processed through the Dáil, there were no more than a dozen qualified town planners in the whole country and crash courses had to be laid on in Bolton Street to make instant planners out of a motley collection of architects, engineers and surveyors. The Corporation's own planning department remained seriously undermanned throughout the 1960s and the harassed staff, operating out of a cramped old building in Christchurch Place, were barely able to cope with the day-to-day flow of planning applications – never mind draw up a comprehensive development plan for the city'.[128]

Patrick Shaffrey wrote in 1985 that 'twenty two years since the planning act was passed, most major local authorities do not employ a planner in a chief officer status, even though planning matters are now among their most important concerns'. Shaffrey suggests that the environment was not as good as it should be and 'future historians may partly attribute this to the lack of professional planning inputs at the highest levels'[129] with more than half of these in Dublin and Cork. In 1983 there were 147 professional planners working in local authorities in Ireland and a year later this has risen to 182 persons in professional planning posts in all local authorities, Minister for the Environment John Boland told the Dáil. In some cases the planning department was a one-person operation and lacking resources.

Reflecting on the state of the profession in 1985 in an edition of the *Pleanáil* journal marking the tenth anniversary of the Irish Planning Institute its president Feargall Kenny questioned why planners were not yet the dominant force in the planning and development process as 'instead the running is being made by others; politicians, semi-state bodies, entrepreneurs, Monsignor Horan, Tony Gregory et al'. Kenny attributed this to the failure of planners to assert themselves and present the objectives and achievements of the profession positively.[130]

As Grist notes, introducing a planning system into a country with a limited tradition of planning outside of Dublin presented certain challenges in terms of skills and public understanding.[131] Minister Blaney understood the importance of public support for the new planning system, saying during a Seanad debate on the legislation 'if we are to improve on the 1934 Act, the first thing we really need is public support … without public support urban renewal and re-development which can and undoubtedly will be a touchy matter will not be possible … on several occasions I appealed to public people, members of the Oireachtas and of councils throughout the country, for this particular public support. It is mainly through members of the Oireachtas and of local councils that we must seek guidance for the public so that they will realise what planning can mean to them. I join fully and wholeheartedly in the view that we do need public opinion behind us if we are to benefit by the proposals in the bill'.

During the Seanad debates Blaney discussed the role of public education on planning with a potential role for his department and the Department of Education in order to 'take every opportunity to get across to the public as full an understanding as possible of what planning really means' with the minister not ruling out the use of films and television for this.[132]

A major programme of public information was launched around the legislation, including the publication of explanatory memoranda, the preparation of planning and development circulars and the publication of a layman's guide to the Irish planning system called *Your Development Plan*. Blaney, discussing the 1963 legislation, acknowledged that 'Good public relations are important and the planning system must ensure that the public, including the land owner, the tenant, the house owner, the shopkeeper and the developer, will be enabled to know with as much assurance as possible how the development of their area is likely to proceed and how that development is likely to affect themselves'.[133]

The UK-headquartered Town Planning Institute held its 1967 annual conference in Dublin and the International Federation of Housing and Planning met in Dublin in 1969s reflecting continued efforts to promote planning and planners.

AN FORAS FORBARTHA

Charles Abrams had discussed the need for research into planning and construction in his report. In the spring of 1963 Padraig Ó hUigínn, an official in the Department of Local Government on secondment to the UN, wrote to Minister Blaney suggesting that the UN Technical Assistance Programme might aid the establishment of a national physical planning institute in Ireland. Ó hUigínn explained that though Ireland's case was weakened by its relatively high national per capita income, the UN accepted that some developed countries such as Iceland and Ireland lacked certain technical expertise.[134]

Ó hUigínn envisaged that the proposed institute would train architects and engineers in physical planning techniques and would prepare development plans for local authorities who were unwilling or unable to fulfil the task. It would also undertake basic research on things such as future population and settlement trends, referencing some of the recommendations of the Abrams report. Ó hUigínn anticipated that the assistance might be similar to the support given to the Economic Research Institute by the Ford Foundation. Blaney's letter to Lemass summarising Ó hUigínn's proposal also referred to the need to draw up construction standards for highrise buildings.[135]

Opposition to the institute emerged from an unlikely quarter with Minister for External Affairs Frank Aiken protesting that he had not been consulted and that the UN was unlikely to provide assistance. Aiken withdrew his objections when the Irish mission to the UN confirmed that assistance had been offered. Aiken's objections appear to have arisen from a fear that accepting assistance would require that Ireland be reclassified as a less developed country.[136]

The United Nations Special Fund agreed to provide expert services, fellowships for further study and the training of personnel, books and equipment to a total value of $725,000 to assist the operation of the institute during its first five years. In its first three years this assistance was estimated at £148,000 with the State providing funding of £183,370 in the same period. Amongst the experts drafted in to provide the necessary skills to the new organisation was architect and urban designer Geoffrey Copcutt who had left Northern Ireland for the UN's Urban Design Special Fund Office after criticising the Stormont administration for its choice of site for the new city of Craigavon.

An Foras Forbartha, the National Institute for Physical Planning and Construction Research, was established by the government in 1964. Ó hUigínn was to become its first managing director and it had a staff of twenty-eight by 1965. One of the 1963 Act's principal architects Gerry Meagher, an assistant secretary in the Department of Local Government, became its first chairman.

An Foras Forbartha's work was divided into four research divisions: Construction, Planning, Roads and Water Resources, with a fifth division looking at Transport and Information. Its aims were to undertake research into, provide training in and advance knowledge of:

a. the physical planning and development of cities, towns and rural areas, including the preservation and improvement of amenities in the context of the Local Government (Planning and Development) Act;
b. various aspects of building and road construction;
c. problems arising from or incidental to physical planning and development, including environmental services and standards, traffic and transportation.

In 1981, foreshadowing Charlie McCreevy's decentralisation policy twenty years later, Minister for the Environment Ray Burke decided that An Foras Forbartha should move from Dublin to Cork but in the face of objections the move never happened. Instead, in September 1987, the government decided to abolish the 200-employee institute that had been set up with UN assistance on cost grounds. Staff took voluntary redundancy or transferred elsewhere, including to the Department of Environment's Environmental Research Unit, the National Roads Authority and the Environmental Protection Agency. According to Martin Mansergh it would 'probably never have been abolished if its staff had agreed to go to Cork'.[137]

An Foras Forbartha has been described as 'the bright star on Ireland's planning horizon'.[138] The Irish Planning Institute called the abolition of An Foras Forbartha 'ill-considered and rash', confirming 'the apparent lack of commitment of the present government towards planning and the environment'.[139] The abolition of the institute had much to do with matters and personnel which ended up under scrutiny of the planning tribunals twenty years later.[140]

CONCLUSION

Frank McDonald is scathing of the 1963 Act's practical impact, concluding that after twenty-two years of planning Dublin was a 'mess'. His 1985 book *The Destruction of Dublin* seeks to establish whether politicians, architects, speculators or planners with 'second-rate minds' were to blame for this.[141]

For some the 1963 Act followed too closely the system imposed by the 1947 British Town and Country Planning Act which operated in a highly urbanised setting and for a more disciplined society 'imposed by war and its aftermath'[142] while Section 77 of the act which enabled a planning authority to develop land, was 'the greatest source of false expectations'.[143] As early as one year after the commencement of the act, however, the press were reporting concerns that planning was overly negative.[144]

Bannon attributes the failure of the 1963 Act to live up to expectations due to the absence of necessary reforms elsewhere and a subsequent policy vacuum.[145] This was to become pronounced in the 1970s, which was a time of growing disenchantment. Under the act planning had developed 'a formidable legal and institutional apparatus' that proved 'extraordinarily sterile ... the great engine found itself operating in a vast intellectual scrubland in which, in a whole generation, virtually no cultivation had taken place'.[146]

In 1983 An Foras Forbartha's report 'Twenty Years of Planning: a Review of the System since 1963' suggested improvements to the post-1963 system. Written at a time of disillusion, it was developed following input from developers, the judiciary, local government, universities and others (unfortunately any politicians invited to participate were unable to) and acknowledged up front that given its genesis it focused more on the negative than the positive. The report noted that planning's core role was to influence decision-making through the development plan rather than spending the money itself and this meant some development plans had an air of unreality which reflected badly on planning as a whole. An Foras Forbartha's report identified key areas in which the 1963 Act was now deficient, namely the need for public participation; the unbalanced nature of urbanisation; the need for energy conservation; the need to generate employment and the need to preserve our ecology and built environment.[147]

5

Garden Cities, Ballymun and Bungalow Bliss

NOTHING NATURAL ABOUT SUBURBIA

For Conor McCabe 'a lot of what we consider to be normal and natural about Irish housing dates from the 1920s',[1] writing 'there is nothing natural about suburbia' and being distant from your employment. Despite this, Irish antipathy to higher density living has deep roots.

In 1898 English reformer Ebenezer Howard published *Tomorrow: a Peaceful Path to Real Reform* followed by a second edition *Garden Cities of Tomorrow* in 1902. This was to prove one of the most influential publications in town planning, leading directly to the development of the 'garden cities' of Letchworth and Welwyn and setting into motion the idea of planned, self-contained communities surrounded by greenbelts, containing proportionate areas of residences, industry and agriculture. The term proved popular and in 1902 the 'Deutsche Gartenstadtgesellschaft' (German Garden City Society) was formed and the book was translated into many languages. For McCabe 'it is not a coincidence that the dominant form of housing in modern Ireland, i.e. one-family occupancy with a garden in suburbia, can be traced back to a small book by an English reformist' as Ireland has frequently looked to Britain on housing and planning matters.[2]

Dating from the latter half of the nineteenth century, the Burnaby estate in Greystones, County Wicklow can be considered one of Ireland's first planned urban housing developments. There, the land agent of the Hawkins-Whitshed family, a Mr Wynne, sought to maximise income from the estate. As early as 1889 it was rumoured that it had 'Been decided by the owners of the Burnaby estate ... to open up a portion of the property, commanding splendid sea and mountain views, for building terraces and villas, and that several handsome roadways will be immediately commenced'.[3] Described as 'Surrey-like', the Burnaby estate was designed by the Dublin practice of James Rawson Carroll and Frederick Bachelor along low density, garden suburb lines, accommodating local families. The streets are laid out as a grid. The plot sizes are large and in the range of 0.2 to 0.8 hectares, often sufficiently large to accommodate tennis courts, with houses set well back from the street.[4]

From the early 1900s low land costs led to the development of very low-density suburbs. The 1919 *Housing for the Working Classes in Ireland* report provided 'plans for the lay-out of typical sites and for various types of houses' on a low-density scale of no more than ten houses to the acre. High densities were associated with the slums and it was argued that by erecting new dwellings in the city centre old slums were merely being replaced with new ones (ignoring the preference of slum dwellers to remain in the city centre though preferably in cottages which could be developed at relatively high densities).[5] The Artisans' Dwellings Company found that its cottages experienced far higher demand than

Burnaby estate in Greystones, County Wicklow is one of Ireland's first planned housing developments. (Reproduced courtesy of the National Library of Ireland: L_ROY_07791)

its flats. Brendan Behan's family was one of those whose accommodation was deemed uninhabitable and they moved from Russell Street
to Crumlin, a move famously derided as 'to hell or to Kimmage' and
dramatised in a RTÉ series of that name in 1978.

Most witnesses at the 1913 housing inquiry that followed the
Church Street collapses favoured suburbanisation. Geddes argued
for a social mix in garden suburbs and emphasised the role of citizen
participation, especially by the poor, who were too often treated 'as if
they were mere passive creatures to be housed like cattle'.

An official report by chief engineering inspector of the Local
Government Board Peter Cowan in 1918 calculated that there was
need to provide improved housing for at least 41 per cent of the city's
population – that is 29,500 families. This translated into a need to
construct 16,500 new houses and to 're-model' 13,000 tenements with
Cowan recommending that at least 12,000 should be built in Clontarf,
Drumcondra, Cabra and Crumlin. These were laid out at low densities
along garden city norms, though schemes such as Capwell and Turners
Cross in Cork were at higher densities.[6] In 1923 the Cork Borough
Restoration Committee said that the city needed at least 2,500 houses
and the same year the Limerick Housing Association called for 3,000
houses, writing 'the housing conditions in Limerick are a perpetual crime
against humanity'.[7] By 1925 it was said that 'Housing in Dublin today is
more than a 'question', and more than a 'problem' – 'it is a tragedy!'[8]

A key figure in planning at the time was E. A. Aston (1873–1949), who
was a zealous garden city advocate and admirer of Geddes and Unwin.
Aston was Honorary Secretary of the Greater Dublin Movement and
the Dublin Citizens' Association and one of the founders of the Housing
and Town Planning Association of Ireland. He was strongly in favour
of 'the development of plantations for city workers in convenient rural
areas' in cooperation with transport authorities.[9] For some Aston was
'undoubtedly the greatest Irish name associated with the promotion of
modern town planning prior to the 1960s'.[10]

Many in Dublin Corporation resisted suburbanisation, prefer-
ring infill development and tenement refurbishment. The State's
emphasis on suburban houses appears to have had Church approval
with the replacement of tenements by individual houses being
attributed to an improvement in morals as well as health.[11] In 1911
Dublin Corporation sent two councillors, Thomas O'Beirne and
Charles Travers, to Birmingham to examine that city's approach to

working-class housing. Upon their return they argued for more parks and amenities and that the 'development of the city and all Irish towns along modern town planning lines should begin immediately'.[12] Despite this, town planning sympathisers were a minority in the pre-war Dublin Corporation. The support of the Irish Parliamentary Party was central to the future of the garden suburb in Dublin and this was not forthcoming.[13] In 1913 the party's housing spokesman J.J. Clancy said that what was wanted was 'not town-planning, or such ornamental development, but something that will house the people afresh in those localities in which now the conditions of life are abominable and intolerable'.

A view that planning had little to offer working-class areas persisted. Many nationalist Dublin City councillors, including W.T. Cosgrave, argued that it was unsuitable as housing should be provided near where people worked.[14] Alderman Thomas Kelly 'the most trenchant opponent of town planning within the Corporation', argued persuasively that because unskilled casual labour was predominant in Dublin, then the municipality must concentrate on providing cheap dwellings as close as possible to sources of work in the city centre.[15] Cheap tram fares for workers existed in some other British cities but were not considered feasible in Dublin where the Corporation did not control the tram system.[16] Kelly arguably was an advocate for sound planning, finding himself against one stream of the early movement that could not see beyond garden suburb living. Kelly's holistic concern for employment, community and transport are certainly principles that are key to modern planning.

The Housing (Ireland) Act, 1919, aimed to compel local authorities to provide adequate housing, though different views remained on whether the main development should be in city centres or in the suburbs. The act accepted the 'Tudor Walters' standard of housing densities or not more than twelve houses to the acre outside urban areas. The British government had commissioned the Tudor Walters Report in 1918. Raymond Unwin served on the Tudor Walters committee and is believed to have written much of its report pressing for standards and densities of housing based on those of the garden city, accommodating houses in culs-de-sac rather than terraces. The Housing and Town Planning Association of Ireland founded in 1911 strongly promoted suburbanisation and garden suburbs. Abercrombie and the authors of the Dublin Civic Survey also promoted this model.

There were complex drivers for suburbanisation. In his book *The Destruction of Dublin* Frank McDonald describes Dublin Corporation's chief planning officer from 1936 to the mid-1970s, engineer Michael O'Brien, as 'the Archbishop's man' in Dublin Corporation.[17] He 'had regular meetings with the Archbishop of Dublin at his palace in Drumcondra to discuss the planning of the city. Thus, when the Corporation proposed building two-bedroom houses on a new estate in Finglas, Archbishop McQuaid put his foot down. As far as he was concerned, Catholic couples needed more breeding space, and that was the end of that. And when the Corporation set about acquiring the Shaw estate in Terenure for what was to become Bushy Park, someone discovered that Michael O'Brien had done a private deal with the Archbishop whereby the best part of the land, where most of the mature trees were, was given to an order of nuns to set up an exclusive convent school'.[18]

In 1922 *The Irish Builder and Engineer* warned that rather than the 'bad old flat system' the future for Dublin lay in 'the small, self-contained detached or semi-detached house on virgin sites'.[19] This was reinforced by a policy that saw flats in central areas let at cheaper Corporation rents than those for suburban cottages attracting the poorest who could not afford to move to the suburbs and meet the associated transport costs. The discussion on higher-density housing was restricted to flats rather than other solutions. The Anglican Archbishop of Dublin argued that the welfare of citizens was linked to their 'ready access to fresh air', suggesting that only suburban dwellings allowed their occupants 'to live healthily and with decency' and that factories would follow workers to the outskirts.[20] Architectural historian Ellen Rowley quotes a planning official of the time as believing lower density allowed a more 'Christian lifestyle'.[21] A 1932 article warned of the 'moral dangers of the common staircase' and that flats were linked to communism.[22]

TUDORBETHAN OUTRAGE

A key figure in the Town Tenants League, Dublin Corporation councillor Coughlan Briscoe, took an interest in town planning and visited schemes in Europe. Returning from representing Dublin Corporation at the Royal Institute of British Architects 1910 Town Planning Conference, he recommended that Dublin should build a garden suburb at Marino.[23] The idea crystalised when the holder of the land, James Walker, indicated his willingness to make his 50 acres available to the corporation for the building of a miniature garden city.[24] A proposal before the corporation in 1910 to progress the idea was met with the protest 'We want no garden city – give us working class dwellings'.[25] Clearly planning was seen as distant from the immediate problems of the day.

In April 1914 Raymond Unwin gave a lecture in Trinity College Dublin entitled 'How Town Planning May Solve the Housing Problem'. Following this lecture he was retained by Dublin Corporation as a housing consultant and during this period he designed a plan for Marino with Geddes. In 1919 city architect Horace T. O'Rourke presented further plans and drawings for the scheme to Dublin Corporation which borrowed heavily from the garden suburb model and had a density of nine-and-a-half houses to the acre. The scheme at Marino begun in 1924 was to be a model scheme of 1,300 five-room houses around green areas and culs-de-sac.

In 1923 the Irish Sailors and Soldiers Land Trust was established for the provision of cottages in Ireland, with or without plots or gardens, for ex-servicemen who fought in the First World War and this was a pioneer in the shift to the suburbs. The Trust sanctioned a total of 3,672 'cottages'. Some were built in ribbon development style in the countryside but many were in small estates near cities and towns along garden suburb lines. The size of the schemes varied greatly; from the 247-house scheme in Killester in Dublin to the two-cottage scheme in Kilkee, from Stranorlar in Donegal to Kinsale in Cork and from Whiteabbey in Antrim to Caherciveen in Kerry, the spread of cottages indicated that volunteers had come from all parts and all traditions.[26] The Killester scheme was laid out as a very low density garden suburb of four houses to the acre by Scottish planner Frank C. Mears and was designed to include the provision of transport facilities. Mears had been an assistant to Geddes as well as being his son-in-law and collaborated with Unwin and Geddes on plans for the Marino estate.[27]

In Dublin in the early twentieth century Public Utility Societies, friendly societies or philanthropic ventures created to provide working-class housing, were set up and in Abercrombie's plan for Dublin they were recognised as a potential solution to the city's housing crisis. In Marino the frontages around the Corporation scheme were reserved for 'better-class' private housing to be built privately and by

Public Utility Societies. These reserved sites were frequently built on to layout plans devised by the Corporation to standards they set down. In a time before planning controls this afforded the local authority some degree of control over the development of housing and allowing for garden suburb style layouts. The policy allowed for some integration of middle-class housing within working-class estates.

Marino has, however, been criticised as too closely emulating British practices and being designed to been seen from the air with its geometry without a human scale on the ground.[28] Manning Robertson attacked the 'Tudorbethan half-timber outrage on the face of Ireland' which was making the suburbs of Dublin 'as nearly as possible like Croydon'.[29]

IRELAND'S WORST PLANNING DISASTER?

The contract for the planning, design and construction of the Ballymun housing scheme was signed on 2 February 1965. The site, which was the grounds of the former Albert Agricultural College owned by University College Dublin, was selected almost by default rather than for its suitability, as Dublin Corporation required land to build housing as part of its slum clearances and the University College Dublin had decided their large site was no longer suitable for agriculture.

Control of the project shifted incrementally to the Minister for Local Government and the depth of Minister Blaney's involvement with the scheme led to some disquiet amongst his cabinet colleagues with the Minister for Finance writing to him 'I hope it will be possible for you to disengage yourself from direct responsibility for Ballymun at an early date'[30] (Blaney's personal preference for the name of the project was Árd Glas, Green Heights).

Prior to the signing of contracts the preferred consortium for the completion of the scheme were required to prepare an outline planning brief between May 1964 and February 1965 based upon the principle of a new and closely integrated community with access to the facilities and amenities of a new town centre. The plan reflected the age's emphasis on private cars with segregation of pedestrians and vehicles, though sunken roads and landscaping were to minimise the visual impact of the car. This was planning along Radburn principles, named for the planned neighbourhood of Radburn, New Jersey, founded in 1929 where the needs of motorists were considered but were not to overwhelm the needs of the community and the principles of garden cities. The aspirations of this plan were not legally binding and the consortium was not obliged to implement these ideas once final contracts were signed. Quickly major landscaping elements were dropped and the Radburn consideration for pedestrians abandoned, along with many promised amenities.

At inception Ballymun was to be a symbol of modern Ireland and of national pride and progress, evidenced by the naming of the seven towers after the Easter Rebellion leaders on its fiftieth anniversary. In 1969 the *Irish Press* optimistically noted that Ballymun was to have shopping facilities, office accommodation, an entertainment centre comprising dance hall, cinema, skating rink, restaurants, bars, community centre, meeting hall and swimming pool,[31] but by 1974 only a swimming pool, snack bar and two pubs had been provided. For Dr Robert Somerville-Woodward who was commissioned to write the history of the area as part of its regeneration in 2002 'there can be little doubt that the inclusion of these ideas in the original plans was more than lip service on the government's part'.[32]

Despite official optimism, the omens were not good. As Ballymun was completed, an explosion at the Ronan Point tower block in East London, built using similar techniques, killed four, due to inadequacies in design and construction. Following Ronan Point, TDs questioned the minister on the robustness of the flats' design in the face of high winds, with one asking that the potential effect of jumbo jets using nearby Dublin Airport be investigated. Similar issues emerged with the new materials and techniques used in housing in Northern Ireland's new town of Craigavon. In contrast, in Cork a deliberate strategy of low-rise public housing was followed at the time. The Ballymun name itself quickly developed negative connotations, with nearby Ballymun Avenue subsequently renamed Glasnevin Avenue after a local plebiscite.

Ballymun has been referred to as the 'state's worst planning disaster'[35] though Sinéad Power notes 'it is arguable as to whether planning was involved at all'.[36] For architectural historian Ellen Rowley, architects were kept at the periphery of the housing debate at the time, with cost concerns predominating.[37] The same could continue to be said of the planning profession.

Exempt from the new planning process, with limited input from a nascent planning profession and with a flexible contract which favoured the developers, Ballymun emerged as a failure of culture and estate management. Expediency rather than sustainability led to the site selection, compounded by political pressures (following a series of tenement house collapses in Dublin) and naiveté, a desire for savings on time and cost, the delivery of housing before other facilities and a focus on construction technology rather than the finished community, all created a perfect storm.

Ballymun has been referred to as Ireland's worst planning disaster though it is arguable as to whether any planning was involved at all. (Courtesy of Bill Hastings)

In 1997 the government approved a proposal for the redevelopment of Ballymun to address decades of social neglect and economic decline exacerbated by the lack of initial planning. Following on from this, Dublin City Council established a company called Ballymun Regeneration Ltd to implement one of the biggest regeneration projects in Europe. The programme of physical regeneration was to be completed by the end of 2014 and saw the construction of around 2,000 new public, private, voluntary and co-operative housing units in the area, and the relocation of 1,500 families from the old flats along with the development of a new main street to form a commercial and civic core.

Ballymun's lessons on the need to provide services and amenities in tandem with housing completion have not always been heeded. The 1972 Dublin County Development Plan, guided by the Myles Wright plan, recommended the development of three new towns at Tallaght, Clondalkin/Lucan and Blanchardstown. Although it was intended that the towns would develop with a strong local employment, it was accepted that commuting to the existing built-up areas of the city from the new towns would be inevitable. With this in mind, rail links between the new towns and the city centre were proposed, though never constructed.[38] The new towns were to be developed at low density, at least in part, as a reaction to the appalling overcrowding of the city's tenement slums, but at twenty-four dwellings to a hectare, with generous open space provision, the approach represented an anti-urban ethos.[39]

For geographers MacLaran and Punch the development of new towns in Ireland following the 1940s echoed the experience in the UK where the aim was to control unplanned suburban sprawl, conserve land and better co-ordinate development. However, using Tallaght as a case study, they conclude that in Ireland, differences in the public-sector funding available for development, in the organisational environment responsible for carrying out policy and in the constitutional position of property owners, produced different results in Ireland than in the UK.[40]

Unlike the British new towns, there were no dedicated development corporations or controlled land prices for Dublin's new towns. Planning and administration for all three were to remain within the control of Dublin County Council, with limited public funding for infrastructure or land acquisition. The process required the co-ordination of a number of service providers, agencies and actors. With Tallaght, apart from the provision of basic infrastructure and public housing, its development 'became primarily an experiment in the ability of a single local authority to facilitate private-sector residential, industrial and commercial development in specified localities'.[41]

Planning permission conditions in Tallaght were not rigidly enforced, leading to inadequate paths, lighting and play spaces in a monotonous residential environment driven by profit maximisation. Ironically while the environment in these areas was designed for the car, as it transpired the persistent low incomes of many residents put car ownership beyond their reach.

As a town of the 1960s Shannon, County Clare, was also designed with the car in mind but its raison d'etre was another form of transport, the aeroplane. Shannon Airport was considered isolated and distant from the population centres of Ennis and Limerick. As transatlantic travel expanded and with the possibility of newer aircraft being able to bypass the airport, it was decided that Shannon must become an industrial centre if it was to continue to grow. The Shannon Free Zone was established in 1958 and the Shannon Free Airport Development Company (SFADCo) was founded the following year. These ambitious plans required a nearby population and housing for workers expected to come to Shannon from abroad. Plans were developed for a new town in connection with an industrial estate. The possibility of developing the existing towns of Newmarket-on-Fergus or Sixmilebridge was considered and rejected on the grounds that commuting to work would become an issue as the number of factories in the industrial estate grew.

By 1960 professional planners were being recruited by SFADCo to work on a development plan for a new town at Shannon on a site connected to the industrial estate described as 'flat and unattractive in winter'.[42] At first ten houses and 137 flats were built, along with a community hall. The town on a 920-acre site was planned by Downes, Meehan and Robson in association with architect Frederick Rogerson, with recommendations from international experts also sought. These included Lord Holford who also advised on the development of the new capitals of Brasília and Canberra. Though there are comparisons to the English new town experience, SFADCo's proposals were more modest, aiming to build a hundred new houses a year compared to the thousands expected of an English new town.

Shannon was also designed along the Radburn principles of separating traffic and pedestrians and included wide avenues, though a less rigid approach was adopted from 1972.

Shannon had international ambitions. In 1965 SFADCo, with the backing of the Irish government, considered making an attempt to persuade the Junior Chamber of Commerce International (JCI) to relocate its world headquarters from Florida to Shannon. Frederick Rogerson was asked to prepare alternative schemes which could be presented at the 1965 JCI congress in Sydney, one with a separate JCI office block and one in which the JCI would share a building with SFADCo. It is not clear whether either scheme was presented to the JCI but the relocation did not take place.

In 1967 a 'New Town Exhibition' took place which was opened by Minister for Transport and Power Erskine Childers who asserted 'the government is determined to ensure that the new town at Shannon will be a model of its kind ... it will lack no desirable amenities'.[43] The reality was to be somewhat different but it was to prove less fanciful than another aspect of Childers's speech where he told those assembled that rocket planes would be flying people to New York in ten minutes by 1985.[44]

Shannon emerged as a town with a young, diverse population but its sustainability was questioned. Just two years later the *Irish Independent* was calling some of the new houses 'slightly jaded', adding that it

Proposal for plaza and office block, in the Shannon new town development, *c.* 1965. (Courtesy of the Irish Architectural Archive)

had 'probably fewer shops per hundred of the population than any
other town, which does give rise to criticism' while noting its other
strong community facilities.[45] In an editorial the west Cork newspaper
the *Southern Star* maintained the wide focus of the *Skibbereen Eagle* it
incorporated (which had famously warned that it was 'keeping an eye
on the Tsar of Russia' over his expansionist plans for China), arguing
'nobody, not even the present-day Shannon dweller, wants to live in an
Irish version of Welwyn Garden City … Like the English "New Towns"
Shannon is socially a graveyard with the inhabitants commuting to
Limerick at every possible opportunity'.[46] In 1970, with a population
of 3,000, plans for a £1 million shopping centre with offices, a hotel
and other facilities were announced to give the town a heart. In 1978
a £3 million extension to the town was announced with a new hotel
and offices and Shannon was to become County Clare's second largest
town. In 2012 Clare County Council prepared a Green Infrastructure
Plan for the town which was commended for 'turning a town of the
sixties' whose 'layout characteristics belong to a period of planning
thought when roads had a distinct prominence' into 'a sustainable,
enjoyable, environment'.[47]

At the same time in Northern Ireland, following the Matthew
Plan for the Belfast region, the New Towns (Northern Ireland)
Act, 1965, provided for the creation of new towns as an answer to
the overcrowding and industrial decline of Belfast and to allow for
a more balanced distribution of development across six key growth
centres. Plans were prepared for Craigavon, which was anticipated to
be five times the size of Shannon though ultimately much of what
was planned was not built.

Writing in 2004 – at the height of the boom – the National
Economic and Social Council (NESC) which advises the Taoiseach
on strategic issues for Ireland's economic and social development
argued that building sustainable neighbourhoods 'bears comparison
with other great challenges that Ireland has faced and met in the
past half century. It is essential to the social and economic future of
Irish society. It requires a widely shared understanding and consistent
action by government and other actors. It challenges many established
approaches to housing, social segregation and urban development'.[48]
During the 'Celtic Tiger' years, when much development was
developer- and incentive-led, this challenge was not always met but
this created an appetite for sustainable communities in the future.

BUNGALOW BLISS?

Dispersed housing in the countryside comprises 'one of the most contested issues facing rural Ireland and contemporary planning policy'.[49] Apart from farms, isolated rural housing in Ireland were traditionally estate houses or the country cottage. The cottage has a long tradition going back to the time of medieval labourers who lived in huts of wattle and clay. Later there were county council cottages on one acre or half-acre plots, while estate cottages were also built by local landlords. Each had particular design elements and all were for people who worked in the countryside.[50]

The vernacular rural house in Ireland is a modest, rectangular, one-storey thatched building, made with local materials and sitting snugly into the landscape. The style was adapted regionally based on climate and land. In the nineteenth century new, two-storey and slated houses became more common alongside larger, formal houses of the gentry and more prosperous farmers.[51]

In the twentieth century a new vernacular, the bungalow, emerged, followed by the dormer bungalow and two-storey houses in a mock-Georgian style. It has been suggested that the wave of 1970s bungalows 'was almost benign by comparison' when one considers the large one-off houses from the mid-1990s whose design bears little relationship to the landscape and whose accoutrements and size do not relate to demographic trends.[52] Numerous rural house-design guides have been published in recent years by local authorities trying to improve design standards, to a lukewarm reception. Councillor P.J. Kelly compared Clare County Council officials to 'the deposed Taliban' for their intended 'suppression of house designs' when the council published its guide in 2002.[53]

Today there are over 400,000 one-off rural houses in Ireland, accounting for around 25 per cent of the national housing stock. The majority are urban generated with no direct economic connection to their immediate rural hinterland. This has resulted in a huge increase in long-distance and time-intensive commuting.

Discussing the history of Ireland since 1970, R.F. Foster writes 'The face of the country has changed, first in the 1990s with subsidised afforestation and setting designated lands aside; now in place of a field of beasts there are likely to be fields with brand-new houses rained down into them … the right of local people to build houses and sell

One-off rural housing with more in common with urban and suburban buildings
than traditional rural building types.

land, without benefit of sustainable planning guidelines or observing
vernacular architectural styles and practice, is fiercely articulated by
county councillors, often to their own profit'.[54]

Concerns over the issue are not new. In 1929 *The Irish Builder and
Engineer* argued: 'Around our cities and even into the heart of the
country, the new bungalow is becoming a menace to beauty. Usually
ill-designed and glaring in colour, it is an eyesore, bad when alone
but hideous when in groups'.[55] A regular visitor to west Cork, well-
known British television journalist Jeremy Paxman has criticised 'ill
thought out' development in rural Ireland saying 'It is just a shame
that Ireland's planning laws are worse than the UK ones. I really don't
understand the way in which beautiful bits of Ireland have been
ruined by unsightly buildings thrown up'.[56]

Geographer Mary Cawley traces the uncontrolled rise in one-off
housing to two main factors: a November 1973 Department of Local
Government circular entitled 'Planning Control Problems' which
facilitated people who wished to live in the open countryside and
Section 4 motions by councillors.[57] Its origins are perhaps deeper.

Fergal MacCabe tells the story of cycling to the most prominent
point in the Midlands plain, Croghan Hill, as a teenager. Seeing two
old ladies at a small house at the foot of the hill he asked them for the
best track to the top: 'One old lady looked at the other and at the hill

she had probably gazed at all her life and said, "Do you know Bridie, I was never up it – were you?"

'To this very day, I am still astonished at the deep incuriosity of that woman and her sublime lack of interest in the local landscape … The old lady beside Croghan Hill said it all – in general we don't really see our rural landscape and we don't care very much if it is compromised.'[58]

Reflecting on Irish values, broadcaster and journalist Olivia O'Leary argues 'the notion that this is "our land" and "our landscape" has not quite yet come into operation. The idea that you can build what you want on your father's land is more predominant than the idea that you are the keeper of the landscape for the nation. We still don't have the attitude that we are only a temporary holder of the land'.[59]

McManus posits that 'Irish people do not generally consider themselves to be urbanites'[60] and suggests that negative attitudes to urban living might be because 'we Irish have never really accepted that we can be both Irish and urban at the same time' due to a 'rural nostalgia' for thatched cottages and turf fires.[61] As the 1963 Act was linked closely to the recommendations of Charles Abrams's work on an 'Urban Renewal Project in Ireland' this perhaps reinforced the disconnect between the push for planning and rural Ireland.

Speaking at the National Planning Conference in 1986, former Irish Planning Institute president Enda Conway discussed the attitude of the Department of the Environment towards rural planning as resembling one of 'planning is all well and good for Dublin but why is it needed down the country', pointing out that the department was not insisting that rural county councils were staffed by planners. At the time four county councils had no planners at all and the average per rural county was 1.5.[62]

Modern rural housing has been associated with the 1971 publication *Bungalow Bliss* by Jack Fitzsimons which provided a manual of plans and contracts for affordable and simple bungalows, dormers and two-storey houses which went through eleven editions (only 10–12 per cent of one-off houses are designed by qualified architects).[63] This title took on a wider meaning for Frank McDonald when he said that 'Bungalow Bliss is not just the title of a book; it encapsulates our social aspirations'.[64] In terms of their design, these houses have much more in common with urban and suburban buildings than with traditional rural building types and traditions.

In 1997 the government published *Sustainable Development: A Strategy for Ireland* which recommended a presumption against urban-generated one-off rural housing adjacent to towns on social, landscape and environmental grounds. In a few years this was diluted. The 1999 White Paper on Rural Development set out the government's vision of rural society, based on 'the maintenance of dispersed, vibrant, rural communities'[65] and suggesting that planning should 'facilitate people willing to settle in rural areas, especially those willing to settle in their own area of origin'.[66]

The National Spatial Strategy did not set out a policy for rural housing but it distinguished between urban generated and rural generated housing, 'shifting the importance of rural housing developments from the development itself to the people and the motives behind such developments'.[67] In 2005 the Department of the Environment published the *Sustainable Rural Housing Guidelines*, which were guided by pressure from councillors rather than evidence.[68] The guidelines state that previous policy, discouraging urban generated one-offs was 'operated over rigidly', signalling a more relaxed approach.[69] Junior Minister Martin Mansergh explained that 'what people want, rather than all the time what different experts determine is good for them, still counts for something'.[70] While the guidelines were being framed Minister Martin Cullen declined to meet the Irish Planning Institute while meeting the IRDA twice.[71]

Many early county development plans under the 1963 Act sought to direct new housing into existing settlements, though they were often diluted with phrases such as 'in as far as possible' and with exceptions for farmers and their families and this dilution continued as the economy developed and the mind-set of owning one's home strengthened. Today most county development plans include rural housing provisions for local people who can demonstrate some sort of 'local need' when applying for permission. The criteria for 'local' vary considerably and the European Commission sought clarity from Ireland on how 'local need' does not break internal market rules and is not discriminatory.

McDonald and Nix have pointed out the contradiction between the RIAI involvement in publications encouraging people to build their own, architect designed, one-off while also warning of the impact dispersed rural dwellings were having on our urban centres.[72]

A blanket ban on all one-off rural housing developments is one alternative[73] but as planner Brendan McGrath has pointed out the issue 'illustrates the gulf that exists between planning theory and practice in Ireland' explaining, 'professional planners contribute to this sense of 'contradictory' planning by persevering with drawing plans and writing policies that signify a rational scientific outlook, in the full knowledge that the reality of rural housing in quite different'.[74] Development plans do not promote ribbon development and the suburbanisation of the countryside near towns and cities 'but they remain characteristic products of the Irish planning regime'.[75]

More bluntly it has been argued that 'every development plan in rural Ireland mouths pious policies restricting rural housing to farmers' children or those with locational needs. But it is as plain as a pikestaff that the amount of rural housing being built bears no relationship to that policy … If such a central plank in the development plan policy is patently a lie, why should anyone believe any of the other policies?'[76]

Cawley contrasts rural planning in the Republic of Ireland with that of Northern Ireland, arguing that while both jurisdictions began regulating rural building in the 1960s 'the application of policy has, however, been much more stringent in Northern Ireland than in the Republic, with the result that notable contrasts exist in the physical appearance of the rural landscape in the two parts of Ireland'.[77] In Northern Ireland a key settlement strategy concentrated housing in existing towns and villages up to the 1970s, whereas in Ireland stated objectives to avoid ribbon development were ignored. From 1964 to 1979 in Northern Ireland planning permission for rural housing required demonstrating a 'need' to live in the rural area. In the late 1970s a policy review concluded that these restrictions were more suited to densely populated Britain and the rule was relaxed outside of certain control areas while also seeking to ensure the viability of existing towns. The Northern Ireland equivalent of the National Spatial Strategy, the 2001 Northern Ireland *Regional Development Strategy: Shaping Our Future* raised the prospect of stricter controls, noting that 'difficult decisions at the local level in relation to the control of individual properties' may have to be taken.[78]

Addressing the Seanad in May 2008 Minister for Community, Rural and Gaeltacht Affairs Éamon Ó Cuív said, 'The planning debate has been very confrontational. I do not want to destroy the visible beauty of rural Ireland and we can avoid doing so by engaging in a rational debate with those concerned. We should be able to have houses and communities without destroying rural areas. Some planning policies have been totally negative. The other interesting point is the myth that, by definition, urban dwellers leave a smaller carbon footprint than those in rural areas. I do not believe that and I am willing to debate the point with the leading experts'.[79] In 2002 An Taisce had called for Ó Cuív's resignation as minister, accusing him of 'embarrassing misunderstandings' and 'voodoo planning theories' in his support of one-off housing.[80]

There is a long-running suspicion of the need for planning and planners amongst some rural representatives. During its passage through the Oireachtas the applicability of the 1963 Act to rural areas was regularly questioned. The main opposition spokesman on the bill, Denis Jones TD, called it a predominantly 'urban bill', addressing Dublin problems. Tipperary South TD Patrick Hogan said, 'it presents … a sort of global approach to town planning … it seems to me that town planning as we understand it is in the first instance necessary for places like Dublin, Cork, Limerick, Waterford and other bigger centres … where there is a case to be made for more elaborate town planning than in the smaller towns and villages'.[81]

The IRDA have criticised 'the extraordinary amount of power bestowed on individual planners by legislation to play God with the rights of Irish citizens wanting to build a home in the country'.[82] In 2010 Ó Cuív quoted IRDA founder Jim Connolly approvingly: 'Humanity is eternally complex, unpredictable, political, highly mobile, multi-cultured and on the whole, little given to bowing to diktats from elitist groups who claim to know what's best for everybody else'.[83] Ó Cuív also claimed the mantle of Martin Luther King in upholding the 'civil rights of ordinary people' to build houses in the countryside.[84]

There may be some foundation to the perception that planners start from a different place. Planning academic Mark Scott contends that planners largely adopt the village or town as the departure point for settlement analysis and questions the usefulness of this approach, quoting a Mayo planner as saying, 'One-off housing development – well it's not really planning, is it? It's just random'.

The criticisms of bad rural planning have become wider, moving from aesthetic concerns that one-off houses were scars on the landscape to looking more deeply at issues of environmental degradation, isolation, service provision and more. The proliferation of one-off houses has also been associated with difficulties finding routes for pylons and even underground electricity cables.[85] This threat had been identified in the early 2000s when it was said that 'it is becoming increasingly difficult to plan rationally for rural Ireland' with any infra-structure project running up against local action groups of residents who live in houses that perhaps 'should never have been there in the first instance'.[86]

The issue certainly inflames passions. Co-founder of Friends of the Irish Environment, Tony Lowes tells of 'a little club of people who've received a bullet in the post' due to their campaign to tighten planning restrictions, particularly on one-off houses.[87] In 2001 Kerry county councillor Jackie Healy-Rae, in a debate about rural planning, warned then county manager Martin Nolan that people were so angry regarding one-off housing restrictions that 'there are places in this county thou dare not travel ... you or other officials'. Councillor Michael Cahill said council officials were like 'the donkey of old. The more we tell you something, the more stubborn you get'.[88]

In his book *Landscape and Society in Contemporary Ireland* Brendan McGrath recalls 'the torrent of verbal abuse' he received from a family while working as a planner in Clare County Council when he told them that their son's preferred site on their family farm was unsuitable for a house for landscape, public health and environmental reasons while other, more suitable, sites were available. McGrath found this surprising not least because they had been friendly acquaintances but also because they had campaigned against the development of the Burren visitor centre on landscape grounds – 'landscape matters to us in different ways', McGrath concludes.[89]

In a study of attitudes to planners and planning policy in rural Mayo and Donegal Mark Scott quotes a Donegal councillor who highlights a similar contradiction. 'The people who have moved in want tighter rules [for restricting new housing], which is naive. People want to move to the countryside, but don't want their views spoiled by someone else building a house in front of them.'[90]

Scott writes that recreational demands and restrictions on rural housing are perceived as 'urban-generated' issues, with groups such as An Taisce and Keep Ireland Open viewed as 'Dublin-based organisations'. Similarly, planners are perceived as 'outsiders', remote from pressing issues such as rural depopulation with an urban bias derived from their professional training and ethos, people who interfere in local issues by restricting housing supply with planning controls. In his study Scott found that there was also an absence of evidence that rural development stakeholders had engaged with planning officials in an attempt to shape rural planning policies but concluded that at the most basic level, local planners should provide information about the rate at which planning permission is granted for rural housing to challenge the perception that 'planners stop things happening' while also engaging more with local needs and aspirations.[91]

For some, the term 'one-off housing' itself is loaded. Dr Seamus Caulfield, originator of the Céide Fields project in County Mayo, advocates a return to the language of the baile fearann, or dispersed townland pattern.[92] The IRDA was formed in 2002 in response to the difficulties experienced with the planning process by people living in rural Ireland. For the IRDA one-offs are a continuation of a Gaelic tradition, though this is tenuous. Actually dispersed housing emerged in the eighteenth and early nineteenth century in response to a rapid population increase that ended with the famine and the sustained haemorrhaging of rural population that has continued to today.[93] The gulf between the painted idealised rural idyll and the car-dependent reality is wide.

Some founders of the IRDA went on to form the Irish Citizens Party which sought to remove An Taisce and its 'secret membership' from the planning process as they saw that organisation as responsible for 'endless suffering and injustice for ordinary families'.[94] They challenge the 'ridiculous denial of the facts' arising from 'planning policy developed from an urban mind-set', suggesting 'a complete disconnect between planners and the cultural and social traditions of Irish life'.[95] For the Irish Citizens Party 'the regime has assumed powers unto itself of mind blowing proportions – powers which are impossible to reconcile with democracy', adding that people had been 'brain-washed' with a trend of urbanisation being enforced. An Taisce, while describing new rural housing as 'a key source of informal patronage for many local and national politicians', argue that they only appeal rural dwellings to An Bord Pleanála where the council is ignoring its own development plan or where there are clear risks to water quality or protected wildlife.[96]

One of An Foras Forbartha's most controversial reports was the 1976 study *Urban Generated Housing in Rural Areas*. Though available by 1983 this still had not been formally published and 'Confidential: Not For Publication' was stamped on copies circulating.[97]

The study was prompted by 'a general belief that an inordinate amount of local authority staff time is consumed in dealing with planning applications for single detached houses required by urban generated dwellers in rural areas'.[98] The study found that the sample of rural dwellers surveyed sought the advantages of urban centres with the benefits of a scenic, private location and concluded that traffic accident rates, accessibility of services, commuting times and service provision were all higher in rural areas compared with urban generated housing. The study promoted clustering future development on serviced sites with flexibility in terms of design, size and layout as a potential way to satisfy the demands of those wishing to live in the countryside along with the implementation of the Kenny Report to reduce the cost of building land. The report is alleged to have been suppressed by then Minister for Local Government Jimmy Tully who deemed it too controversial and unpalatable.[99]

Ironically An Foras Forbartha had a reputation for engaging positively on rural issues. For example, in 1970 it considered a report they had commissioned from former Dublin City Architect and town planner Daithi Hanly which explored how planning could be used to preserve and extend the Irish language in Connemara while encouraging economic development.

The 2014 draft Mayo County Development Plan included the objective, 'the sustainability of rural communities will only occur if rural population densities are restored to 1951 levels and this objective should be supported by Mayo County Council' (a benchmark year the *Ireland After NAMA* blog suggests, tongue in cheek, might have been selected as it is the last year County Mayo won the all-Ireland). According to *Ireland After NAMA* in 1951 the population of County Mayo was 117,181, with the 2011 equivalent being 82,808. 'Mayo councillors are therefore seeking to increase the population of the rural part of the county by 35,000 people. This is despite the fact that, according to the draft plan, the total (and now extremely optimistic) additional population target for the entire county by 2020 is 17,500' and necessitating the removal of any restrictions on one-off housing. Mayo County Council's own independent environmental assessment of the proposed amendments states, 'With respect to population, it is not clear if it is sustainable to restore the rural population to 1951 levels. This material alteration to the Settlement Strategy is predicted to result in significant effects on landscape with mitigation not deemed feasible

... is considered to weaken control and management of housing in rural areas and consequently is also considered to have significant effects ... with no likely mitigation to reduce, offset or prevent these effects'.[100]

In 2011 senior planning engineer Paul Stack with Kerry County Council warned that the county's 35,000 one-off houses (averaging seven one-off houses per kilometre of road) were impacting on Kerry's vital tourism industry, saying '80 per cent of the visitors to County Kerry come here for the quality of the landscape and the unspoilt scenery and we have destroyed it in parts of this county'. Mr Stack was speaking to a Killarney Area Council meeting in response to criticism from councillors after planning was refused for an undisclosed house. According to Stack, 'We are destroying our county with one-off houses and people are now suffering for the sins of others,' adding that there had been 'incredible damage' caused as the vast majority of the terrain in Kerry was not suitable for on-site effluent disposal, pointing to the fact that 2 million gallons of effluent a day flows into groundwater.[101]

Planning consultant Diarmuid Ó Gráda cites the example of Roscommon, where 30 per cent of the homes in the county must boil their water before drinking, explaining 'Roscommon is formed like a geological colander, shot through with sinkholes and springs. Foul effluent quickly finds its way into domestic wells (more than 75 per cent of its water supply comes from springs). The council has continued to grant planning permission for houses where the ground conditions cannot deal with septic tank effluent'.[102] In 1986 a paper was presented to the Irish Planning Institute's national planning conference which outlined emerging evidence that septic tanks were responsible for contaminating groundwater. The paper recommended a regular inspection process.[103]

In October 2009 the European Court of Justice ruled that Ireland had failed to fulfil its obligations under the Waste Directive's require-ment that member states take the measures necessary to ensure that waste is disposed of without endangering human health, air, soil, water, animals, plants and the countryside. The court held that domestic waste waters treated by septic tanks and other individual waste water treatment plants constituted waste under the Directive and required an appropriate system of monitoring. The Court held that Ireland did not have an appropriate system of inspection and that the guidance on septic tank standards was not suited to the geological and soil characteristics of most of Ireland. They rejected Ireland's contention that with over 400,000 septic tanks there were significant difficulties in implementing any inspection system. The notable exception was Cavan County Council whose inspection regime by-laws met the requirements of the directive. By February 2013 all owners of septic tanks were required to have registered them.

Mark Scott has identified a complex set of motivations regarding housing in rural areas, asking if those most critical of planners are concerned with local affordable housing need and maintaining rural services or if they are driven by a market agenda, supportive of development interests in selling sites and housing to people with little or no attachment to the place in which they live.[104] According to long-time TD Noel Davern 'Planning never was a problem, up to the late 1990s. You went in. You compromised on it. There was no question of a family not getting a planning permission for a farm. If a farmer needed money …you'd tell the planning officer that he was in financial trouble and he badly needed the permission. And they'd give it to him'.[105]

Ian Lumley has claimed that in many cases planning permission was being sought in a child's name (some as young as six years of age) with the intention of immediately selling the site as soon as permission was granted.[106] Former chairman of An Bord Pleanála John O'Connor said it would not be unusual for its inspectors dealing with appeals on one-offs to find 'for sale' signs, even in cases when occupancy conditions were being imposed.[107]

In Kerry the issue of farmers selling sites can dominate council debates, with the majority of councillors believing that farmers should be entitled to sell a site in order to subsidise their income while management argue that farmers should be in the business of farming and not selling land. In a debate about a new development plan, Independent councillor Billy Leen described the door of the planning office at Kerry County Council as 'the most harrowing door in Ireland', saying 'there's no logic in telling a man that he has to sell his farm instead of selling a site. We'll create more landlords than Cromwell'.[108]

In their 2002 analysis of one-off housing in the countryside Clinch, Convery and Walsh argued that financial motives for the landowner and house owner are perhaps the most important explanation for the phenomenon, with agricultural land with planning permission fetching higher prices and a one-off house cheaper to build when compared to buying a new house in an estate: 'This dynamic of cheaper housing for buyers and large capital gains for landowners, mainly farmers, goes far to explain the popularity of the one-off'. Other factors suggested include snobbery (fear of social housing on estates), cultural preference, and limited awareness of the long-term landscape and environmental implications. [109]

In 2012 the chairmanship of the Kerry branches of the IRDA, the Irish Farmers Association and the Gaelic Athletic Association produced a report titled *The Rural Challenge* which asserted: 'people are key to the attractiveness of Ireland, and planning regulations should aim to assist individuals to live in the country. It is widely accepted that the visual appearance of the landscape is of vital importance but as the saying goes, "beauty is in the eye of the beholder" meaning we must work together to determine a happy medium in the pursuit of a vibrant populated countryside. This remains visually attractive using natural landscaping and trees to assist in blending in houses'. [110] This suggests that there may be a developing understanding of the landscape implications of dispersed rural housing and the potential for dialogue, though the other consequences are still considered less pressing.

One clear issue is the limited range of alternatives for some to building a one-off house in the countryside. Though it is cheaper for those building, the societal impacts are not factored in. For many years planning was passive, rather than proactive in the matter. Many rural dwellers would have preferred to live in towns and villages if sites were available at reasonable cost and these settlements could have taken more housing. Brendan McGrath notes the 'accomplished execution' of places like Adamstown which represent the potential of attractive suburban living today but warns that they 'are unlikely to be more than footnotes in the history of Irish settlement given the scale of dispersed rural housing development that is taking place'. [111] An Taisce recommends the implementation of the Kenny Report because providing sites at fair value in serviced areas rather than in the open countryside is the best solution. [112] Any future policies to restrict building in the countryside must be accompanied by policies to strengthen the centres of villages and towns. Much new building in small settlements has been of a suburban style, with little respect for neighbouring buildings and the characteristics of the village street. The failure to grasp the potential of the significant network of small villages or hamlets around Ireland has been a glaring failure of planning policies.[113]

Planning has a wider role in the future of rural communities that can be separated from the housing debate. Undoubtedly many small rural settlements have experienced huge development to an extent that inhabitants experience an eroded sense of place and identity. Patrick Kavanagh wrote extensively of life in rural Ireland and especially of his family's small holding in Mucker, outside the village of Inniskeen, County Monaghan. Locations mentioned in the poet's most loved verses are still intact and are visible from the adjoining roadways. The sites are well-known locally; however, there was no formal documentation to identify them, no scaled map to locate them, and few of the sites have statutory protection. Beginning in 2012 Inniskeen Enterprise Development Group and The Patrick Kavanagh Rural & Literary Resource Centre developed a *Kavanagh Country Literary Landscape Character Assessment and Management Plan* aiming to define the ordinary elements of the landscape that inspired Patrick Kavanagh and the project demonstrates the potential scope and diversity of planning in the future. The objective of the *Character Assessment and Management Plan* was to assist the enterprise group in engaging and informing the public of the built and natural landscape that influenced Kavanagh.

The plan was developed by architects and planners through a participatory planning process that identified the sites relating to the life and work of Kavanagh, recorded how they would have appeared at the time of his writing, identified works to conserve and protect them and explored how they could be made accessible to visitors. It provided a clear path for the future direction and development of Kavanagh Country but more importantly raised public awareness of the importance of this landscape and the need to secure its sustainable future.

Amongst the sites analysed, as if they were urban spaces, was Billy Brennan's farmyard and barn (with its 'parallel farmstead' design with house and buildings separated by a narrow yard or 'street'). The barn was immortalised by Kavanagh's poem 'Inniskeen Road: July Evening': 'There's a dance in Billy Brennan's Barn tonight'.

The surveys include a description of each site as it exists today and maps its location and presence in the literature. Each site was appraised in terms of its visual contribution, and its value was assessed in terms

Planning can work with rural communities to build a sense of place. *The Kavanagh
Country Literary Landscape Character Assessment* engages the public in the built and
natural landscape that influenced Patrick Kavanagh. (Courtesy of Sheridan Woods
Architects and Urban Planners & Inniskeen Enterprise Development Group)

of its contribution to the understanding of the literature. The pressure
to change was assessed, in order to identify its potential vulnerability
and its sensitivity to change, should change occur.

Planning can work with rural communities to capture local characteristics they deem worth preserving and can build a sense of place
in a more sustainable way that considers socio-cultural and economic
factors as well as the environmental ones that often dogmatically come
to the fore.

SECTION 4

The introduction of the local authority management system was
unpopular with councillors and Section 4 of the City and County
Management (Amendment) Act, 1955 gave councillors the power to
direct the manager how to perform any of the executive functions.
This power achieved notoriety and was regularly used to require the
manager to grant planning permissions.

Ferriter argues that Section 4 motions in relation to rezoning 'were abused by a minority for clientelist purposes or to create personal wealth at the expense of co-ordinated planning'. In 1983 An Taisce published *Your Guide to Planning and Use and Mis-Use of Section 4 of the City and County Management (Amendment) Act, 1955 in Relation to Planning*.[114] In some of the most grievous cases, council planners, knowing they could not do it themselves, asked the Irish Planning Institute to appeal against Section 4 motions.

By 1985 the Irish Planning Institute was recommending that Section 4 should not apply to the planning acts as it 'was never intended to apply and it is abused extensively throughout the country to bestow preferential treatment on selected individuals contrary to the common good'.[115] The profession also warned that the use of Section 4 for one-off houses was threatening tourism.[116]

Most Section 4 resolutions were viewed negatively by all local residents except the beneficiaries and this saw controversial Section 4 resolutions proposed by councillors from outside the electoral area in question, allowing them to 'escape subsequent retribution at the polls'.[117]

The power was restated in Section 140 of the Local Government Act, 2001. The 1991 Act set limits on these powers, requiring them to be signed by at least three-quarters of the members of the electoral area containing the site in question and to be passed by three-quarters of the total members of the authority. Speaking after councillors voted in favour of a Section 140 motion to contravene the development plan to enable the granting of planning permission for a house, County Louth Senior Planner Gerry Duffy told councillors that Section 140 'calls the whole planning system into disrepute if you are continually seeking to vary the plan in this way' and expressing concern that members of the public were being told that it didn't matter if they didn't get planning permission as they could always get a Section 140.[118]

In 2004 there was a warning that planners did not want to work in County Kerry any more because there was too much conflict with councillors and the public following the debate of sixty Section 140 motions for one-off and multi-unit developments at one meeting.[119] A councillor at the time called planning in the county 'a simmering cauldron of discontent,'[120] though privately some councillors admitted they felt under enormous pressure to secure planning permission for constituents, regardless of whether or not the application constituted good planning. Discussing the matter MacCabe suggests that 'it would appear that many county councillors regard it as their aggressive duty to see that as many one-off houses as possible are provided in the countryside'.[122]

The final report of the Mahon Tribunal recommended the restriction of Section 140 and the Local Government Act, 2013 meant that this power no longer applied to planning functions.

6

Planning
Drift

The 1970s and 1980s have been described as an era of 'planning drift'.[1] Writing at the time, British planner Gordon Cherry declared, 'we are [now] much less sure about the future … in some planning circles we have almost forgotten to think about it'.[2] However, in Ireland there was much activity. An Bord Pleanála was established as an independent appeals body in 1977 and significant work was done regarding private property rights and their relationship to planning. To understand the sequence that gave rise to this it is first necessary to explore decision-making in planning from the 1960s more closely.

CHEQUE-BOOK PLANNING

A system of enforcement against unauthorised development is intended to underpin a basic principle of planning in Ireland: that permission must be obtained from the planning authority before commencing development. Unfortunately too often enforcement has been considered the ignored 'Cinderella' of the planning process.

Frank McDonald has described 'the Gouger Factor. Either we have planning laws or we don't. If we do then they should be rigorously enforced'.[3] Discussing the lack of enforcement proceedings against developments that did not comply with their permissions in the 1960s, 1970s and 1980s, McDonald says, 'in cases like this, the planners behave like brass monkeys. They see, hear and speak no evil. Little wonder then that the planning laws are held in such contempt'.[4]

Dublin in the 1960s was a time of significant office development, facilitated by the demolition of a raft of historic buildings despite the protests of conservationists. A leading figure in this trend was architect Sam Stephenson who strongly defended what his clients were doing. In an interview with Uinseann MacEoin, the editor of *Build* magazine, Stephenson said: 'A city must live. It must evolve and keep changing'.

'But why start with the best parts of it, Mr Stephenson?' he was asked.

'Because developers are primarily interested in a return for their money' he replied. 'But this is cheque-book planning!' exclaimed Mac Eoin.

'That is so, but it is inevitable in a democratic society,' Stephenson responded.[5]

In *The Destruction of Dublin* McDonald recounts the story of the development of a nine-storey block of offices at the corner of Lansdowne Road and Northumberland Road by businessman Stephen 'Stepho' O'Flaherty in 1963: 'The Corporation had rejected this blatantly speculative scheme, but O'Flaherty had friends in high places – and one of those friends was Sean Lemass himself. Thus, before Neil Blaney had even made the order granting permission on appeal, Stepho threw a champagne party to celebrate his famous victory. Lemass had promised to "fix him up". Blaney's decision was made against the strong advice of his own planning officials.'[6]

In 1969, Dublin Corporation was dissolved by the Minister for Local Government for refusing to strike a rate. The Commissioner appointed to carry out the functions of the city council, John Garvin, confirmed the Corporation's original draft development plan without amendment, despite over 2,000 objections and submissions from the public. For McDonald 'the whole process of "public participation", beginning with the first exhibition of the plan … was shown to be an elaborate charade'.[7]

McDonald also recounts the development of the eight-storey Central Bank office building on Dame Street from the mid-1960s where it was discovered when under construction that the building was almost 30 feet higher than it should have been: 'Here was one of the great institutions of the state caught in the act of breaking the law, and in such a flagrant fashion. It was of course a major scandal'[8] and 'the most flagrant ever breach of the planning act'.[9] The original

proposal for a thirteen-storey building was refused permission by the
Minister for Local Government Kevin Boland in 1969 in the face of
intense political pressure to grant. Revised plans were granted permission but frequent revisions to elements of the design and layout of
the scheme and hasty decision-making by Dublin Corporation meant
that the unauthorised increased height went unnoticed until it was
spotted by Dublin's Chief Planning Officer, Charles Aliaga Kelly.

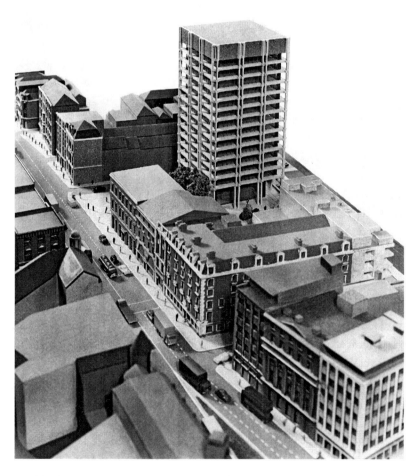

Model of early design for the Central Bank. When construction got underway it
was found that the building was almost thirty feet higher than permission had been
granted for. (Credit: Stephenson Gibney Collection, Irish Architectural Archive)

McDonald describes Kelly as 'a gentleman in a job that – unfortunately – required a roughneck', saying 'Kelly found his role
increasingly usurped by hard-nosed bureaucrats who knew nothing
about planning except what they had absorbed by osmosis. Their
main concern was to avoid claims for compensation, so they looked
at most developments from a narrow viewpoint, circumscribed by
zoning and plot ratio requirements. Architecture and civic design
took a back seat – and the city suffered as a result'.[10] The Central
Bank's application for approval for the new height was refused by
the Corporation and was appealed, leading to a public hearing.
The Dublin Civic Group declared that this was the test case on which
the whole future of planning in Ireland would stand to fall.[11] Architect
Sam Stephenson told the inquiry that planners should not meddle
in the aesthetic work of architects and that a planning permission
'was merely a licence to develop an architectural concept, therefore
if the height of the Central Bank had been increased by 25 per cent,
this was the unavoidable outcome of a creative design process'.[12]
As McDonald points out, if the Central Bank's appeal succeeded,
any developer could obtain planning permission for a building, add
substantially to its height during the course of construction and then,
after this was discovered, call in 'experts' to testify that it was a 'work
of art'.[13] The bank lost its appeal and it had to go through another
planning application and another appeal before permission was finally
granted for a 'compromise' solution in 1975.[14]

During the 'Celtic Tiger' years the Ombudsman noted a 'marked
reluctance' to tackle errant development as the 'thrust of economic
and political pressure is towards the completion of developments in as
short a timeframe as possible' explaining that this led to public cynicism
and allegations of corruption and conflicts of interest.[15] In recent years
a structure very different to the Central Bank emerged as a famous
enforcement case. On Achill Island, County Mayo, developer Joe
McNamara (who blocked the main entrance of Leinster House with
a cement mixer emblazoned with 'toxic bank' and 'Anglo' as a protest
against the behaviour of banks following the collapse of the banking
system in 2007) built a Stonehenge-style structure thirty metres in
diameter. Mayo County Council requested a court order to force
McNamara to remove the edifice as it had been built without planning
permission. McNamara claimed that the structure was exempt from
planning rules as an 'ornamental garden'. The High Court required

The unauthorised 'Achillhenge'. Enforcement has been called the 'Cinderella' of the planning system. (Courtesy of Brendan McGrath)

McNamara to cease further work on the site, and as he was found to be in breach of this, he was jailed for three days for contempt of court. The court referred the planning decision to An Bord Pleanála, which in July 2012 upheld the council's decision, but over eighteen months later the structure remained in place.

Labour's James 'Jim' Tully was Minister for Local Government from 1973 to 1977. Writing in 1985, when there had been nine ministers in office since the 1963 Act, Frank McDonald declared 'in terms of planning, Tully was the worst Minister for Local Government in the history of the state. Almost every county in Ireland is littered with the consequences of his decisions,' describing his four years in office from 1973 to 1977 'as the very nadir of planning in Ireland'.[16] Tully's term as Minister for Local Government has been linked to an extremely relaxed attitude to rural housing in County Meath at the time.[17]

According to McDonald: 'Tully persistently rejected the advice of his own planning advisers. One of his officials has vivid recollections of Tully's modus operandi. "You would be standing in front of his desk arguing that such-and-such an appeal should be rejected out of hand on all sorts of planning grounds, but he would just sit there, smiling malevolently at you, while he signed an order granting permission," he said. "Almost every appeal that came from Meath was granted, especially for bungalows in the countryside, because he apparently saw this as part of a service for his constituents." As a gutsy anti-intellectual, Tully had no time for planners and their often abstruse arguments.'[18]

Years after this time in office, local authority planners, especially in Dublin, would still be trying to cope with the fallout of inexplicable 'Tully permissions' and their 'devastating results'.[19]

McDonald describes Tully as making 'increasingly bizarre planning decisions', citing the May 1975 case where he granted retrospective permission for a half-finished bungalow at a beauty spot in the Dublin mountains – despite the fact that the owner had built it without county council's permission, had been fined in court for breaking the law and had then defied an order to demolish it. Tully's explanation did not reassure outraged conservationists: 'As far as I saw that, it was an opportunity for someone who had never owned a house to own their own house'. He declared, 'I am following policies in relation to planning control which command the support and approval of the great mass of the general public'. While this was a highly publicised case that has parallels to a case in Wicklow in 2013 when the High Court found that a woman who built a chalet without permission did not have to demolish it, McDonald raises the issue of the many Tully decisions that received no media coverage at all.[20]

Another notorious case involving Tully was the development of an office block at the rear of 39 Northumberland Road, in Ballsbridge, Dublin. The scheme was rejected by Dublin Corporation in July 1976. The developers, Isanof Investments, appealed to Tully who, on the advice of his own planning staff, confirmed the Corporation's decision. McDonald continues: 'The Minister's decision shocked auctioneers Geoghan O'Rourke, who were the owners of No. 39 Northumberland Road, because they had been assured that Tully would fix them up. But he didn't realise that they were trading under an assumed name so, when the file arrived on the desk, he failed to make the connection between them and "Iansof Investments". Thus reassured, the boyos now felt confident that Tully would not make the same "mistake" again. Three weeks later, they resubmitted their scheme to the Corporation, using exactly the same set of plans as before, and they were promptly refused permission yet again for exactly the same reasons. But this time, when it went to appeal, the result was quite different'.[21] On 14 March 1977, the day before he handed over appellate jurisdiction to An Bord Pleanála, Tully granted full planning permission without giving any reasons and without setting down any conditions to reduce the impact of a development which he had found seriously deficient months earlier. In another case on the junction of Eglinton Road and Donnybrook Road in Dublin, Tully granted permission for an office building in the face of local and councillor opposition. McDonald quotes Sean Moore as calling the case 'a cynical disregard for all town planning ideals and principles'.[22]

In 1971 plans for a major shopping development at Blackrock in south Dublin requiring the demolition of the eighteenth-century residence of Lord Edward FitzGerald, Frescati House, were announced to outrage. Actor Michael MacLiammoir declared, 'We should struggle and protest, even if we go down under the wave of vulgar bullying. If we are careful, vociferous and violent enough, Frescati will be saved. Man does not live by bread alone, nor does a nation live by supermarkets alone'.[23] What ensued were several years of controversy, during which conservationists wanted to save the house and developers wanted to build a Roches Stores, an office block and a 700-vehicle car park. As Frescati was zoned commercial, the risk of a £1.3 million compensation claim hung over the Council. The dispute continued for years and the house continued to deteriorate. The house was vandalised and many of the fittings were stolen, which made the house more and more difficult to restore. The shopping centre was finally built and the main part of the house continued to deteriorate following the demolition of its wings and it was completely demolished in 1983 after a battle of thirteen years. Much blame was placed on Dún Laoghaire Corporation for failing to ensure that the vacant building was kept in proper repair and that conditions relating to the house were adhered to.

A member of the Frescati Protection Society, Marie Avis Walker applied for, and obtained, planning permission for a development that would preserve the house. This was using a mechanism whereby anyone could apply for permission to redevelop property without the owner's knowledge. The law was changed as a direct result of Walker's action to require that the applicant submit a letter of consent from the owner.

This mechanism first came to light in 1971 when planner Fergal MacCabe applied for permission to build 'a small cabin of clay and wattle construction, nine bean rows, and a honey-bee hive' on the Isle of Innisfree (this was refused by Sligo County Council, who claimed that it would hinder public amenities). MacCabe went further and appealed the decision to the minister asking for an oral hearing on the grounds that the council's decision was *ultra vires* as the bean rows were agriculture development and that notice of intent to

The loss of Frescati House confirmed the weakness of the 1963 Act when it
came to conservation. (Reproduced courtesy of the National Library of Ireland:
L_ROY_05948)

develop the site had been public since the poem's publication in 1888.
The department considered using MacCabe's appeal as a test case for
charging for oral hearings and the appeal was ultimately denied but
not without wags in An Foras Forbartha reporting that their tests of
the load-bearing properties of clay and wattle construction suggested
MacCabe's hut was just a stalking horse for a taller development!

At the time MacCabe also considered applying for permission to
construct a bungalow on Rockall, encouraged by Donegal County
Council who felt that their processing of the application might
assist Ireland's territorial claim to the islet. This was scuppered when
The Irish Times refused to print the required public notice.

McDonald attributes much of the blame in the Frescati affair to
Sean Gibbons, the most senior planning official in Dún Laoghaire
Corporation. He played a very active role in the whole process,
though the nature and extent of his involvement did not come
to light until March 1981 when Ray Burke, then Minister for the
Environment, ordered an inquiry into the affairs of the borough
planning department. This followed a court case during which a
resident of Dún Laoghaire recalled approaching Gibbons for advice

on a planning application, to which Gibbons replied, 'Would you give the job to my son? He is an architect'. His son, John T. Gibbons received a large share of work in Dún Laoghaire while his father was the borough's senior planning official and an investigation by the RTÉ programme *Today Tonight* uncovered that 52 per cent of all successful planning applications over a two-year period were handed by J.T. Gibbons and Associates. Gibbons was suspended and subsequently resigned.[24]

McDonald provides a story outlining the pressures of the period where representatives of a British property investor alleged that they had met Taoiseach Jack Lynch through a Fianna Fáil intermediary to discuss their difficulties in obtaining planning permission for a shopping centre in Crumlin and they received planning permission the following afternoon. Lynch was very concerned about this allegation, saying he had no recollection of anyone coming to see him about property in Crumlin and that if anyone mentioned a planning matter to him while he was Taoiseach he always advised them to use the proper channels.[25]

British developers and architects attempting to develop in Dublin took to publishing notices in newspapers in Irish, leading *Build* magazine to ask whether one such company intended to transact all of its other business through Irish or if it was an attempt to conceal 'a classical piece of urban butchery?'[26] In 1981, just after its ILAC centre in Dublin's Henry Street opened, Irish Life Assurance Company property manager Michael Lucey addressed the Architectural Association of Ireland and suggested the removal of all planning controls, asking 'how much worse would we be in a free-for-all situation?' with McDonald pointing out that at the time the shape of Dublin was almost entirely determined by business forces and 'pin stripe vandals' anyway.[27]

LEANING OVER BACKWARDS

The first party in planning is the applicant for planning permission and the second party is the local authority. Third parties are anyone else with a view on a planning application. Ireland is unique in Europe in that it has a national planning appeals system, available to both first and third parties, operated by an independent body, An Bord Pleanála. The third party right of appeal mechanism has been modified as the numbers and proportions of appeals have increased and development interests have lobbied for its diminution; however, the right to appeal goes back to the 1934 Act.

In the Town and Regional Planning Act, 1934 and the amending Act of 1939, there were several forms of appeal allowable. First, the resolution of a local authority that decided to make a planning scheme was subject to a confirmation order made by the minister which was laid before each House of the Oireachtas. There was also a right of appeal under Section 5 of the 1939 Act for the annulment of the initial resolution by a local authority to make a planning scheme. In addition to that, the property owner affected by a planning scheme had a right under Section 31 to apply to the High Court for an annulment of the whole of the planning scheme or part of it.

Under the 1934 Act any person aggrieved by the grant or the refusal by a planning authority of permission could appeal to the minister. Section 59 of the 1934 Act provided that any person aggrieved by the decisions of a planning authority during the period of interim control, that is, during the period between the passing of a resolution to make a planning scheme and the coming into operation of the planning scheme, could appeal to the minister and the minister could confirm, revoke or alter the decisions of the planning authority as he or she thought proper. By January 1963, the total number of valid appeals under Section 59 of the 1934 Act was 4,037: 790 appeals were allowed; 435 were allowed subject to conditions; 1,425 were disallowed, and 1,030 appeals were withdrawn.[28]

Third parties did not have any express right to make objections to planning applications to the local authority but there was no prohibition on taking them into account either. In 1961 Deputy Patrick Byrne asked the relevant minister if he could restrain Dublin Corporation from allowing the ESB to demolish a terrace of Georgian houses on Fitzwilliam Street for its new headquarters. The minister advised the deputy, 'In theory, any citizen who feels aggrieved by what is proposed can appeal. In practice, it is usually some person with adjoining property. I do not imagine it would be impossible to have an appeal. In fact, I am sure there will be appeals'.[29]

The 1963 Act introduced an unrestricted right of appeal against all local planning decisions (permissions or refusals) for owners wishing to develop their own property; those affected by neighbouring proposals; and the public at large, empowering the Minister for Local

Government to decide appeals against decisions by the applicant (first party) or by third parties. The minister promoted the option of an appeal to him rather than the courts as being cheaper for the citizen saying, 'There will be nothing to stop him from employing advisers or experts but I hope it will be possible for him to present his case without having to employ the costly advisory personnel that would be necessary if he were to have recourse to the courts'.[30]

The 1963 Act's grant of rights of appeal to third parties seems to have been well ahead of its time and the principle received little attention during its passage through the Oireachtas. Before the bill was introduced into the Dáil, officials and the minister extensively toured Europe and North America studying their varied planning systems, and they took on the working of the British system. It has been argued that they concluded they could improve on current British practice.[31]

At the time Neil Blaney stressed that 'every interested person' would have a right of appeal, 'if anything, we are leaning over backwards for the third party's interests and at the same time, there is the danger that we may be forgetting the interests of the owner of the property'.[32]

Future minister Jimmy Tully warned, 'A crank by acting as a third party could hold it up for a considerable period. Is there anything to ensure that that cannot happen?' and was assured by Blaney, 'Where there is a crank operating, it will not be long before we get to know him. There is provision here in case of frivolous appeals so that that type of person will be discouraged on the basis that the Minister can apportion costs. Taking it by and large we are going a very great distance to protect the interest even of the cranks or semi-cranks'.[33]

Under early planning legislation any appeals went to the Minister for Local Government. Shortly after the 1934 Act the Local Government Tribunal suggested that a special tribunal be established to consider appeals under the legislation. Minister for Local Government and Public Health Seán T. O'Kelly introduced the 1938 Town and Regional Planning (Amendment) Bill to the house in October 1938 for its second reading. Outlining the rationale for the proposed amendments O'Kelly did not discuss Section 12 of the bill which gave additional appeal powers to the minister, including the power to impose costs. This was raised by leader of the opposition, W.T. Cosgrave, who suggested that the minister was appointing himself as a court in an unprecedented way.[34]

The appeal to the minister was far more contentious than the idea of third-party appeals during the 1962 bill's passage through the Oireachtas. In the Seanad Fine Gael spokesman Thomas Fitzpatrick warned, 'In my experience, appeal to the Minister is never satisfactory because it is not an appeal in open court. At best, the evidence is given to an inspector appointed by the Minister … I know the Minister's answer is that, if he is to preserve uniformity, he must keep control. There is something in what the Minister says, but I think he could restore, or preserve, public confidence by appointing an arbitrator to deal with this sort of thing'. Fitzpatrick added, 'The Minister cannot but be influenced by the fact that he may have already directed a planning authority to do that against which appeal is taken'.[35] Deputy Patrick Hogan warned that the appeal to the minister could 'arouse in the public mind suspicions that it is a measure which lends itself beautifully to political patronage'.[36] Deputy Mark Clinton said the appeal powers gave 'an opening to a Minister to use that power for party political purposes' and particularly referenced promoters of petrol stations who he felt might bring substantial pressure to bear.[37] Deputy Thaddeus Lynch, an auctioneer, felt the right of appeal to the minister was 'the law of the jungle' with the possibility of 'inhuman' officials in the department assessing appeals.[38]

There was also criticism from the cabinet. Minister for Health and former Local Government Minister Seán MacEntee called for an independent appeals procedure given the pressure that might come to bear on the minister in appeal cases, claiming that when he was Minister for Local Government he had intended introducing legislation proposing that they be handled by a member of judiciary.[39] The Department of Local Government quadrupled its technical staff to deal with the expected increase in planning appeals.

In 1970 the planning committee of the RIAI began a study into the operation of the 1963 Act. The findings attributed delays in planning decisions to staff shortages in planning departments rather than the process itself with broad support for the third-party appeals system.[40]

In 1978 the Construction Industry Federation (CIF) was calling Ireland 'the happy haven for development obstruction' with delays at local authority level and the appeals system to blame.[41] Writing in *Construction* magazine in November 1980, former president of the CIF Sean McKone called planning the 'Achilles' heel' of the construction industry, arguing that it artificially inflated land values and delayed construction, compounded by the appeals system. When the 1982 Local Government (Planning and Development) Act provided for fees for appeals and submissions (previously a refundable £10 deposit applied) a public protest was called against their imposition.

The 2000 Act tightened up the process, requiring that for a third party to appeal a decision they must have made an observation to the local authority on the application. It remained open for any member of the public to become involved in the process and newspaper and site notices contained this information.

AN BORD PLEANÁLA

Dissatisfaction with the minister's handling of planning appeals built quickly. In his 1961 report Charles Abrams had recommended a planning appeals tribunal. The constitutionality of the right of appeal to the minister, not to the courts, in the 1963 Act was challenged. In 1967 Fine Gael introduced a private member's bill providing for a planning appeals board amid suspicions 'that money was being passed into the coffers of the Fianna Fáil party for favours under the Planning Acts'.[42]

A 1968 Dáil debate on the Planning Appeals Bill turned into a prolonged exchange between Minister for Local Government Kevin Boland and Fine Gael TD Gerald L'Estrange over suggestions that donors to Fianna Fáil's fundraising operation Taca received favourable planning decisions on appeal to the minister. L'Estrange said of one developer, 'This man will ultimately get permission because he is a head member of Taca … I will have a little bet on it. The Minister is making the case for him now because he will be giving him permission shortly … Does the Minister deny that this man gave £2,000 to Taca and gave it because he wanted something in return and said he would get it?'[43] The bill was rejected by a vote of sixty-four to fifty-four in March 1968.

In February 1969 the Minister for Local Government Kevin Boland introduced the Local Government (Planning and Development) Bill 1969, providing for the establishment of An Bord Achomharc Pleanála; however, the planning appeals board was not created until 1977. The Fine Gael/Labour coalition's manifesto of 1973 (its statement of intent 'There is an Alternative') included a commitment to transferring the planning appeals function from the minister to an independent body. The resultant Local Government (Planning and Development

Bill), 1973 saw almost 200 amendments considered before it became law in July 1976.

On 1 January 1977 An Bord Pleanála was established as an independent body. Initially the chairman of the board was required to be a High Court judge or someone who had previously held judicial office. Its first chairman was Mr Justice Denis Pringle, a former High Court and Special Criminal Court Judge. Pringle had presided over some high-profile cases, including the trial of the kidnappers of the Dutch industrialist Tiede Herrema, where he received a letter bomb the day before the trial, and he imposed the death sentence in the initial trial of Noel and Marie Murray for the murder of Garda Michael Reynolds. The principal officer in the Department of the Environment, Brendan O'Donoghue, was responsible for the preparation of the bill, was also appointed and became de facto chief executive.[44] In a controversial move at the time, Jim Tully appointed one of his associates Seán O'Brien, a former bread salesman from Navan, to the six-person board, though he 'proved to be able and effective'.[45, 46] Its first non-judicial chairman was former Dublin senior planner Frank Benson in 1984.

For Oliver Flanagan TD the real reason the Fianna Fáil government pressed ahead with an independent body to administer planning appeals was pressure from local representatives who were at the mercy of constituents demanding that they take an interest in their planning applications with the credit (deserved or otherwise) in successful applications and appeals to the minister balanced against the unpopularity arising from refusals.[47] The buffer of the board conveniently allowing politicians an opportunity to blame bureaucrats in Dublin when required.

An Bord Pleanála considers all appealed developments 'de novo', that is as if the application had been made to it 'in the first instance'. Unlike the minister who did not have to give their reasons for a planning decision, the board is required to make public its reasoning for every decision. However, it has been encouraged to provide a greater level of detail as part of this.

The board's early years were not without controversy. In June 1977 it rejected an appeal by a developer for planning permission for a three-storey office building in Dublin's Harcourt Terrace. In line with the act's requirement that the board gives reasons for all decisions in a highly controversial addendum, it proceeded to offer advice on how the office block might be redesigned to win approval at a later stage. This gave rise to accusations that the board was usurping the role of the local authority. Within weeks developer Desmond FitzGerald submitted a revised set of plans – drawn up to comply with 'the requirements of the planning board'.[48] On 28 July 1978 the Supreme Court issued its first decision relating to an appeal decided by the board, confirming that a decision on an asbestos waste dump was not beyond its powers.

Establishing the board had unintended negative consequences – the secondment of the majority of the Department of Local Government's planning staff to the board diminished the importance of the planning function within the department and further limited its effectiveness in terms of policy-making or co-ordination.[49]

Further legislation in 1983 provided for a reconstitution of the board and an 'arm's length' system for appointing board members. The collapse of the Fianna Fáil government at the end of 1982 revealed that outgoing Minister for the Environment Ray Burke had appointed five members to An Bord Pleanála who had little relevant qualifications or experience. R.F. Foster puts it more bluntly, saying that Burke had 'packed An Bord Pleanála … with five apparently unqualified nominees'. Incoming Tánaiste and Minister responsible Dick Spring 'was gravely concerned at this, especially in view of information that suggested that some appeals were in effect being delegated to groups of board members that might include no non-political appointees'[50] and prepared a bill curbing the potential for political appointments to the board. For Taoiseach Garrett FitzGerald the existing board was replaced 'to protect the planning appeals system from political influence which, given the amounts of money at stake, could be open to accusations of corrupt use'.[51]

Fianna Fáil leader Charles Haughey responded with 'undisguised fury', calling the legislation 'spiteful' and 'a mean, debasing piece of legislation. It has no motivation except party political vindictiveness'. He went on to state, 'this business of physical planning and our environment is essentially a social matter. Because it is a social matter it must be a political matter. We totally reject this idea of depoliticising the planning process'.[52] For Foster 'spiteful, dirty, mean and debasing' were words that might be better applied to Haughey and Burke's 'manipulation of patronage and planning'.[53] It has been suggested that some of Haughey's outrage was an attempt to delay the legislation while the 'old' board considered applications in which he had an interest.

Though internationally unusual and generally well respected, some are less than enthusiastic about the board to this day. In a report in 2009 the IRDA described An Bord Pleanála 'as the most powerful institution in the country – more powerful than the Oireachtas'.[54] The Irish Citizens Party challenged An Bord Pleanála's independence, concluding that it made the Irish planning system the 'most undemocratic in the world'.[55]

PRIVATE OWNERSHIP OF PRODUCTIVE PROPERTY

The Constitution of the Irish Free State of 1922 contained no general provisions dealing with property rights, while the Constitution of 1937 was notable in that it contained two separate provisions dealing with the right to property. Irish journalist Vincent Browne has traced the insertion of these private property clauses to the Jesuits, whose submission to the constitutional drafting committee proposed the modest distribution of private property, an allowance for some property being held in public ownership, with a strong endorsement on 'private ownership of productive property, as understood in Christian teaching'.[56]

The 1934 Act provided for compensation and betterment, the latter of which was later omitted from the Local Government (Planning and Development) Act, 1963. Section 72 of the 1934 legislation provided that the local authority could require property owners to pay the authority 75 per cent of the increase in value of land, where the increase arose from a provision of the local authority's planning scheme for the area. The landowner could avoid this liability for a period of fourteen years or until the property changed hands by undertaking not to change the use of the property involved. It was felt that the payment of betterment to local authorities was likely to offset claims for compensation. However, while there was widespread fear of onerous demands for compensation, the provisions relating to betterment were completely ignored by local authorities.

The idea of compensation can be traced back to the Lands Clauses Consolidation Act, 1845 and a patchwork of other Victorian legislation, which conferred on each householder the right to connect up to the public water and sewage systems. This was a time before zoning and planning permission and 'It is not surprising, therefore, that these statutory rules reflected the idea that a landowner should receive compensation where he was denied the right to do as he pleased with his property'.[57] The 1890 Housing of the Working Classes Act entitled the owners of unhealthy tenements to compensation. The 1908 Clancy Act placed the cost of clearing an unhealthy tenement building on the owner rather than the Council but owners still made large compensation claims and there is indirect evidence that slum property may have been acquired in the expectation of profiting from compensation when it was cleared.[58]

As planner, barrister, lecturer and former member of An Bord Pleanála, Berna Grist explains the principle of planning compensation is 'if the value of an interest in land is reduced as a result of a planning decision, the person having such an interest in entitled to be paid an amount representing this reduction in value by way of compensation'.[59] The reductions may arise from a refusal of permission or onerous conditions which are seen to interfere with a landowner's rights to develop their land. Therefore Part VI of the 1963 Act, which had to be drafted in accordance with the rights to private property in the Bunreacht na hÉireann, included 'generous provisions with regard to eligibility for compensation and amounts awardable' though 'these have been made more restrictive over the years in line with the developing attitudes of society towards private property rights'.[60] There were limited exemptions (primarily on traffic or public health grounds).

In 1967 legal proceedings were issued by a number of Dublin city-centre property owners (the Central Dublin Development Association) who called aspects of the legislation 'inhumane', claimed the powers given to planning authorities were unconstitutional and that the provisions for compensation were 'completely inadequate'. The challenge failed, largely because of the provisions for compensation provided for in the act.

Grist describes a 'culture of compensation' in the 1970s, encouraged by High Court judgements. In the 1976 Viscount Securities case it was held that a refusal for permission to build houses on land zoned for agriculture created a liability for compensation. This sparked interest in the property industry since in a worst-case scenario any purchase of land might lead to compensation while planners recognised that any refusal could trigger a compensation claim unless non-compensatable

reasons were included.[61] Frank McDonald attributed fear of compensation claims to the Minister for Local Government's controversial
1969 decision to allow a modern office development at the corner of
Hume Street and St Stephen's Green in the face of preservationists'
ire. McDonald also argues that compensation caused local authorities to do deals with developers, sometimes leading to permission for
'appalling schemes'.[62]

By the mid-1980s a number of large compensation payments
increased awareness of this cost to the public purse and calls for limi-
tations on compensation increased. Reformers in the Irish Planning
Institute and local authorities argued that compensation could
constitutionally be eliminated for developments which contravened
the zoning of the development plan made in the common good.
In the X.J.S. Investments case, 24 acres in Killiney which had been
bought for £40,000 in 1981 were the subject of a compensation claim
of £2.375 million when permission for residential development was
refused. In his judgement Judge McCarthy asked 'whether or not
legislation which appears to authorise such a use of public funds is
constitutionally proper?'[63]

The 1990 Planning Act enlarged the non-compensatable reasons for
refusal – for example if permission was refused on the grounds that it
would contravene the zoning of the development plan, compensation
was no longer payable. Some protection was offered to landowners
in the event of 'downzoning' but new valuation rules for assessing
compensation were introduced. No constitutional challenge was
brought against these provisions and the result was abrupt. In 1990
twenty-three claims for compensation valued at £41 million were
lodged, but by 1999 no claims were recorded though provisions
regarding compensation remain in the 2000 Act.[64] From 2002 to 2012
there were nineteen compensation claims totalling €68,095,005. Four
were paid to a total value of €1,869,813.

Effective planning is largely dependent upon the availability of a
supply of development land at a reasonable cost. In 1971 the government established a committee of experts, chaired by Mr Justice J. Kenny,
'as a response to the anarchic explosion of badly-planned housing
during the previous Irish boom of the 1960s'.[65] The committee was
to consider measures for controlling the price of land required for
urban development and securing a substantial part of the increase in
the value of serviced land for the benefit of the community.

The 1974 Kenny Report on the Price of Building Land proposed a Designated Area Scheme whereby land likely to be required for urban expansion over the following ten years or land benefitting as a consequence of public works could be 'designated' by a High Court Order. The local authority would then have the right to acquire such designated land at existing use value, plus 25 per cent. There was also a minority report that disagreed with the majority report on a number of grounds, including possible unconstitutionality. This recommended giving local authorities a right or pre-emption to buy land at an agreed market rate, rather than compulsory purchase at existing use value, plus 25 per cent.

The Kenny Report concluded that 'a situation should [not] continue where dealings in building land can result in large unearned profits for individuals and where local authorities have to compete with private interests in order to acquire land required for the expansion of towns and cities and to pay inflated prices for it'. The policy was almost unanimously in the public interest, and in fact 'threatened just one small group of people – the speculators and developers who controlled the large land banks'.[66] According to Fintan O'Toole of *The Irish Times* every government has agreed with the Kenny Report while managing 'to believe that this conviction was like agreeing with Pythagoras's theorem – it was clearly right but you didn't have to do anything about it'.[67]

In 1981, seven years after its publication, it was still being debated with the Minister of State at the Department of Finance, Barry Desmond, telling Dublin county councillors that the Constitution should be amended to enact the Kenny Report if required as the windfall profits given to landowners by some re-zonings made it 'very hard to tell the ordinary people to exercise moderation and not to look for too big a share of the national cake'. The response of the councillors present at Desmond's address was mixed with one saying 'what happened after they rezoned it was not their problem'.[68] In 1982 a bill 'to provide for the better control of the supply and price of building land' failed to pass and was followed by a joint committee on building land.

Discussing the failure of successive governments to implement, or even test the constitutionality of the Kenny recommendations (which could be addressed by a referendum if necessary), Professor Dennis Pringle concludes that 'it is difficult to avoid the suspicion that neither Fianna Fáil nor Fine Gael have any real interest in curbing property speculation'.[69] Though for Ciarán Cuffe the 2009 NAMA Act in essence introduced the Kenny Report by creating an 80 per cent tax for windfall profits arising from rezoning.

According to Dennis Pringle the Republic of Ireland failed to respond to the planning problems associated with urbanisation due to its 'prevailing rural ethos' with this 'traditional rural outlook' reflected in the private property rights of the Irish constitution which he blames for inappropriate development (to ensure there are no compensation claims) and property speculation.[70]

REGENERATION

American historian, sociologist and chronicler of cities Lewis Mumford was invited to Dublin in 1971 by An Foras Forbartha. In a lecture Mumford argued that Dublin displayed 'the worst aspects of the collapse of twentieth-century urban structure and was on its way to becoming a non-city' with lifeless suburbs, 'boring' office developments and town planners with second-rate minds.[71]

Encouraged by policies focused on the development of the suburbs from the 1930s until the early 1990s, large numbers of individuals left the inner city of Dublin. By the early 1980s the inner city area was characterised by widespread dereliction, rising unemployment, population loss and a range of other social problems. Policymakers came to the conclusion that the level of investment required to remedy urban decay was well beyond the resources available to Dublin Corporation, so in the mid-1980s they sought to induce the private sector to invest in the inner city.

The first impetus for urban renewal emerged from the 'Gregory Deal' where Taoiseach, Charles Haughey agreed in 1982 to allocate an extra funding for housing development in the north inner city, in return for the critical support of Tony Gregory TD.[72]

The main drivers of urban renewal in Dublin from the mid-1980s to the late 1990s were the Urban Renewal Act and the Finance Act, both enacted in 1986. A 1982 Urban Development Areas Bill proposed the establishment of two special commissions within Dublin city. The first would oversee renewal at the Custom House Docks, and the second in the Liberties area of the city. The commissions would be exempted from the traditional planning process, and this was heavily criticised by city councillors and An Taisce as undemocratic. The collapse of the Fianna Fáil government in November 1982 saw the bill lie dormant until the Urban Renewal Bill 1986 which closely resembled the 1982 bill, passed all stages of the Oireachtas.

The Urban Renewal Act established designated areas, which were to become the prime focus of urban renewal policy, while the 1986 Finance Act outlined a broad range of financial incentives which were to be applicable in these areas.[73]

The Custom House Docks Development Authority (CHDDA) was set up in 1986 to redevelop the 27-acre Custom House Docks site. It had its own planning powers and could enter public-private partnerships. For some this represented a shift to more 'entrepreneurial' planning influenced by 'neo-liberalism and Thatcher-style policies of privatisation'.[74] The model exposed a tension in Irish planning regarding the role of the State as 'rather than the local authority mediating the relationship between central government and the market, this middle tier was removed' with central government funding and taking responsibility for the development through the 'provision of fiscal and other financial incentives as well as through the creation of a new regulatory environment to facilitate private investment and development'.[75]

In 1997 the CHDDA was dissolved and the Dublin Docklands Development Authority was set up, overseeing a 520-hectare area north and south of Dublin's River Liffey. It produced its first overall master plan for the area in 1997, under which more detailed planning schemes were made. Development carried out the by the DDDA which was consistent with the adopted planning scheme or which was certified by the DDDA to be consistent with the scheme, did not require permission. Following a report from the Comptroller and Auditor General in 2012 the government decided to wind up the DDDA and return the planning of the area to Dublin City Council, much of it as a Strategic Development Zone.

The creation of a new living and working community in Dublin Docklands represented a considerable achievement comparable to other major waterfront regeneration projects elsewhere in Europe. The award-winning Grand Canal Square is the location for the Studio Libeskind-designed Grand Canal Theatre, a hotel and other supporting businesses. The design for the public realm project in Grand Canal Square was selected following a competition won by American

The Custom House, home of the Department of Environment, Heritage and Local Government which is responsible for national planning policy. It was not until 1946, twelve years after the first planning legislation, that a planning section was formed within the then Department of Local Government. (Courtesy of Bill Hastings)

landscape architect Martha Schwartz. This emphasis on quality place-making has been widely recognised and the docklands are now the site of discerning multinationals like Google and Facebook, leading to it being dubbed 'Silicon Docks'.

The fundamental aspect of any regeneration is community involvement. During a 1988 Urban Renewal Week organised by the Goethe Institute, in association with the Irish Planning Institute and University College Dublin, German and Irish practitioners drafted an agenda of principles for future urban renewal schemes in Dublin and other Irish centres. These centred on community participation and inclusion. Twenty-five years later upon the publication of Dublin City Council's proposed scheme for the Strategic Development Zone in Dublin Docklands, Irish Planning Institute president Joanna Kelly reiterated this agenda, emphasising, 'that the creation of sustainable and vibrant communities must be at the heart of any planning scheme ... we should ask where is the evidence of community engagement or influences on the scheme? Is the built environment, as envisaged in the scheme. What the current population within the Docklands want or will existing communities be displaced?'[76]

In 1986 Minister for the Environment, John Boland established the Dublin Metropolitan Streets Commission. The commission, evoking the spirit of the Wide Street Commissioners of the eighteenth century, was entrusted with the task of improving the public image and physical, economic and social qualities of Dublin city centre, including St Stephen's Green, Grafton Street, College Green, Westmoreland Street, D'Olier Street, O'Connell Street and Parnell Square. The commission had wide powers to control day-to-day planning, land use, traffic and maintenance. It recommended major traffic-calming proposals in O'Connell Street, with significantly widened pavements and a tree-lined central mall; College Green was to become once again a major civic space with reduced traffic; D'Olier Street and Westmoreland Street were to be tree-lined boulevards with wide pavements and the Grafton Street area was to be totally pedestrianised.[77] A change of government meant the commission was disbanded after fewer than six months, meaning it had no time to implement its policies. Though many were subsequently adopted, it has been suggested that its only direct achievement was a new Eason's street clock on O'Connell Street.[78]

From the 1980s new mechanisms and agencies were put in place to oversee development and planning in areas such as the Dublin Docklands. (Courtesy of Bill Hastings)

Temple Bar is one of the oldest parts of Dublin but by the 1960s it had become severely run down. Córas Iompair Éireann (CIÉ), the State transport company, began buying up property there in the 1970s with the view to building a large bus depot with an underground DART railway connection. Delays in financing led CIÉ to rent out the buildings at nominal rents, many of which were taken up by small businesses and a growing number of artists seeking cheap studio space in the city centre. This produced a nascent 'cultural quarter'. In July 1987 councillors voted for the preservation and redevelopment of the area. For John Montgomery, a planner who advised the Irish Government on the development of Temple Bar as a cultural quarter under the Temple Bar Area Renewal and Development Act, 1991, one of the area's assets was the potential for variety and diversity of uses and activities rather than neat zoning schemes, saying 'the tragedy of town planning is that it has, since its early days, sought to thin out the city and separate activities from each other'.[79] The success of the area remains contested.

CONCLUSION

In 1991 the Irish Branch of the Royal Town Planning Institute held a conference in Dublin to mark its fiftieth anniversary. Amongst the speakers was Fintan O'Toole whose paper *Planning and the Irish Psyche* asked 'are the Irish people amenable to planning?' O'Toole suggested that in Ireland the problem about planning was that it attempted to predict an uncertain future and 'in Ireland, not only is the future unpredictable, even the past is unpredictable. We keep revising our history. If we can't even trust the relationship of the present to the past, how much less can we trust the relationship of the present to the future'. O'Toole suggested that Irish happy fatalism and easy pessimism where 'we expect calamity so that we can be pleasantly surprised if things turn out to be barely tolerable at all' means a culture of 'if nothing can ever really get better, then there is not much point in working and planning for change' prevails. O'Toole concluded that there were three reasons for this fatalistic belief in the inevitable failure of planning: Catholicism; poverty; and the sense of the impermanence of our political and social institutions. For him 'It is only when we move away from these things that we will begin to be able to commit ourselves to the notion that planning might be about bringing about the best rather than preparing for the worst'.

Ireland was shortly to experience a boom that should have addressed O'Toole's poverty thesis but instead economic success may have accentuated, rather than lessened, apathy towards planning for a sustainable future. Meanwhile the reasons and consequences of much 1980s rezoning were to emerge.

Boom
and Bust

NEW LEGISLATION, NEW HOPE

Under the 1963 Act each planning authority was obliged to make a development plan by 1967 and thereafter to review the plan at least every five years, but by 1999, 43 per cent of development plans were more than five years old.

The programme for government agreed by Fianna Fáil and the Progressive Democrats, 'Action Programme for the Millennium', following the 1997 general election committed the parties to 'updating and consolidating our planning laws to prepare for the challenges of the new millennium'. This was in order to 'ensure the planned and orderly development of all areas', to 'facilitate maximum participation in the planning process' and to 'ensure the principle of sustainable development is at the centre of the planning process'. This began with a public consultation from August 1997, culminating in a 'convention on the Irish planning system' entitled 'Continuity and Change' in November 1997. Grist notes that this was an innovative approach to legislative reform which was essential in the circumstances as planning was the local government activity which was in contact with everyone.[1]

For Minister for the Environment Noel Dempsey the legislation was to create a 'planning system of the twenty-first century' which must be 'strategic in approach, be imbued with an ethos of sustainable development and deliver a performance of the highest quality'.[2]

Speaking on the bill, Conor Lenihan TD called the existing legislation a 'crank's charter' in need of streamlining. Planners did not escape ridicule. In a Dáil debate Denis Naughten TD complained that the 'latest planning officer' in his electoral area was 'only just out of college and when she is making a decision on whether to grant planning permission, she refers to her textbook. It is not acceptable for somebody just out of college to have the responsibility of a planning officer and to use a textbook to decide whether to grant planning permission or to decide the conditions she will impose'.[3]

The Planning and Development Act, 2000 was brought into force in five phases between 1 November 2000 and 11 March 2002. The act had an emphasis on 'sustainable' development, with the adjective qualifying development throughout.[4] For Noel Dempsey sustainable development was 'woven into the fabric of the bill' and while on first glance 'proper planning and development' of an area was replaced with 'proper planning and sustainable development' it went deeper than a change in terminology.[5] Despite this focus on sustainable development, the term was deliberately not defined as in the minister's view 'it is such a dynamic and all-embracing concept, and one which will evolve over time, that any legal definition would tend to restrict and stifle it. Weaving it into the fabric of the bill, as we have done, gives effect to the concept in a holistic and comprehensive way'[6].

For Berna Grist the 2000 Act consolidated, modernised and amended complex planning legislation and brought clarity to the area, though this was short-lived. Soon domestic and European-driven changes were to return planning legislation to a 'labyrinth to be negotiated solely by the valiant and then with considerable trepidation'.[7]

The 2000 Act introduced detailed binding timeframes for the review and preparation of development plans. This was to address the issue of out-of-date plans. A 1983 An Foras Forbartha study showed that 75 per cent of planning authorities were not keeping to the then five-year reviews of their development plans.[8]

The act required planning authorities to 'have regard to' regional planning guidelines. The judgement in the case of McEvoy and Smith *v*. Meath County Council meant 'this phraseology was rendered innocuous'. Tony McEvoy, an elected member of Kildare County

Council, and An Taisce chairman Michael Smith mounted a legal
challenge to the Meath County Development Plan, which had over-
provided zoned lands compared to the projected regional population
growth. The High Court held that the phrase did not require the
planning authority to comply with the relevant guidelines but merely
to give them 'reasonable consideration'. The judgement held that
'to have regard to the guidelines when making and adopting the development plan does not require it rigidly or "slavishly" to comply with
the guidelines' recommendations or even necessarily to adopt fully
the strategy and policies outlined therein'.[9] The population of County
Meath was to grow to 139,500 by 2006 but councillors rezoned so
much land that the population could reach 242,000 by 2011, with
minutes of council meetings showing that the regional guidelines
were rarely discussed while councillors were considering submissions
to have land rezoned for housing. Instead, the decisions 'appear to have
been influenced more by pressure and lobbying exerted by interested
parties' with 'local interests' overruling 'local needs'.[10]

In Berna Grist's words 'the legislation does not see planning
authorities or An Bord Pleanála as the sole repository of knowledge
on planning matters', hence there are 'prescribed bodies' who may
be statutory consultees, depending on the type and location of the
proposal.[11] For Grist the 2000 Act reflected the changes in Irish
society since the 1963 Act in other ways, with emphasis on recreational amenities and landscape in the 2000 Act reflecting the needs
and priorities of an urbanising society, for example.[12]

In the 1990s Ireland suffered a housing crisis with demand
outstripping supply, especially in and around the cities. Sustained
household growth, house price inflation and a rise in the cost of
living saw the Department of the Environment commission a series
of housing studies (referred to as the 'Bacon Reports' after their
economist author Dr Peter Bacon) and introduce Part V into the
Planning & Development Act, 2000. This required all local authorities to adopt a housing strategy in their development plan and to
allocate up to 20 per cent of all new residential developments of
four or more dwellings in zoned land for social and/or affordable housing. A key goal of Part V of the act was to disincentivise
residential segregation and encourage integrated, mixed housing
(in social and tenure terms). This part of the act was challenged
by developers and construction industry leaders who claimed that

the State was intervening beyond its remit in the private housing market.[13] The Planning and Development Bill, 1999 was presented to the President for signing into law on 26 June 2000. The President referred Part V of the bill to the Supreme Court for a decision on whether it was repugnant to the Constitution. By referring Part V to the Supreme Court its validity could not subsequently be disputed though the rest of the act remained open to scrutiny. The matter was heard on 24 and 25 July and the Supreme Court delivered its judgment upholding the constitutionality of Part V on 28 August; the bill was signed into law later that day. In its judgement the Supreme Court accepted that the social problems arising from the housing crisis of the time warranted interference with consti-tutionally protected property rights and that the housing strategy mechanism constituted a restriction of those rights proportionate to the desirable social objective of providing both affordable and public housing integrated with private housing.

In December 2002 the Minister for the Environment Martin Cullen introduced a bill amending Part V of the 2000 Act, allowing developers additional ways to comply with their obligations to provide social and affordable housing. Now developers could provide land, sites or houses at a completely different location within the functional area of the planning authority or pay to discharge this obligation. This undermined the emphasis on integrated housing developments underpinning the original provision and fore-grounded the developer-led nature of the construction industry and housing sector at the time. NIRSA suggest that this 'ability of vested interests to routinely overturn strategies designed to support the public benefit is indicative of the loose and mutable arrangements in the Irish policy sphere'.[14]

The 2000 Act introduced the concept of Strategic Development Zones (SDZs) for which there would be a streamlined planning process. The 1999 Bill envisaged SDZs as a mechanism to develop economic projects by overseas companies investing in Ireland. This was to counter suggestions that the planning application process was discour-aging inward investment.[15] SDZs are essentially an adaptation of the UK's Simplified Planning Zones (SPZs), which were introduced by the Thatcher government in 1986. During the bill's passage through the Oireachtas with the housing crisis beginning to bite, their use was extended to residential schemes. This gives an indication of the shift regarding which planning issues were of national economic and social importance. An SDZ is designated by the government on the proposal of the Minister for the Environment and once designated, planning schemes are prepared by development agencies such as the local authority or the Grangegorman Development Agency. The SDZ must be of economic or social importance in the view of government. A detailed draft planning scheme is submitted to the planning authority for adoption in a procedure modelled on the development plan. The planning scheme can be appealed to An Bord Pleanála. Applications for planning permission in an SDZ are made in the same way as elsewhere but must be granted if they are consistent with the planning scheme and cannot be granted if they are inconsistent with it.

Following the 2000 Act three sites in the Dublin area were designated as SDZs from 1 July 2001. These included Adamstown and Hansfield. Subsequently designated SDZs include Clonburris, Cherrywood and Grangegorman in Dublin and Monard in Cork (refused by An Bord Pleanála in 2013). Following the decision to dissolve the Dublin Docklands Development Authority parts of the Dublin Docklands area were designated as a Strategic Development Zone in 2012.

The 223-hectare Adamstown Strategic Development Zone has sought to provide community facilities and public transport alongside high-quality housing. (Courtesy of South Dublin County Council)

Adamstown, on a 223-hectare site to the south-west of Lucan, has been the most successful and advanced SDZ to date, seeking to efficiently use space with a high standard of design and material finishes while providing community facilities and public transport alongside housing. However, some residents have expressed a sense that the area is 'unfinished' with promised facilities yet to materialise, in significant part due to the financial crisis of recent years.

NATIONAL SPATIAL STRATEGY

As early as 1919 *The Irish Builder and Engineer* carried calls for a hierarchy of plans guiding development saying: 'No housing scheme should be embarked upon unless it forms part of a town-planning scheme, and no town-planning scheme should be decided upon unless it forms part of a regional planning scheme, and one would like to say that all regional planning schemes should form part of one general national scheme.'[16]

In September 2001 Noel Dempsey specifically chose to launch the final stages of the public consultation paper on the National Spatial Strategy in Charlestown, County Mayo, given the town's links to journalist John Healy whose series of newspaper articles 'Death of an Irish Town' – later published as *No One Shouted Stop* in 1968 – discussed rural decline and the need for a response. Dempsey linked the strategy to solving issues of rural decline and isolation by leading to more balanced regional development. In his address Dempsey warned that parochial outlooks and local self-interest could not hamper the 'once in thirty year' chance to adopt a considered and realistic spatial strategy prioritising certain areas for growth.

The National Spatial Strategy was published on 28 November 2002. The National Development Plan 2000–2006 had identified the five main cities as 'gateways', driving growth in the regions. The National Spatial Strategy added Dundalk, Sligo and the 'linked gateways' of Letterkenny/Derry and Athlone/Tullamore/Mullingar to the mix along with nine regional 'hubs' supporting the gateways.[17] The aim was to develop a critical mass in these locations to drive growth. Following its publication much of the discussion focused on the selection, or lack of selection, of particular places as either gateways or hubs. At the time there was an optimistic view that, despite previous resistance to focusing development on key centres rather than seeking its equal distribution around the country, 'Irish society was now mature enough to "buy" into it'.[18]

The government's decentralisation programme for the Civil Service was announced in December 2003 by the Minister for Finance Charlie McCreevy's budget. This programme anticipated over 10,000 civil servants and eight government departments relocating from Dublin to fifty-three centres in twenty-five counties, many outside of designated gateways and hubs. According to Ciarán Cuffe, 'The decentralisation programme filleted the National Spatial Strategy'.[19]

For Berna Grist, a closer look at the chosen towns revealed that, for the most part, they were in constituencies of various ministers, constituencies which had not been allocated a gateway or hub. For example, the administrative headquarters of the Department of Defence was moved to Newbridge in the constituency of the Minister for Finance while the Office of Public Works was relocated to Trim, County Meath, in the constituency of the Minister for Transport.[20]

Professor Brigid Laffin, principal of the College of Human science at the University College Dublin, told the MacGill Summer School in Glenties, County Donegal, on 20 July 2010, that 'it wasn't decentralisation. Decentralisation is a very good thing. This was a dispersal of public jobs throughout the country in the most extraordinary fashion and it went completely against the government's own spatial strategy. Decentralisation was costly. It increased the fragmentation of our public institutions. It is a charter for mileage claims and a high cost to the Irish public.'

For Grist, another factor which undermined the National Spatial Strategy was the steady relaxation of controls on new rural housing contained in a series of national policies.[21] The strategy was not given statutory, legislative status and was viewed as merely a framework document that offered guidance to policymakers. Dr Edgar Morgenroth of the ESRI attributes the failure of the National Spatial Strategy to its lack of engagement with economics and the market.[22] This drive to spread development despite what the economy can sustain can first be seen in Norman times when of 270 sites that adopted town charters, only fifty-six developed into significant towns. Morgenroth attributes this to a tendency to plan for existing patterns and behaviour rather than asking if there are more sustainable or desirable ways of doing things.[23] In 2013 Minister for the Environment

Phil Hogan told an Oireachtas committee that the National Spatial Strategy had been scrapped. It was then hastily explained that the policy remained in force until a successor had been developed.

EVIDENCE THAT THE STATE IS BECOMING A DICTATORSHIP

In 2006 Labour's then Environment, Housing and Local Government spokesperson Eamon Gilmore criticised Fianna Fáil and the Progressive Democrats for not doing enough to speed up infrastructure development saying: 'Fianna Fáil was founded by a mathematician, so I have a mathematical conundrum for the Minister. If the Victorians could build a railway line from Dublin to Cork and from concept to completion in only four years, why in the twenty-first century did it take Fianna Fáil and the Progressive Democrats nearly three years to write a bill about speeding up the construction of railways and roads?'[24]

In their book *Chaos at the Crossroads* McDonald and Nix argue that the government was determined to make it easier for big projects to get the go-ahead and criticise the then strategic infrastructure bill as allowing private sector, profit driven ventures quicker passage through the planning consent process. McDonald and Nix write that 'behind all of this is Bertie Ahern', claiming that Ahern's visit to China in January 2005 was a significant point in the evolution of the legislation. While in China, Ahern – using characteristically jumbled syntax – said that he would like to have the powers of Han Zheng, the Mayor of Shanghai: 'When he decides he wants to do a highway and if he wants to bypass an area, he just goes straight up and over. I know that that is not going to happen at home. I would just like when I am trying to put it on the ground that we can put it through the consultation process as quick as possible.'[25]

However, the Strategic Infrastructure Act's gestation and the possibility of revised planning consent procedures long preceded Ahern's visit to China in January 2005, going back to the cabinet committee on housing, infrastructure and public private partnerships which was established in June 1999 and its 'Framework for Action' to implement its infrastructure programme.[26]

In April 2004 a memorandum proposing the establishment of a National Infrastructure Board was submitted to the government. However, the plans set out in the memorandum by the then Minister

for the Environment did not come to fruition due to cabinet resistance, mainly from the Minister for Justice Michael McDowell who
was concerned about the implications for his own constituency where
it had been proposed to locate an incinerator.[27]

Minister for the Environment Dick Roche announced a new
proposal in 2005 that would create a strategic infrastructure
division within An Bord Pleanála. The Planning and Development
(Strategic Infrastructure) Bill was published in February 2006.
The bill was debated for four weeks in the Oireachtas with an
above average number of contributions. But an examination of the
Dáil debates reveals that a number of these contributions seem to
have had little to do with the bill and were mainly concerned with
one-off housing.

During the parliamentary debates as the bill passed through the
Oireachtas, Michael Ring TD specifically denounced the legislation
saying: 'I do not support this dangerous bill, which provides evidence
that the state is becoming a dictatorship. The time has come for people
to march in the streets in protest at the denial of their rights in a range
of areas … This is the most dangerous legislation that has ever come
before the House because it seeks to deprive people of the power
to make observations and objections in regard to planning matters.
We are told its provisions relate only to critical infrastructure but we
can be certain it will only be critical for developers … Developers
may be given such extensive powers that they will no longer require
planning permission for building projects. This is dangerous legislation
and it should be opposed.'[28]

According to then Green Party TD (and professional planner) Ciarán
Cuffe the bill represented: 'an attack on democracy, it emasculates local
authorities, sidelines little people and turns the Fianna Fáil tent at
the Galway Races into a permanent pavilion and institutionalises it.
The Minister may well argue there is nothing wrong with the tent.
He will argue that the big boys and girls need access to power and
privilege, but so do the little people. This bill will look after the big
guys but will sideline the communities and the people who need
support from the planning process. Perhaps we need to speed up
some of the major infrastructure projects. I agree with the Minister
that things should move more quickly in certain circumstances
but, curiously, even he tiptoed very carefully around the suggestion
that planning is the problem. He merely stated that planning could

potentially act as a barrier. What is the problem? Is it that the planning process is not moving quickly enough or is it that the Minister and his pet projects are not moving quickly enough?'[29]

Instead Cuffe laid the blame for delays or problems with large infrastructure (such as separate Luas lines which did not connect in Dublin city centre) on poor management, ministerial incompetence and 'a lack of "coglioni", as the Italians would say … that is not an issue of planning but is an inability to tackle the difficult issues at the outset'.

For architect and independent TD Paddy McHugh the proposed legislation could be interpreted as a 'macho' response to delays 'at the hands of cranks, do-gooders and other idealists' but instead it risked 'riding roughshod over all and sundry'.

Arthur Morgan TD considered the proposed amendments to the planning legislation as 'the practical expression of the government's opposition to democracy' suggesting that the bill was 'the brainchild of those irked by delays resulting from what they regard as annoying democratic input to the planning process. It is designed to facilitate ramming through unwanted infrastructure, such as incinerators, against the democratic wishes of communities and regardless of genuine concerns of those likely to be affected by such developments. One wonders whether the government came under pressure from vested interests, such as Indaver Ireland, to publish this legislation.'[30]

The Strategic Infrastructure Act, 2006 was signed into law on 16 July, introducing a system of direct application to An Bord Pleanála for permission for certain projects. It has been argued that the original objective of the proposed legislation was pragmatic, based on the perception that in effect all major applications were decided by An Bord Pleanála as applicants or third parties appealed planning authority decisions. Under the act the applicant applies first to the board's Strategic Infrastructure Division, which decides whether or not the project is of strategic importance under a number of criteria. If the board decides it is not of strategic importance the proposer can apply to the relevant planning authority as a 'regular' planning application. If the board agrees that the project is of strategic importance an application is made directly to the board.

One of the earliest pre-application consultations sought was for a cable car along the Liffey. The board found that this was not strategic infrastructure.[31] Proposals for the 'Suas' re-emerged in spring 2014.

SUSTAINABLE DEVELOPMENT OR SUSTAINED DEVELOPMENT?

In a 2004 feature headlined 'The Concrete Isle', Mark Lynas wrote: 'Ireland is used to violent change. Over the centuries, scores of armies of conquest, from the Danish hordes to Oliver Cromwell, have left their brutal mark on this soft and beautiful land. Today Ireland is threatened again. But this time no armies are massing on its border, nor are foreign fleets preparing to invade. This threat is an internal one. It comes from home ... Forget what you've seen in the tourist brochures. Do not be deceived by the glossy pages of mist-wreathed mountain vistas, wild open bogland and friendly, brightly painted little towns. Many of these are stock publicity photographs, already several years old. Today's reality is altogether different. If you want a tamed landscape dotted with off-the-shelf mock-Georgian houses, congested with nose-to-tail traffic and suffused by an ugly suburban sprawl, then céad mile fáilte – welcome to Ireland. This is the land of the bulldozer, where Tarmac, churned-up mud and shopping malls are as likely to greet the visitor as historic castles and windswept bays.'[32]

This trend did not go uncriticised with the Irish Planning Institute (IPI), for example, warning of the relegation of the common good in the Irish planning process. Speaking in 2005 the IPI president Iain Douglas stated, 'The vision and the promotion of the "common good" is what sets planners apart from the other actors involved in the development process and for far too long the "common good" has been relegated or downright ignored in our planning system'.[33] Douglas continued by asking whether political expediency or 'base self-interest' were responsible for this.

In his presidential address to the National Planning Conference in 2008 Andrew Hind forcefully argued that the planning system, combined with the taxation system, facilitated the accumulation of wealth by landowners and developers while depriving communities of basic social and transport infrastructure. According to Hind the planning system at the time seemed to give a higher priority 'to the making of private fortunes' than the needs of communities and concluded that sustainable development requires the protection of the public interest or the common good but '... during recent years of economic growth, individual interests too often won out in battles against the common good'.[34]

Writing at the time, Dr Mark Clinton, chairman of An Taisce's National Monuments and Antiquities Committee, argued that 'those entrusted with our nation's future display not only ignorance, lack of imagination and ill-planning in the name of progress, but present such deficiencies as a "heritage or development" ultimatum. This is a lie. It runs directly contrary to their espoused policies for sustainable development in the internationally-recognised definition of the term'.[35]

Then Green Party TD Eamon Ryan observed, 'The definition of sustainable development here is sustained development'.[36] Development Management Guidelines for Planning Authorities were published by the Department of the Environment, Heritage and Local Government in June 2007, which appear to justify this suggestion. In his foreword to the consultation draft Minister for the Environment Dick Roche wrote, 'We have higher expectations of planning authorities. We expect that they will support economic growth'.[37] The Irish Home Builders Association (IHBA), a constituent of the CIF, made a submission on the draft in February 2006 which characterised the planning system as failing to respond effectively to economic and social changes in Ireland and argued for reducing the role of prescribed bodies in the planning application process, seeing it as a source of unnecessary duplication and delay.[38]

The language of assessing planning applications shifted from 'Control of Development' described in the 2000 Act to 'Development Management'. In the minister's foreword to the final Development Management Guidelines in 2007 Roche wrote that the guidelines 'reflect the changes in the planning environment that have taken place in Ireland over the past 25 years with a shift in emphasis from Development Control to a more pro-active focus on Development Management. At the launch of the draft guidelines I referred to a new approach to planning that required the ambitious implementation by planning authorities of the positive vision for their areas set out in the development plan and the adoption by all of a pro-active approach towards development proposals which help achieve plan objectives. I encouraged everyone working within the planning system to adopt the positive Management Development term and the attitude it reflects'.

In the period Ireland became one of the most car-dependent countries in the world. Writing in 2004 economist Colm McCarthy concluded: 'It is time to accept that Dublin, unfortunately, now resembles a US sunbelt city, irreversibly car dependent, and that the sprawl which has already occurred severely limits the potential of rail-based public transport solutions. There is nothing to be said for compounding the errors in land-use policy by proceeding as if they had not happened'.[39]

In 2006 *The Irish Times* reported that Dublin's sprawl was being used by the European Environment Agency as a 'worst-case scenario' of urban planning so that newer EU member states such as Poland might avoid making the same mistakes.[40] An Taisce's heritage officer Ian Lumley described Ireland of the period as 'an American country ... we're individualistic, not strategic in planning, and there's no concern for the long-term consumption of resources. There's one word that describes it all: sprawl'.[41] McDonald and Nix have condemned the government's response to Dublin's sprawl as 'limp', despite it being at odds with government policy.[42]

Geographer and retail expert Tony Parker describes different approaches to retail planning in the Republic of Ireland and Northern Ireland in the period, arguing that in the Republic planning was 'reactive rather than prescriptive, planning for trends long gone rather than in tune with current social trends' with retail applications often 'judged on engineering and traffic criteria rather than social and commercial needs'.

Researcher Sunnhild Bertz quotes a senior planner in Dublin City Council as suggesting that local authority planners at the time came under pressure to allow commercial development at locations which might be regarded as unsustainable in order to secure commercial rate income. In the research, estate agents identified 'blatant competition between the local authorities around Dublin for rates income and I'm not convinced that the way in which they organise their zoning or planning has been in the good of the locations. I think that it's almost transparently obvious that it's to gain rates income' with a developer telling him 'planning authorities strive to keep development within their own jurisdictions and will not give up development opportunities just because the zoning is wrong'.[43] For Ciarán Cuffe the division of Dublin into four local authorities has led to competition for development and rates, not the planning required.[44] This had been summed up in one of the slogans of the Greater Dublin Reconstruction Movement in the 1920s when they demanded a unitary council for Dublin: 'One problem! One authority'.

Discussing attitudes during the so-called 'Celtic Tiger' bonanza, journalist Olivia O'Leary said 'we go on a mad spending spree instead of investing our wealth in the things that will make life better for the long term – better education and health services, better public infrastructure, better planning'.[45] It was an exuberant time for many. In his account of Anglo Irish Bank, 'the bank that broke Ireland', Simon Carswell of *The Irish Times* tells how developer Johnny Ronan celebrated receiving planning permission for one of his developments by flying fifty friends to Italy where Luciano Pavarotti sang for them in the garden of Ronan's villa.[46] This atmosphere was not unprecedented. Frank McDonald's *The Destruction of Dublin* gives an account of the swashbuckling developers of the 1960s, '70s and '80s, describing 1960s Ireland as 'an almost ideal setting for property speculation' with a flood of overseas investors coming to Dublin where, according to *Plan* magazine, 'a patriotic government was allowing them to make a quarry out of the city'.[47]

Despite rising national confidence and brashness at the time of the 'Celtic Tiger' it has been said that Ireland reverted to 'poor mouth' mode when it came to meeting international environmental obligations.[48] Ireland's record of respecting EU environmental laws at the time was one of the worst in Europe. Eighty-five 'first warnings' were issued to Ireland by the Commission in the five years up to 2002, more than the number issued against Austria, Denmark, Finland, the Netherlands and Sweden combined.[49]

INCREASED SCRUTINY

Planning came under increasing scrutiny in the 2000s. In September 2005 the Centre for Public Inquiry published its first report titled 'Trim Castle: A Monument to Bad Planning', written by its executive director, journalist Frank Connolly. The body was established in February 2005 to investigate matters of public importance in Irish political, public and corporate life and its board included Mr Justice Feargus Flood, the former chairman of the Planning Tribunal.

In the Trim report Connolly alleges that the planning system and Minister for the Environment failed in their duties and allowed the construction of a hotel in close proximity to the recently-restored

Trim Castle, leaving the national monument (and film set for the blockbuster *Braveheart*) 'defaced'. The report arose from complaints from councillors, citizens and An Taisce to the Centre for Public Inquiry about the project. Connolly alleges that by granting planning permission for the development at the scale sought, Meath County Council ignored heritage concerns and the views of councillors without sufficient impact assessment. The report also alleges that by not objecting to the development the Minister for the Environment Martin Cullen (who has been described as 'Minister against the Environment' or the 'Minister for No Environment' by some) ignored the advice of his senior heritage officials. In its second report published in November 2005 the Centre for Public Inquiry traced the history of the Corrib gas project, concluding that there were too many unknowns regarding the operation of the proposed pipeline to justify planning permission.

Originally to have been funded by Atlantic Philanthropies to the tune of €4 million over five years, the Centre for Public Inquiry closed in April 2006 following the withdrawal of this funding amidst allegations that Connolly had used a fake passport to gain entry to Colombia and a dispute with Minister for Justice Michael McDowell. The Irish Planning Institute subsequently moved into the office block vacated by the centre upon its wind up.

The general statutory right of appeal available to third parties from 1963 onwards was removed in March 2002, when Section 37 of the 2000 Act came into force. It limited the possibility of appeal to the applicant and 'any person who made submissions or observations in writing in relation to the planning application to the planning authority in accordance with the permission regulations and on payment of the appropriate fee'. The 2001 Planning and Development Regulations set a fee of €20 for making observations at local level. Prior to the enactment of the 2000 Act, third parties had a general right to make submissions on an application, free of charge, which could be taken into account at the evaluation stage.

The Aarhus Convention, a United Nations treaty, lays down a set of basic rules to promote citizens' involvement in environmental matters and to improve enforcement of environmental law. It has three pillars: access to information, public participation in environmental decision-making, and access to justice. It was ratified by Ireland and came into force on 18 September 2012.

Since ratification, public authorities, including semi-State companies are now required to provide environmental information on request at little or no cost and to involve the public in all decision-making that impacts on the environment. The Irish Planning Institute has recommended removing many fees in light of Aarhus's commitment to access to information and participation.

CATACLYSMIC MONEY

During the 'Celtic Tiger' years the total value of mortgage debt increased from €47.2 billion in 2002 to over €139.8 billion at the end of 2007, with house prices peaking at €322,634 for the average new home (a 382 per cent increase since 1991). The period of real economic growth from 1995 to 2000 was followed by a property-led bubble period collapsing in 2008.

From 2000 growth was driven by population rises and an extraordinary credit boom, which financed speculation and construction activity in the residential and commercial property sectors. Writing in the mid-1990s planner Nicholas Mansergh drew an analogy between the relationship of the construction industry and the State and Eisenhower's military industrial complex, given that the State simultaneously promotes and regulates the industry.[50] Social Justice Ireland have persuasively argued that at the time the government had reached the false conclusion that economic growth was a good in itself and could be pursued through the construction sector 'putting considerable faith in the ability of a highly incentivised property and construction sector to maintain the high growth levels enjoyed in previous years'.[51]

According to Social Justice Ireland a key factor to this was 'unsustainable house price and commercial property price inflation and profiteering. Ireland's largest developers and senior bankers formed strong alliances, and their perceived successes were highly praised by the media and prized by politicians'.[52]

Some 15 per cent of the national income came from house building and 6 per cent from other forms of construction at the peak in 2006. This is compared to approximately 6 per cent during the 1990s. The sector jumped from about 7 per cent of all employment in the early 1990s to over 13 per cent, the highest share in the OECD.

The total stock of dwellings – which had stood at 1.2 million homes in 1991 and had gradually increased to 1.4 million homes in 2000 – exploded to 1.9 million homes in 2008. There were warning signs. In the 2006 Census, 15 per cent of the housing stock was found to be vacant (predominantly speculative purchases rather than holiday homes). House completions went from 19,000 in 1990 to 50,000 in 2000 to 93,000 in 2006. Economist Karl Whelan has compared Irish house completions per capita with their equivalent in the United States, showing that while Ireland's rate of housing completions during the 1970s and 1980s had been comparable to that seen in the United States they exploded to the point where per capita completions were four times as high in Ireland as in the US.[53]

The international credit crunch in September 2008 exposed the huge involvement of the country's banks in borrowing short-term funds on international money markets to fund property investments and purchases. Ireland's decade-and-a-half of growth ended with the bursting of 'the steepest and longest of the several national property bubbles around the world in the late 1990s and early 2000s'.[54]

Unlike what happened previously in other Europeans countries such as Sweden and Iceland, Ireland's banks were not allowed to collapse under the debt burden created during the boom. In order to introduce liquidity into the Irish banking system the State undertook a two-track approach which involved guaranteeing all domestic bank liabilities in September 2008, along with direct recapitalisation where the State took a stake in the banks for preferential shares or took direct ownership, using the national pension reserve and finance procured on the international markets, and relieving the banks of their toxic assets by purchasing all property loans of €5 million or more issued before 1 December 2008 and placing them in a new State agency to manage on behalf of the taxpayer. This State agency is the National Asset Management Agency – or NAMA.

Explaining the climate that ultimately led to the creation of NAMA, its chairman Frank Daly sets out how, between 2004 and 2008, 'credit for households and non-financial institutions expanded by an average of 30 per cent each year in Ireland compared to a Eurozone annual average of 8 per cent over the same period. Over 80 per cent of this new lending in Ireland was property-related. The growth in Irish property lending was characterised by high-risk lending practices, including lending to individuals with little or no supporting corporate infrastructure, poor quality credit appraisal, a total absence of rigour in terms of analysis by banks of the sustainability of the property price bubble and, of course, serious regulatory failure. In layman's terms, the balance sheets of AIB and Bank of Ireland doubled to €200 billion each and that of Anglo quadrupled from €25 billion to €100 billion within the space of five years.'[55]

Published in 1961, *The Death and Life of Great American Cities* was the first and most influential book by Jane Jacobs, a writer and city activist from New York. The book is a reaction to post-war American urban renewal where Jacobs warns of the dangers of 'cataclysmic' development money. Jacobs classifies money into three forms: credit extended by traditional, non-governmental lending institutions; money provided by government; and money from the shadow world of cash and credit. Jacobs argues that despite the differences, these three kinds of money behave similarly in one regard: they produce drastic changes when poured into an area. Such influxes 'behave not like irrigation systems, bringing life-giving streams to feed steady, continual growth. Instead, they behave like manifestations of malevolent climates beyond the control of man – affording either searing droughts or torrential, eroding floods'.[56] The supply of easy credit during the 'Celtic Tiger' and its consequences proved Jacobs right.

8

Picking up
the Pieces

A HAUNTED LANDSCAPE

For An Taisce 'there is a clear and direct link between bad planning practice and the austerity resulting from Ireland's financial difficulties' as 'the unfettered zoning of land for new development by councils was a critical component of the toxic mix that created Ireland's property bubble and financial crisis'.[1]

In 2010 the National Institute for Regional and Spatial Analysis, NUI Maynooth (NIRSA) produced a paper provocatively titled 'A Haunted Landscape: Housing and Ghost Estates in Post-Celtic Tiger Ireland' which sought to consider the role of the planning system in creating 'a haunted landscape' where 'a new spectre is haunting Ireland – the spectre of development run amok' leading to ghost estates and idle shopping centres and hotel developments. This echoes a 1962 Oireachtas debate where the Minister for Local Government was challenged to address the development of a 'superabundance' of 'luxury hotels and luxury suites of offices' built at the expense of affordable houses in a situation akin to 'South American republics'. This led to people 'beginning to ask themselves: "Who are going to occupy the office blocks and luxury hotels?"'[2]

The NIRSA researchers argued that banks could have lent all the money they desired, but if zonings and planning permissions were not

Post-Celtic Tiger reports spoke of 'a haunted landscape' of 'ghost estates and idle shopping centres and hotel developments.'

forthcoming then development could not have occurred in the way that it did. They trace this to the non-implementation of the Kenny Report.

The NIRSA paper describes two levers through which the government can seek to regulate property development. The first is fiscal, such as regulating access to credit and determining taxation rates and the second is through planning policy and the zoning of land and the granting of planning permissions. NIRSA argue that there was 'a catastrophic failure of the planning system' due to a laissez-faire approach which did not see planning as a counter-balance to the pressures of development or providing checks and balances to the excesses of development and in favour of the common good, even if that meant taking unpopular decisions.

Frances Ruane, director of the Economic and Social Research Institute, notes the abolition of An Foras Forbartha in 1987 and suggests that since then development has been market driven, adding 'there are some who may be glad that we do not have an independent institute covering this area'.[3] It is regrettable that the ESRI did not see a role for itself in combating the trend identified.

NIRSA identify an unsustainable pattern of development that saw local authorities that had the most vacant stock in 2006, subsequently building the most housing and now having the highest surpluses, and the most land zoned for future use.

As early as 2006, David McWilliams had coined the term 'ghost estates' for the dozens of unfinished developments across Ireland. NIRSA defined a ghost estate as a development of ten or more houses where 50 per cent of the properties are either vacant or under-construction and suggested that many properties in rural areas will remain empty for quite some time, questioning whether these will be fit for purpose by the time the market returns. Beginning in 2010 the Department of Environment, Community and Local Government has undertaken National Housing Surveys to monitor unfinished developments. In the first survey, conducted in 2010, the number of unfinished estates were reported as 2,846, rising to 2,876 in 2011. The 2013 survey shows a decrease of 56 per cent in the number of unfinished developments since 2010 and a €10 million Site Resolution Fund was announced, principally to address deficiencies in public infrastructure, such as roads, footpaths, public lighting and open spaces. It is estimated that all or part of at least forty unfinished estates will be demolished.

For *Irish Times* environment editor Frank McDonald unfinished estates were 'the most visible legacy of over-building during the boom years and provided suitably grim images for articles on the collapse of the property bubble. Abandoned by developers who realised they would no longer cover their costs in a depressed housing market, they stood as gaunt reminders of planning and housing folly'.[4] As McDonald points out, the suggestion that the schemes would be a ready source of social housing was misplaced as many are remotely located from nearby towns.[5]

One of the normal conditions attached to a planning permission for a housing estate is the provision of adequate security for completion of the development but this has not always been adhered to. Every permission for a housing development will include a condition requiring a payment under the planning authority's development contribution scheme. The adoption of the development contribution scheme is a reserved function and, for Berna Grist, in the past elected members may have pressed for low contributions. This was compounded by inadequate monitoring of security and contributions in some authorities.[6] Grist argues that though the 1963 Act and subsequent legislation cite the common good as underpinning planning 'too often in the recent past, planning has been carried out for the enrichment of individual landowners and, as unfinished estates demonstrate, to the detriment of the common good'.[7]

This is directly linked to many of the issues of the 'Celtic Tiger', with Grist arguing that thereafter 'planning authorities throughout the country overzoned with impunity, which of course laid the foundations for unfinished housing estates, inappropriately located developments on the periphery of towns and other related land use problems'.[8]

NIRSA identify housing and planning policy as a driver of the property bubble, encouraging development through tax incentives and a focus on development levies while failing to integrate plans and provide checks and balances, arguing that the Irish planning system is 'undermined by elements of clientelism, cronyism and low-level corruption at play in the system at all levels' because of the 'division of legislative and executive functions between councillors and planners' which sees elected representatives having the final say on zoning and development plan matters while 'double jobbing as planning agents (or consultants)'.[9] The NIRSA paper and Mahon Tribunal report both singled out Section 140 of the Local Government Act, 2001 (formerly Section 4 of the City and County Management (Amendment) Act, 1955) which allowed elected members to override a specific planning decision as a manifestation of this.

OVERZONING AND THE 2010 ACT

One of the most frank assessments of the weaknesses and the failures of planning during the boom came from the chairman of An Bord Pleanála John O'Connor as he reflected on his eleven years in the role. Speaking at the Irish Planning Institute's National Planning Conference in Galway in 2011, O'Connor said his biggest regret was that the appeals board had not taken a strong stand against badly located, poorly designed, residential development during the 'Celtic Tiger' years, adding that land rezoning was the issue that brought Ireland's planning system most into disrepute. O'Connor maintained that excessive and unsustainable zoning of land had been a contributor to the property bubble but explained 'the board often found itself in a difficult position because in our planning system if the land is properly zoned in the development plan and serviced there is a presumption in principle that development will be permitted and to refuse could mean local authorities being faced with claims for compensation by landowners'.

For O'Connor 'The zoning of land for appropriate and sustainable uses is at the heart of planning and if this departs from proper
principles the whole system is in difficulty and this extends to the
property and land market and the construction industry'. O'Connor
argued 'The Celtic Tiger era clearly indicated that the demand for
property and in particular residential property was determined more
by financial considerations than by population projections or demo-
graphics. The land-use planning system cannot determine or control
that demand in a free market economy. It is essential if we are to avoid
a recurrence of the boom/bust cycle that demand is not artificially
inflated by financial incentives and considerations'.

The Planning and Development (Amendment) Act, 2010 moved
to address these issues, particularly the arising issue of residential
over-zoning, by requiring a more evidence-based process with core
strategies co-ordinating development plans with the National Spatial
Strategy and regional planning guidelines. The 2010 Act obliged
councils to ensure their plans are 'consistent with' national and
regional guidelines, rather than 'have regard to' them as was the case.

Ciarán Cuffe, who was Minister for Planning at the time of the 2010
Act, calls it a 'camel' comprising both aspirational, positive planning
aspects but also practical items that had to be included to regularise or
fix issues. For Cuffe the possibility of reform crystallised when a senior
Fianna Fáil TD led a delegation of traders from a border town to meet
him to discuss retail planning and risks to their town centre. For Cuffe
this showed that there was an opportunity to build support and act to
improve planning.

Village magazine has argued that loopholes in planning law allowed
for the complete absence of planning and chronic over-zoning during
the boom.[10] Planning law expert Yvonne Scannell attributes blame
to consecutive Ministers for the Environment and the department
itself for failures of oversight and poor policy formulation during the
period.[11] For the University College Dublin Urban Institute 'land
zoning and rezoning policies have badly failed and require replacement. In particular excessive and inappropriate rezoning, including in
floodplains, has served to undermine the legitimacy and accountability
of the development and planning process throughout the country'.[12]

Minister for Planning from 2011 to 2014 Jan O'Sullivan identified a prevailing 'addiction to zoning as opposed to real planning for
communities' in the Celtic Tiger period.[13] By 2009 there were 42,058

hectares of land zoned for housing, representing an oversupply of 4.5 times actual need. Then Minister for the Environment John Gormley attributed this to 'serious, excessive and inappropriate re-zonings' over the previous decades which had been 'a big factor in inflating development land prices around the country' and suggested that Fine Gael and Labour councillors bore some of the responsibility, saying Fine Gael councillors in particular had been 'embroiled in re-zoning controversies across the country, and have embarked on nothing short of a re-zoning frenzy in some cases'.[14]

In 2006 planning was criticised for failing to deliver sufficient permissions even though in the Greater Dublin area, there were over 26,000 housing units granted permission. The Irish Planning Institute suggested 'with so many housing units already granted planning permission out there waiting to be built, is the building trade getting cautious to avoid an over-supply in the face of rising interest rates by reducing the amount of 'starts'? The amount of grants of new housing in any year has a very strong relationship to the amount applied for. The decline in permissions cannot all be laid at the door of planning authorities'.[15]

In October 2006 the Irish Planning Institute again defended planners saying 'the decision to zone land in any county lies solely with the elected councillors. Sometimes a decision is made by councillors to place a residential zoning on a parcel of land against clear recommendations by planners and engineers that the land is totally impractical to service and should not be zoned … The problems resulting from this should be placed at the door of those responsible, rather than tarring "the planners" for bad decisions made in the Council Chamber'. The institute suggested that the decisions of elected councillors on zoning be subject to independent scrutiny by a national inspectorate, in the same way as decisions on planning applications can be appealed to An Bord Pleanála saying 'Such a mechanism, while preserving local democracy, would ensure that incoherent zoning decisions are highlighted in the public arena, and councillors forced to give full reasons for such decisions. At present, the only person with the power to over-rule zoning decisions of county councils is the Minister, and it is unlikely in practice that a national politician would interfere with decisions of local councillors, often from his own political party'.[16]

The minister is to be consulted at each stage in the making of a development plan. If the elected members decide not to comply with any recommendation made by the minister, the Department of the

Environment must be informed and given reasons for this decision. If a development plan fails to take sufficient account of the minister's observations the minister can, following a consultation process with the local authority, issue a direction requiring them to take specific measures in relation to the plan.[17] These ministerial powers were contained in the original 1963 Act and are restated in the Planning and Development Act, 2000.

Mayo County Council published its draft development plan for 2008 to 2014 in April 2007. As part of the draft plan's public consultation process, the Department of the Environment wrote to the council in June 2007 expressing concern that the amount of land zoned for residential development was approximately six times the level that would be needed to service forecasted population growth over that period. The draft plan provided for a population increase of almost 80,000, through zonings scattered countywide. In Claremorris, where a population increase of approximately 1,100 was projected to the year 2013, the plan indicated that some 27 hectares of land would be needed to meet this demand. However, a total of 157 hectares of land was zoned, capable of increasing the town's population by more than 10,000 people, almost ten times the need. This pattern was repeated in many of the smaller towns and villages throughout the county. Planning practice allows for some headroom in terms of zoning to allow a certain amount of choice while prioritising where growth should happen.

The amended draft plan contained no change to the unfocused over-zoning for residential development across the county and watered down the evidence-based rural housing policy framework set out in the original draft plan. The manager's report to the elected members in April 2008 outlined not only the department's concerns, but pointed out to the members that the proposed plan was in conflict with the advice from the council's planners and environmental staff and was contrary to the findings of the strategic environmental assessment, carried out by the council under European Union requirements. The council adopted the plan on 8 May 2008, and the finalised plan failed to deal with the minister's concerns and a direction to vary the plan to 'prioritise and develop residentially zoned lands in the Castlebar–Ballina hub over other locations in the county' was issued.

Gormley's direction to Mayo County Council led to heated exchanges in the Oireachtas environment committee in November 2008. For Fine Gael TD Pádraic McCormack there was 'nothing wrong with zoning more land than was required, because it brings down the cost of land in many cases as there is more zoned land available. Therefore, I would not agree with the submission made here that more land than was required was zoned and that this is necessarily a bad thing'.[18] One councillor later acknowledged that it was unacceptable: 'at the time of the plan, against the advice of the planners, we were just doing what politicians do – which is to try and make everyone happy'.[19]

In the committee the Senator and future Minister of State for Housing and Planning Paudie Coffey criticised the 'audacity' of the department saying, 'We are trying to shoe-horn our populace into towns and villages'. In his evidence to the committee chairman of Mayo County Council councillor Paddy McGuinness rebutted perceptions that councillors were 'buffoons', referencing an online survey and email which 'requested people to answer "Yes" to the survey on the website below and forward it to anyone from Mayo and then it is stated in bold print "retarded Mayo councillors". We suspect, although we have no proof, that this emanated from people in or associated with planning in Ireland'. McGuinness also criticised the language of planners. saying 'focused development' was another way of putting 'herding of people'.[20]

In the 2000 Act planning authorities were given scope to prepare local area plans. This was to be a simple procedure to allow local flexibility in meeting the county development plan objectives, for Grist they 'have been problematic in operation'.[21] This was due to extensive material amendments by elected members and the inclusion of zoning in local area plans with the potential for conflict with the hierarchy of plans above it.

The 2010 act also addressed issues regarding quarries and EU Habitat and Environmental Impact Assessment Directives. Lawyer Yvonne Scannell is critical of the failure to act on obvious weaknesses in planning law regarding quarries, noting that as early as 1966 complications arose regarding the planning obligations of quarries but nothing was done until 2000 when poorly drafted legislation opened up new issues and cost quarry owners millions in legal fees.[22] For Ciarán Cuffe the quarry provisions in the 2010 Act were a 'sticking plaster on, literally, a very large hole' to address a very complex issue.

The regulation of quarries since 1963 has created a substantial volume of case law and subsequent amending legislation. The Planning and Development Act, 2000 introduced a new system for the control and regulation of quarries within Section 261. The section applied to two categories of quarries: those which received planning permission more than five years before the section came into force; and those which did not receive such planning permission but which were in operation on or after Section 261 came into force. This latter category included both pre-1964 quarries which may not have required planning permission and quarries illegally operating without planning permission. By April 2005, the owner or operator of any of these quarries was under an obligation to provide certain information relating to the operation of the quarry to the planning authority. Issues arose in relation to certain aspects of the registration system as it did not confer legitimacy on the operation of a quarry as unauthorised development or beyond the confines of the development's original boundaries and different local authorities interpreted the legislation in different ways. Proceedings tied to Section 261 have generated more case law that any other sections of the Planning and Development Act, 2000, despite efforts in the 2010 Act to address the situation by requiring planning authorities to undertake a review of all quarries in its administrative area and decide in respect of each quarry whether an environmental assessment was required.

PLANNING TRIBUNAL

Zoning contributed to the speculative development of the 'Celtic Tiger' but in recent years a darker underbelly has been exposed. The Mahon Tribunal found that corruption in Ireland was 'both endemic and systemic' and its 'existence was widely tolerated'. In 2012 An Taisce reported that 'endemic parochialism, clientelism, cronyism and low-level corruption' existed during the boom.

Unfortunately, such suggestions were not new, though corruption reached its nadir in the 1980s. For Hanna in the 1960s it became 'abundantly clear that figures from within the highest echelons of Fianna Fáil, particularly Charles Haughey, were profiting from this building boom, while also aiding property developers through rezoning and the dismissal of planning appeals'.[24] Describing the period, Hanna highlights 'the populist-cynical moves of development companies which were often given names derived from Irish mythology and which frequently published its planning notices solely in Irish, both in order to construct the property boom in terms of 'national' rejuvenation, and also, more pragmatically, because so few people could read the national language'.[25] R.F. Foster notes that a 1979 *Magill* magazine carried rumours that Ray Burke was arranging 'suspect planning permissions'.[26] Discussing the period, Foster argues that the connections between planning permissions, land development and political influence can be 'directly and crudely drawn'.[27]

By 1981 the Irish Planning Institute was expressing grave concerns regarding some planning decisions, raising the 'spectacle of ill-judged re-zonings in County Dublin' leading to 'a strained relationship between the officials and the public representatives' along with some public disquiet.[28, 29] For the institute the rezoning of hundreds of hectares of agricultural land was 'neither necessary nor justifiable' and would leave premature communities without services and facilities.[30] The institute subsequently made a submission to Dublin County Council to this effect, setting out planning reasons why a number of sites should not be zoned and discussing the 'sinister precedent' the proposals might set by encouraging developers to buy un-serviced land at agricultural prices and 'persuade' the Council to rezone it.

Then councillor and future TD the late Liam Lawlor, who was to come to prominence in the planning corruption tribunal beginning in the late 1990s, responded to the institute's concerns by letter in November 1981, expressing disappointment at such criticism and stating the institute should play a more positive role and participate in the process and explaining that 'the lobby for additional residential development comes from people who are natives of the areas wanting to secure a local authority house in their original home area'.[31] Subsequently Lawlor addressed the Irish Planning Institute's National Planning Conference outlining his thoughts on how land was brought forward for zoning and concluding that in the future a team effort was required in planning with the 'practical politician tempering the theoretical planning view, counter balanced by the community input'.[32]

In the editorial of the 1982 edition of its journal *Pleanáil* the Irish Planning Institute warned of 'a very ominous turn' in the pressures placed on planners and highlighted the 'unedifying spectacle of wholesale and unco-ordinated land rezoning in Dublin County; the spectre of Section 4 continues to stalk the system, and members of this institute have been subjected to personal vilification for taking a principled stand in appealing such decisions'.

In 1983 An Foras Forbartha warned 'the magnitude of gains in
the value of land after zoning for development means that elected
members of planning authorities are subjected to extraordinarily
heavy pressures from landowners when a development plan is being
adopted'.[33] This emerged in the Tribunal which saw that given the
financial opportunities arising from rezoning, planning was vulnerable to corruption though this was recognised long before the
Tribunal first sat.

Writing in the 1980s on local authority law, Mr Justice Keane
commented that the management system was created because 'it was
recognised that entrusting the elected councils with responsibilities
now exercised by managers would have encouraged the bringing to
bear of pressures of every kind on councillors'.[34]

In 1985 political scientist Lee Komito wrote 'Where the officials'
criteria for judging planning matters is the long-term planning
good, councillors have more immediate criteria. There are no votes
in the long-term good, but there are votes in assisting individuals'.
Flagging what would emerge in the Planning Tribunal, Komito
continued, 'The rewards which politicians receive by getting planning
applications approved are significant … There are different ways in
which an individual rewards a councillor who uses his influence to
get through a financially rewarding planning permission. Straight
financial rewards are one way, though this is dangerous for all
concerned. It seems to happen when major rezonings take place
during the five-year development plan review, and people sometimes
contribute to party headquarters rather than to individual councillors.
Instructions are then issued to local councillors to support a particular
rezoning proposal (without the councillors knowing why they should
support the proposal). Other rewards are equally helpful, but not
as risky; favours done by councillors are 'cashed in' at election time.
They include: small financial assistance, providing canvassers, helping
organise the campaign, or delivering blocks of votes. Councillors have
been known to get campaign contributions from specific builders,
and benefit from builders' workers canvassing on the councillor's
behalf. Since the benefits to the individual are so great in planning
matters, it is obvious that the benefits returned to the councillor will
also be great'.[35]

Explaining the unsustainable attitude of some, Komito writes
'Planning permissions do not require capital expenditure and constitute

"cheap" patronage'[36] if they are willing to ignore the long-term social and environmental implications.

In 1989 the Gardaí investigated allegations of bribery and corruption in the planning process, which led to one unsuccessful prosecution. A 1993 investigation resulted in no action by the Director of Public Prosecutions due to insufficient evidence.[37]

In 1995 whistleblower James Gogarty came forward when a £10,000 reward was offered by former An Taisce chairman Michael Smith and barrister (and now High Court judge) Colm MacEochaidh through a firm of Newry solicitors, Donnelly, Neary and Donnelly, for information relating to what they believed was extensive corruption in the rezoning of tracts of land in Dublin. In a statement to the solicitors Gogarty said that he had given a prominent politician money for planning favours on behalf of a company called JMSE (Joseph Murphy Structural Engineers). He named then Fianna Fáil Foreign Affairs spokesman and former environment Minister Ray Burke in his statement and subsequently stories appeared in newspapers including the *Sunday Business Post* about the matter, though Burke was not named. At a press conference in the middle of the 1997 general election campaign Geraldine Kennedy of *The Irish Times* asked Bertie Ahern about the allegations, who denied them without naming Burke. The incident merited only a brief mention in the following day's *The Irish Times* and was not referred to in the media for the remainder of the campaign. After the election and before Burke's appointment as Minister for Foreign Affairs, Fianna Fáil chief whip Dermot Ahern was despatched by Bertie Ahern to London to meet with JMSE chief executive Joseph Murphy junior who denied the rumours. Subsequently it emerged that Bertie Ahern had made his own inquiries, asking builder Michael Bailey who Gogarty claimed had been present when money was handed over to Burke. Subsequently this led to Ahern's infamous line that he had been 'up every tree in North Dublin' to find out about any payments before appointing Burke to the cabinet.

In the summer of 1997 Burke admitted to receiving a political donation of £30,000 from Gogarty on behalf of JMSE in 1989 and under mounting pressure he resigned from the cabinet and the Dáil in October 1997. The government agreed to opposition demands for a tribunal into payments to Burke which included the whole issue of planning in north County Dublin, chaired by Mr Justice Feargus Flood. This was to establish the facts behind a number of planning matters in the Dublin area from the mid-1980s to 1997. Public sessions began in Dublin Castle in January 1998. Further revelations saw the tribunal's terms of reference widened in July 1998 to investigate payments to any other politician.

The Flood Tribunal was not the first planning-related tribunal of inquiry. Allegations in the Dáil in 1974 by deputies Bobby Molloy (a former Minister for Local Government) and Brendan Crinion that the then Minister for Local Government Tully rezoned land improperly and had dealings with a builder named Robert Farrelly or Farrell led to the appointment of a tribunal of inquiry in July 1975 under the auspices of the Oireachtas committee on procedure and privilege. This tribunal into 'allegations made by two Members against the Minister for Local Government in the Dáil' found that the two TDs were in grave breach of privilege in making allegations against the Minister, who denied any wrongdoing. The TDs refused to make statements to the committee as it was unclear if Dáil privilege extended to its deliberations.

In December 1998 the Flood Tribunal issued a warning that it was concerned that 'confidential information connected with the Tribunal is being deliberately and systematically drip fed to elements of the media' – and that it had made a formal complaint to the Gardaí on this matter.

In January 1999 former Minister for Trade, Commerce and Tourism, Minister for the Environment, Minister for Justice and Minister for Industry and Commerce, Pádraig Flynn gave an astonishing interview to Gay Byrne on *The Late Late Show* about his 'class act' daughter Beverly Flynn, the expenses involved in running three households and the Flood Tribunal. Flynn referred to claims by developer Tom Gilmartin that he had given Flynn a £50,000 donation when Flynn was Environment Minister during a period when he was trying to develop a shopping centre at Quarryvale in west Dublin – a development which later became Liffey Valley. Flynn's denial and his comments about Gilmartin's health angered Gilmartin to such an extent that he decided to alter his previous stance of non-cooperation with the tribunal. Flynn was ultimately found to have 'wrongly and corruptly' sought the payment from Gilmartin and then to have 'proceeded to utilise the money for his personal benefit'.

In March 1999 former assistant Dublin County and City Manager George Redmond was arrested at Dublin Airport by the Criminal Assets Bureau (CAB) where was found to be carrying £300,000 in cash and drafts. The Tribunal revealed that he was lodging sums of money equivalent to multiples of his legitimate income in off-shore bank accounts and in 2002 it found that he had received corrupt payments in exchange for favourable planning decisions, a finding he disputed. Redmond's conviction for corruption was quashed in 2004.

In April 2000 former government adviser and Fianna Fáil press secretary Frank Dunlop made several revelations to the Tribunal about money he paid to politicians on behalf of developers in return for favourable rezoning decisions in relation to land at Carrickmines. Developer Owen O'Callaghan – who took over the Quarryvale project from Tom Gilmartin in 1992, denied that he knew of any such payments. In early 2001 Liam Lawlor was jailed for the first time for contempt of court for not co-operating with the Flood Tribunal.

The second interim report, published by Mr Justice Flood in September 2002, found that Ray Burke received bribes from various business people, including property developers during the 1970s and 1980s. In June 2003 Flood resigned as head of the Tribunal and was replaced by Judge Alan Mahon, assisted by Circuit Court judges Mary Faherty and Gerald Keys. Following the publication of the second interim report of the Tribunal Irish Planning Institute President Rachel Kenny cautioned that 'rezoning is not a victimless crime. It is the general community that has to pay the bill, whether in direct monetary terms or in the poor quality of development and lack of community that has characterised many of our suburban areas' and warned that it could happen again if the law was not amended.[38]

In March 2004 Gilmartin gave evidence to Mahon, alleging that Flynn had taken the £50,000 and that former Minister Ray MacSharry had introduced him to several Cabinet members in relation to the development of a shopping centre. He said Bertie Ahern was one of those people – both Ahern and MacSharry denied Gilmartin's claims. It is during this evidence that Gilmartin claimed that a man – whose identity was never revealed – cornered him in a corridor at Leinster House and told Gilmartin he could 'end up in the Liffey' for refusing to pay £5 million to pave the way for the shopping centre. In November Bertie Ahern was ordered to bring forward all documents relating to any accounts he might have in financial institutions either here or abroad. (This later led to the claim that Ahern had no bank account between 1987 and 1993. He was a government Minister, first for Labour and then for Finance during this time.) Ahern's affidavit to the Tribunal assured that he didn't avail of a tax amnesty and had no outstanding tax liability. The Tribunal demanded more documentation from him. In September 2006 *The Irish Times* published leaked claims from the Tribunal about financial 'digouts' Ahern allegedly received. Six days later, Ahern told Bryan Dobson in an RTÉ interview that the money had been a loan – although he hadn't made repayments at the time. Here too, he remembered getting £8,000 from a group of Irish businessmen, collected for him at a dinner in Manchester.

In March 2005 Liam Lawlor admitted to the Tribunal that he got £350,000 from beef baron Larry Goodman for the purchase of land at Coolamber but denied that he participated in any deal for the rezoning of Carrickmines. Lawlor died in a car crash in Moscow in October of that year. The Tribunal found that Lawlor's involvement with landowners and developers rendered him 'hopelessly compromised'.

In July 2006 the Criminal Assets Bureau stopped the sale of lands owned by Jackson Way Properties at Carrickmines due to Frank Dunlop's allegations that councillors were bribed to rezone the land. In October of that year Ahern made a statement in the Dáil on the 'digouts', apologising to the Irish people for 'the bewilderment' caused to them by the payments but insisting he had breached no laws nor code of conduct. From September to December 2007 Ahern appeared at the Mahon Tribunal where Mr Justice Mahon appeared to grow frustrated by 'significant gaps' in Ahern's explanations for his finances. This rumbled on into 2008 when Grainne Carruth, Bertie Ahern's former secretary at his constituency office called St Luke's in Drumcondra, broke down while giving evidence at the Tribunal, admitting that she made sterling lodgements into Irish Permanent Building Society accounts in his name and those of his daughters in 1994. Ahern said he won the money on the horses. In May 2008 Bertie Ahern officially resigned as Taoiseach.

In May 2009 Frank Dunlop was sentenced to two years in prison for corruption, with the final six months suspended. He was released in July 2010.

The fifth and final report of the Tribunal published in 2012 states that for some councillors in Dublin County Council, corruption had become a regular aspect of their public role. Findings of corruption were made against eleven councillors. The report continues: 'Those councillors exercised their public powers in their own interests rather than in the interests of the public and bartered that power in exchange for cash and/or other benefits. There was apparently no shortage of persons prepared to pay for the corrupt exercise of public power and large tracts of land were ultimately rezoned because of the making and receipt of corrupt payments rather than in the interests of proper land use and development.'[39] In July 2013 the final chapter of the final report from the Tribunal was published, following the collapse of a corruption trial against four former politicians. The chapter had been held back in case it would interfere with the prosecution but after star prosecution witness Dunlop fell ill, the case could not continue.

The overall cost of the Tribunal is estimated at €159 million. For commentator Pat Leahy the most striking feature of the Tribunal was the 'mafia-like quality' to planning corruption, complete with capos and omertà against the outside world while systematically privatising parts of the public realm for private gain.[40]

Public interest was such that its first substantive tribunal report in 2002 sold out its print run in a few days. Regrettably in the climate of the tribunal, planning became linked with corruption in the public mind. In a small victory against this perception in 2001 the Irish Planning Institute lodged a complaint with the Advertising Standards Authority of Ireland against a radio advertisement for OKI printers. The OKI advertisement linked planning and 'brown envelopes' which the institute claimed 'pandered to the basest and most ill-informed prejudices about the planning system' in a complaint that was upheld by the Authority.

This confusion regarding planning and corruption in the public mind can extend to other professions. In 1997 the RIAI raised what they considered corruption in the planning process, complaining of local government officials acting as planning consultants on applications to their own authority. At the same time *Phoenix* magazine included details of one such case. Though it was not clear in these public statements, it was not intended to suggest that professional planners were engaging in this type of practice, rather it was other professional grades, something that was subsequently clarified.[41]

For the profession the Tribunal's findings were seen as vindicating planners who recommended refusal of many ill-considered zonings and no professional planner was found to be corrupt.

The final report contained sixty-four recommendations to counter corruption across public life, with ten specific planning recommendations. These can be summarised as:

1. Placing the National Development Plan and the National Spatial Strategy on a statutory footing.
2. Directly elected members of the Regional Authorities.
3. Facilitating documentation of Regional Authority considerations in making draft Regional Planning Guidelines.
4. Independent Appointments Board to appoint members of National Transport Authority.
5. Increase transparency in the planning process by publishing motions and submissions on the development plan and requiring councillors to give reasons for departing from a manager's recommendation.
6. Provide for advance notice to the Minister and regional authority of material contravention of development plans.
7. Restrict procedure set out in Section 140 of the Local Government Act, 2001.
8. Provide for documentation of submissions/interventions made by elected members on applications for planning permission to be noted on the file and published online.
9. Introduce requirement to identify relevant political donations to members of the planning authority when making application for planning permission.
10. Establish an independent planning regulator who would receive the Minister's supervisory powers to make directions in respect of plans.

The government accepted recommendations 6 and 7 and stated it would make them by legislative amendment. It accepted 9 and 10 in principle but said they required investigation. Recommendation 1 was accepted with regard to the National Spatial Strategy but not the National Development Plan. Recommendation 4 was rejected. The government stated that recommendation 3 had been substantially addressed by the 2010 Act while recommendation 5 was already substantially provided for. Recommendation 2, regarding directly elected regional authorities was to be considered as part of wider local government reforms but was not included in the reform package 'Putting People First' when it was published in October 2012. For Grist the least satisfactory government reaction was to recommendation 8 which interpreted interventions by politicians to be formal submissions similar to those made by the public, rather than attempts at exerting informal influence in confidential conversations.[42]

The recommendation with the most obvious potential to alter the planning landscape is that of a regulator. The Tribunal recommended: 'The Minister for the Environment's enforcement powers should be transferred to an Independent Planning Regulator who should be charged with carrying out investigations into systemic problems in the planning system as well as educational and research functions.'

The Mahon Report does not provide a descriptor of the likely powers or structure of the Office of the Planning Regulator. By spring 2014 the precise role and remit of the proposed Office of the Planning Regulator (OPR) and its obligations with regard to the evaluation of plans and issues within the planning system was still unclear with a new planning bill due in order to give effect to the proposal.

In the Irish Planning Institute's view in order for the Office of the Planning Regulator to result in meaningful change in public confidence in the planning system, it must be clear that the OPR is independent and that the OPR must be afforded some genuine power to 'regulate' specified elements of the planning system rather than just make recommendations. In 1990 An Taisce suggested an independent National Planning Authority which has similarities to the roles proposed for the regulator by Mahon, including directing local authorities to consider certain matters in their development plans and a research role.

The adoption of the development plan is the most significant local government function remaining with councillors, and their focus of interest remains on two aspects – zoning and rural housing policy. Identifying that a significant number of councillors have their 'day jobs' in the property sector, often auctioneering, and are concerned with the sale of land, Ciarán Cuffe has suggested that ethics rules for elected members must be strengthened to ensure 'Caesar's wife is above suspicion'.

For Cuffe 'the people of Dublin are still picking up the tab for mad rezoning decisions that took place in Dublin County Council in the 1980s. Councillors were allowed to rezone land without any sense of responsibility and without a mayor who had the bigger picture about what the city might be'.

9

Places for People
or Pension Funds?

Planning touches everyone. It involves place-making and design, heritage, economic development and retailing, landscape, transport, urban and rural development, housing, renewable energy, flooding, waste management and communications infrastructure. It is chiefly concerned with places – how they change and develop over time and how competing needs can be reconciled.

Just like places change over time, planning and planners are adapting. Kavanagh Country in County Monaghan is an example of how planners and planning skills (such as surveying, mapping, site appraisal and the long-term focus on place) can be used to look at spaces in new ways and give communities a strong sense of identity and secure our physical and cultural heritage. Technology opens up the potential for better decision-making on developments and buildings as their impacts can be visualised and modelled. Interactive 3D digital models can show how towns and cities have developed, identify patterns of development and accurately explore height, lighting and distance implications in ways that were not possible before, leading to better decision-making.

Reflecting on recent developments affecting the country's largest local authority and planning department, Dublin City Planner Dick Gleeson says, 'The last few years could not be described as business as usual either for the country or for the Dublin City Council and the planning department'. Part of the planning department's response

Interactive 3D digital
models and technology
open up the potential
for better decision
making on the impacts of
proposed developments.
(Courtesy of RealSim)

to this was 'extending out horizons and renewing a sense of purpose
about our collective role in the making of a better city' and examples
are captured in its *Planners Workbook* publication. The dublinbikes
scheme is a Dublin City Council planning department project and
has seen the implementation of one of the world's most successful city
bike share schemes with planning ideally placed to lead a multidis-
ciplinary team changing infrastructure, sustainable transportation and
the public realm in the city.

Sometimes Ireland has been at the forefront of planning theory
and practice. In 1976 An Foras Forbartha held a conference titled
'Streets for Living' which explored how residential estate layout
could be improved to cater for pedestrians and residents rather than
for the car. This was subsequently set out in a report of the same
name, though its recommendations were not always incorporated
in development plans. This approach was reflected almost forty years
later in the award-winning *Design Manual for Urban Roads and Streets*
which brought road design up to date with planning's focus on
sustainable communities. The design manual set out a new approach
to streets as more than just corridors for traffic and more as multi-
functional spaces in which people want to live and spend time. There
are long-term benefits to this. As William Brady from University
College Cork's Centre for Planning Education and Research notes
'the poor design of pedestrian routes and the distances people have

to travel to get to basic amenities' has a part to play in growing health problems.[1]

Climate change is the greatest long-term challenge facing human development. Planning can make a major contribution to tackling climate change by shaping new and existing developments in ways that reduce carbon-dioxide emissions and positively build community resilience to problems such as extreme heat or flood risk. Planning has the potential to deliver the right development in the right place in a sustainable, fair and transparent way.[2]

The Intergovernmental Panel on Climate Change (IPCC) Working Group III released a paper in 2014 which starkly described the potential consequences of climate change for human settlements, infrastructure and planning, warning that choices around land use, transport and housing now might mitigate some future consequences of rising temperatures and energy use. This is a clear challenge and opportunity to make the best use of land and reduce future energy requirements. The links between energy and planning were being explored by the profession as early as 1979 when a conference on the topic was held and it was also the subject of an Irish Planning Institute policy paper at the time.

The world class dublinbikes scheme is a Dublin City Council planning department project, showing new opportunities for planning. (Courtesy of Dublin City Council)

RESOLVING COMPLEXITY

From the Wide Streets Commissioners to model towns to the independent third-party appeals system there have been significant innovations in Irish planning. Rooted in concepts of social and spatial justice, planning in Ireland has sought to define, target and direct development and determine the objectives and resources required to achieve it. But how effective has that system been and has it delivered for the common good?

The cost of bad or absent planning has an immediate effect on the State's bank balance with the imposition of European fines. For example by the end of 2013 Ireland had paid €3,648,000 in fines imposed by the European Court of Justice over septic tanks and Environmental Impact Assessments. These arose following Ireland's failure to translate a European wastewater directive, which requires each member state to regulate septic tanks and similar systems, into Irish law, and a finding that Ireland had not complied with a directive about Environmental Impact Assessments for developments. There are a number of other cases against Ireland in the earlier stages of proceedings relating to habitats protection and other infringements.

Planning mediates between competing and sometimes conflicting demands for land. Discussing opinions of planning in the 1980s Berna Grist notes that parties to the planning process – public, developers, councillors and planners themselves – were dissatisfied with the system, indicating that it might not be functioning correctly.[3] The opposite may however be the case, with the role of planning in resolving complex issues perhaps meaning that it is inevitable that every party does not get it all their own way.

Michael Bannon draws some clear conclusions from his two-volume work on planning in Ireland from 1880 to 1988 – one is that the success of any planning movement is dependent upon its social relevance, public perception and acceptability. Another is the folly of attempting to solve Irish problems by replicating concepts from other countries rather than developing indigenous policies informed by international practice. Irish planning has been deeply influenced by the UK model but also by international thinking. Some of this has been successfully applied, some less so.[40]

In Ireland planning is largely a socio-political activity, governed by legislation and the structures of central and local government. Planning is a child of this situation and much of its subsequent character was influenced by the conditions of its formative years. The prioritisation of economic growth, the failure of regional planning and the absence of positive planning led to a focus on planning control by limited staff who were 'junior' in terms of age and experience to some other local authority professions.[5]

Bannon suggests that in the 1970s and 1980s planning became 'preoccupied with planning control', leading frustrated project promoters to point out that the legislation was the planning and development act, not the 'planning and no development act'.[6] Allegations of a lack of imagination amongst the profession can be traced back to its earliest years. In 1938 General Richard Mulcahy TD deplored the fact that town planners did not have objections to a housing development he thought unsuitable in Clontarf as it complied with the letter of the requirements.[7]

The detail and procedure that local authorities insist upon when assessing planning matters may be attributed in part to the fear of legal action and the weight of case law which arises from operating planning in a more individualist society where its merits are not broadly accepted. It has been ruefully observed that planning legislation, case law and regulations form far thicker volumes when compared to some comparable areas and planning has created a significant industry in legal textbooks, conferences and training. Yvonne Scannell attributes part of the difficulty to the impenetrability of planning legislation passed by the Oireachtas, suggesting that this is facilitated by the lack of 'meaningful scrutiny of planning legislation' in a parliament characterised by rushed debates of poor quality. As an example Scannell cites the 119 pages of amendments made by the government to the original thirty-four-page Planning and Development (Amendment) Bill, 2009 at a late stage.[8] For Scannell 'one of the defining characteristics of Irish planning law is its lack of transparency' being buried in legal sources and numerous acts and regulations in a way that is inaccessible to the public as well as practitioners.[9]

This negative perception has hampered planning and drowned out more positive examples but it may have its roots in wider attitudes to property and the common good. Dublin City Hall features a statue by John Hogan, erected by public subscription, of Thomas Drummond who was a reforming under-secretary for Ireland in the 1830s. Supporters of a vacant land levy in Dublin city have taken to quoting the epigram inscribed on the statue's base, that 'property has its duties as well as its rights' which Drummond used to chastise Irish landlords for neglecting their tenants. Concerns around private property rights have hampered much innovation in Irish planning. They were cited unchallenged as the reason for shelving the Kenny Report for example and continue to be cited in debates on rural housing restrictions, but the Supreme Court has made clear that interference with constitutionally protected property rights can be justified for desirable social objectives.

This is not to suggest a paternalistic sense that the public would like planning if only they understood it as this unhelpful attitude can be traced back a long way with little positive results. The planning exhibitions of the 1900s were an early attempt to achieve this. The 1914 *Dublin of the Future* competition was intended to raise awareness of planning issues. In 1931 the Civics Institute sought broadcasts on town planning to little avail and public education campaigns at the time of the 1934 and 1963 Acts did little to rouse support.

In the bleak economy of the mid-1980s, it was emphasised that 'in an era of scarce resources the careful ordering and proper planning of physical investments becomes a vital necessity'.[10] At any point in the economic cycle land is a valuable resource and its misuse and exploitation comes at a cost. Despite failures, challenges, changes in best practice and advances in technology and lifestyle, the key precepts of planning remain sound. Though it occurs in an increasingly multi-disciplinary environment, planning can facilitate dialogue with an emphasis on securing the common good.

For NAMA chairman Frank Daly 'The planning system will loom large in our deliberations for the foreseeable future. Delivery of a number of projects within our portfolio, and by extension NAMA funding, is contingent on securing viable planning permissions. In the case of residential housing, some of our projects will become viable only if the densities approved as part of the original planning permissions are lowered.'[11]

Many planning authorities were criticised in the past for having excessive levels of zoning. Since the 2010 Act, zonings are now at a more sustainable level, derived from projected population growth calculated at national and regional level.

In 2014 as the economy continues to recover from the post-'Celtic Tiger' crash, there remains zoning and planning permission for more than 30,000 homes across the four Dublin local authorities alone, with land for over 500,000 new homes zoned nationally. The Irish planning system can be strategic in its broad-ranging perspective but also efficient, accountable and transparent by providing the market with confidence and certainty through sound, evidence-based reasons for its land-use planning decisions.

IRELAND OF THE FUTURE

Speaking in 1982, the head of the planning division at An Foras Forbartha Gerry Walker said 'planning has failed because we were never really serious about planning – we have always stopped short of fully and publicly committing ourselves to taking the sometimes harsh actions necessary to achieve our social, economic and physical goals'.[12]

Planning has taken certain roles over the course of its history and has been received enthusiastically when it was seen as answering the pressing problems of the day. Just as the Wide Streets Commissioners sought to build an imperial capital and enhance property values, it has been suggested that in twentieth-century Ireland there were three periods when the commitment to planning was particularly strong – post-First World War, the early 1940s and the 1960s – with it being seen as having a role in addressing particular problems of the time (poor housing and urban decay, post-Emergency renewal and the need for economic expansion respectively). However, each time as planning 'became the perceived prerogative of a narrow professional elite or lost its direct relevance to socio-economic issues, its popularity waned'.[13] In early twenty-first-century Ireland planning was seen as an obstacle to the growth imperative of the so-called 'Celtic Tiger' and something to be got around. Today planning must respond to the socio-economic climate while remaining open and inclusive. The planning solutions to the significant social, environmental and economic issues facing Ireland today must be more open, responsive and responsible, not less.

For the Irish Planning Institute two key concepts underlie planning: the common good and sustainable development.[14] Planning should work on the principle of supporting the common good with the aim of achieving sustainable development. For the institute representing the profession, these are supported by some key principles:

1. Transparency: The planning system must be transparent in how
    it operates and makes decisions. Transparency is fundamental to
    ensuring public confidence, credibility and legitimacy in the system.
2. Evidence-based decision-making: Transparency is facilitated and
    decision-making is improved where there is a clear reasoning for
    decisions and where they are supported by up-to-date, relevant
    research and evidence.
3. Public engagement: The planning system seeks to improve the
    quality of life of all citizens. To do this, it must engage with
    people and communities to ascertain their views and require-
    ments and ensure that statutory development plans reflect the
    needs of the communities they are meant to support.
4. Plan-led development: Planning should be on the basis of robust
    spatial plans, which are founded on up-to-date information
    and research.
5. Consistency and certainty: These two items are directly related
    as consistency in decision-making will enhance certainty for
    participants in the planning system. Evidence-based and plan led
    decision-making will facilitate consistency in decision-making.
6. High quality: This should be a hallmark of the operations of the
    planning system and visible in all of the outputs from planning,
    including in the built environment and places that are created
    and standard of living that results, the plans that are produced
    and the decisions that are made.

Dublin of the Future closed by commending planning as a way of
ensuring 'the real health and happiness of the people'.[16] This is
not to downplay its functional roots in Ireland. The Wide Streets
Commissioners began their work to remove street congestion and
projects were undertaken to increase property values; model villages
were developed to maximise the output of workers and as we have
seen the 1963 Act was heavily premised on planning for economic
growth. Either way, as emphasised in a 2007 Combat Poverty Agency
working paper on planning, participation and disadvantaged communities, planning matters.

Frank McDonald has asked if fundamentally we wish to make places
for people or pension funds.[17] Speaking as Irish Planning Institute
President, Mary Crowley was unequivocal saying that 'parachute
planning', that is, dropping large, unsuitable developments tailored

to the needs of developers rather than the community in the wrong places must not occur again. For Crowley 'Today we have a more comprehensive suite of policy guidance and learning than ever before which clearly demonstrates the aspiration at national level to deliver quality places. We must implement these, avoid the mistakes of the past and get on with the job of building high quality, sustainable places'.

Successful planning creates urban and rural places that people can relate to and that they feel positive towards. In Ireland planning for the future has a long and rich history to draw from, in terms of achievements as well as missteps, in this regard.

Notes

INTRODUCTION

1   From the Irish Planning Institute, see 'About planning' on
    www.ipi.ie.
2   Michael Bannon, 'Irish Planning from 1921–1945:
    An Overview', in M. Bannon (ed.), *Planning: The Irish
    Experience 1920–1988* (Wolfhound Press, Dublin, 1989), p.68.
3   *Cork Town Planning Report and Sketch Development Plan*, 1941,
    p.5.
4   Ibid., p.6.
5   Michael Bannon, 'Introduction', in M. Bannon (ed.),
    The Emergence of Irish Planning 1880–1920 (Turoe Press, Dublin,
    1985), p.14.
6   Nigel Taylor, *Urban Planning Theory since 1945* (Sage, London,
    1998), p.102.
7   *Southern Star*, 10 November 1962.
8   Brendan McGrath, *Landscape and Society in Contemporary Ireland*
    (Cork University Press, Cork, 2013), pp.84–85.
9   Michael Bannon, 'Forty Years of Irish Planning: An Overview',
    Journal of Irish Urban Studies, vol.3, no.1 (2004), p.12.
10 Fergal MacCabe, 'Spatial Planning in Ireland 1910–2010' in
    J. Teixeira (ed.), *A Centenary of Spatial Planning in Europe*
    (ECTP-CEU, Brussels, 2013), p.137.
11 Bannon, *Planning: The Irish Experience 1920–1988*, p.9.

12 Jim Connolly, address to Irish Rural Dwellers Association
    Annual Conference (2005).

13 *Fortnight*, 30 November 1973, cited in Erika Hanna in *Modern
    Dublin: Urban Change and the Irish Past, 1957–1973* (Oxford
    University Press, Oxford, 2013), p.14.

14 Frances Ruane quoted in Paul Sweeney, *Ireland's Economic
    Success: Reasons and Lessons* (New Island, Dublin, 2008), p.58.

15 Ibid.

16 John O'Connor, address to Irish Planning Institute National
    Planning Conference (2011).

17 *Village Magazine*, 'Sweet – but perhaps vicious',
    February – March 2013.

18 *Sunday Times*, 7 November 2004.

19 Lewis Keeble, *Principles and Practice of Town and Country Planning*
    (Estates Gazette, London, 1952), p.2.

20 Bannon, *Planning: The Irish Experience 1920–1988*, p.12.

21 Peter Clinch, Frank Convery, Brendan Walsh, *After the Celtic
    Tiger: Challenges Ahead* (O'Brien Press, Dublin, 2008), p.18.

22 Bannon, *The Emergence of Irish Planning, 1880–1920*, p.14.

23 *The Irish Times*, 17 August 2011.

24 Andrew Kincaid, 'Response,' *Irish Geography*, vol.39, no.2
    (January 2006), p.202.

25 Andrew Kincaid, *Postcolonial Dublin: Imperial Legacies and the
    Built Environment* (University of Minnesota Press, Minneapolis,
    2006), p.14.

26 Brendan Bartley, 'Planning in Ireland' in B. Bartley and
    R. Kitchin (eds), *Understanding Contemporary Ireland* (Pluto
    Bartley, London; Ann Arbor, 2007), p.33.

27 *Dáil Debates*, vol.197, col.1762.

28 Diarmaid Ferriter, *The Transformation of Ireland 1900–2000*
    (Profile Books, London, 2004), p.546.

29 Berna Grist, *Twenty Years of Planning: A Review of the System
    Since 1963* (An Foras Forbartha, Dublin, 1983), p.4.

30 Brendan Bartley and Kasey Treadwell-Shine, 'Competitive City:
    Governance and the Changing Dynamics of Urban
    Regeneration in Dublin' in Moulaert, F., Rodriguez,
    A. and Swyngedouw, E. (eds) *The Globalized City: Economic
    Restructuring and Social Polarization in European Cities* (Oxford
    University Press, Oxford, 2003).

CHAPTER 1

1   Liam De Paor, *St Patrick's World* (Four Courts Press, Dublin, 1996), p.23.

2   Clare Crowley, *The Origin of the Curvilinear Plan-Form in Irish Ecclesiastical Sites: A Comparative Analysis of Sites in Ireland, Wales and France* (PhD Thesis, DIT, 2008).

3   P.F. Wallace, 'Town Layout and its Possible Regulation in Viking age Dublin', *Pleanáil: Journal of the Irish Planning Institute*, no.6 (1986).

4   Gilbert Camblin, *The Town in Ulster* (Wm. Mullan & Son Publishers Ltd, Belfast, 1951), p.17.

5   Ibid., p.18.

6   John Hendry, 'The Control of Development and the Origins of Planning In Northern Ireland', in Bannon, *Planning: The Irish Experience 1920–1988*.

7   Arthur Young, *A Tour of Ireland 1776–1779* (Irish University Press, Dublin, 1970), p.21.

8   Colm Lennon, *Irish Historic Towns Atlas, 1610 to 1756* (2008), p.3.

9   Ibid.

10 Finnian O'Cionnaith, *Land Surveying in Eighteenth and early Nineteenth-century Dublin* (PhD Thesis, NUI Maynooth, 2011), p.316.

11 Ibid., p.318.

12 Maurice Craig, *Dublin 1660–1860: The Shaping Of A City* (Liberties Press, Dublin, 2006), p.199.

13 Fergal MacCabe, 'Spatial Planning in Ireland 1910–2010', p.137.

14 Michael Gough, 'The Dublin Wide Streets Commissioners (1758–1851): An Early Modern Planning Authority', *Pleanáil: Journal of the Irish Planning Institute*, no.11 (1992–93), p.135.

15 Ibid., p.138.

16 Kevin Hourihan, 'The Evolution and Influence of Town Planning in Cork' in P. O'Flanagan and C. G. Buttimer (eds), *Cork History and Society: Interdisciplinary Essays on the History of an Irish County* (Geography Publications, Dublin, 1993), p.946.

17 Antóin O'Callaghan, *Cork's St. Patrick's Street: A History* (Collins Press, Cork, 2010), p.27.

18 Ibid., p.37–39.

19 Petition of Wide Streets Commissioners of Cork city, Requesting Funds for Public Works, National Archives CSO RP 1822 3332.

20 Gina Johnson, *The Laneways of Medieval Cork* (Cork City Council, 2002), p.184.

21 *Limerick City Development Plan 2004–2010*, Appendix 2.

22 For a fuller account of the background of the individual commissioners see Gough 'The Dublin Wide Streets Commissioners'.

23 Gough 'The Dublin Wide Streets Commissioners', p.127.

24 Ibid., p.128.

25 Ibid., p.131.

26 Ibid.

27 Hubert Butler, 'The Story of New Geneva Part 1', *Irish Press*, 21 May 1947.

28 Hubert Butler, 'The Story of New Geneva Part 2', *Irish Press*, 22 May 1947.

29 New Geneva is in the parish of Crook, commonly suggested as the origin of the phrase 'by hook or by crook' referring to Cromwell's assertion that Loftus Hall would be taken by the ports at Hook Head or Crook.

30 O'Cionnaith, p.323.

31 Ibid., p.336.

32 Frank Gibney, 'Dublin "Castles in the Air"', *Dublin Historical Record*, Vol.17, No.3 (June, 1962), p.95.

33 Gough 'The Dublin Wide Streets Commissioners', p.150.

34 Ibid., p.152.

35 Ibid.

36 O'Cionnaith, p.337.

37 Ibid., p.338.

38 Edel Sheridan-Quantz, 'The Multi-Centred Metropolis: the Social Topography of Eighteenth-Century Dublin', in P. Clark & R. Gillespie, *Two Capitals: London and Dublin, 1500–1840* (Oxford, Oxford University Press, 2001), p.275.

39 Ibid., p.276

40 *Freeman's Journal*, 22 March 1830.

41 *Freeman's Journal*, 2 May 1846.

42 Ibid.

43 Thomas Hall, *Planning Europe's Capital Cities: Aspects of Nineteenth-Century Urban Development* (Alexandrine Press, Oxford, 1997), p.2.

44 O'Cionnaith, p.343.

45 Gough 'The Dublin Wide Streets Commissioners', p.133.

46 O'Cionnaith, p.342.

47 Gough 'The Dublin Wide Streets Commissioners', p.129.

48 Craig, *Dublin 1660–1860*, p.201.

49 Ibid.

50 Gough 'The Dublin Wide Streets Commissioners', p.153.

51 R.F. Foster, *Modern Ireland 1600–1972* (Penguin, London, 1989), p.192.

52 Kevin Whelan, 'Town and Village in Ireland: A Socio-Cultural Perspective', *The Irish Review*, no.5 (Autumn, 1988), p.34.

53 Ibid., p.35.

54 F.H.A. Aalen, 'The Rural Landscape: Change, Conservation and Planning', in F.H.A. Aalen (ed.), *The Future of the Irish Rural Landscape* (Department of Geography, Trinity College Dublin, 1978).

55 National Inventory of Architectural Heritage, Department of Arts, Culture and the Gaeltacht.

56 Heritage Council, *Heritage Conservation Plan for Portlaw* (2003), p.8.

57 Mary E. Daly, *Dublin: the deposed capital. A social and economic history, 1860–1914* (Cork University Press, Cork, 1984).

CHAPTER 2

1 Mary E. Daly, 'Housing Conditions and the Genesis of Housing Reform in Dublin' in Bannon, *The Emergence of Irish Planning 1880–1920*, p.78.

2 Frank Cullen, 'The Provision of Working and Lower-Middle-Class Housing in late Nineteenth-Century Urban Ireland', Proceedings of the Royal Irish Academy (2011).

3 Ruth McManus, 'Blue Collars, "Red Forts", and Green Fields: Working-Class Housing in Ireland in the Twentieth Century', *International Labour and Working Class History* (2003), p.38.

4 Daly, in Bannon, *The Emergence of Irish Planning 1880–1920*, p.77.

5 'To Hell or to Kimmage: Planning Outcomes of the 1913 Church Street Disaster', History Ireland Hedge School, 21 January 2014.

6 J.J. Lee, *Ireland 1912–1985* (Cambridge University Press, Cambridge, 1989), p.72.

7 Mary E. Daly, in Bannon, *The Emergence of Irish Planning 1880–1920*, p.91.

8 Cullen, p.227.

9 Ibid., p.251.

10 F.H.A. Aalen, 'The Working Class Housing Movement in Dublin, 1850–1920' in Bannon, *The Emergence of Irish Planning 1880–1920*, p.175.

11 Ruth McManus, 'Housing in Post-Colonial Dublin', *Irish Geography*, vol.39, no.2 (2007).

12 Fergal MacCabe, 'Spatial Planning in Ireland 1910–2010', p.137.

13 Lady Aberdeen certainly had a full life, for example she also was a strong promoter of Irish lace, received the Freedom of Limerick and is credited with introducing the Golden Retriever to Canada.

14 Michael Bannon, 'Dublin Town Planning Competition: Ashbee and Chettle's "New Dublin" – A Study in Civics', *Planning Perspectives*, vol.14 (1999) p.148.

15 Ibid.

16 Murray Fraser, *John Bull's Other Homes: State Housing and British Policy in Ireland, 1883–1922* (Liverpool University Press, Liverpool, 1995), p.134

17 *The Irish Times*, 13 April 1911.

18 *Freemans Journal*, 8 June 1911.

19 *The Irish Times*, 25 May 1911.

20 *The Irish Times*, 25 May 1911.

21 *The Irish Times*, 16 November 1914.

22 *The Irish Times*, 8 March 1915.

23 Fraser, *John Bull's Other Homes*, p.134

24 Ibid., p.136.

25 Ibid.

26 Ibid.

27 Patrick Geddes, 'Two Steps in Civics: Cities and Town Planning Exhibition and the International Congress of Cities', *Town Planning Review*, vol.4. no.2 (1917), p.78.

28 Fraser, *John Bull's Other Homes*, p.137.

29 Bannon, 'The Genesis of Modern Irish Planning', in Bannon, *The Emergence of Irish Planning 1880–1920*, p.215

30 Fraser, *John Bull's Other Homes*, p.137.

31 *Irish Worker*, 10 July 1914 to 8 August 1914.

32 Bannon, *The Genesis of Modern Irish Planning*, p.220.

33 Ibid., p.218.

34 Fraser, *John Bull's Other Homes*, p.137.

35 *The Irish Times*, 23 September 1916.

36 Bannon, 'Ashbee and Chettle', p.150.

37 Cited in Bannon, 'Ashbee and Chettle', p.151.

38 Ibid.

39 Ibid., p.151.

40 Patrick Abercrombie, Sydney Kelly, Arthur Kelly, *Dublin of the Future: The New Town Plan* (Civics Institute, Dublin, 1922), p.v.

41 Ibid., p.viii.

42 Ibid., p.ix.

43 Ibid., p.x.

44 Ibid., p.xi.

45 A reproduction of the work was presented as part of the 'Me Jewel & Darlin' public artwork on O'Connell Street in 2011 where artist Sean Lynch selected artefacts that evoked various memories of the city.

46 Kelly Sullivan, 'Harry Clarke's Modernist Gaze', *Eire-Ireland: An Interdisciplinary Journal of Irish Studies* (November 2012), p.7.

47 Kincaid, *Postcolonial Dublin*, p.13

48 *The Irish Times*, 21 July 1972.

49 *Dáil Debates*, vol.49 No.2271.

50 Civics Institute, Executive Committee Minutes, 13 October 1925.

51 Michael Gough, 'Socio Economic Conditions and the Genesis of Planning in Cork', in Bannon, *Planning: The Irish Experience 1920–1988*, p.315.

52 Aodh Quinlivan, *Philip Monahan: A Man Apart* (Institute of Public Administration, Dublin, 2006), p.69.

53 Cork Town Planning Association, *Cork – A Civic Survey, 1925* (University Press of Liverpool and Hodder & Stoughton, London, 1926), p.v.

54 Kevin Hourihan, 'The Evolution and Influence of Town Planning in Cork', p.958.

55 Kincaid, *Postcolonial Dublin*.

56 Ibid., p.20.

57 Ibid., p.29.

58 Bannon, *The Emergence of Irish Planning 1880–1920*, p.15

59 Fraser, *John Bull's Other Homes*, p.145.

60 Ibid., p.146.

61 Ibid.

62 Ruth McManus, 'Housing in Post-colonial Dublin', *Irish Geography* vol.39, no.2 (January 2006), p.190

63 Kincaid, *Postcolonial Dublin*, p.5.

64 Ibid.

65 *Dáil Debates*, vol.199, col.125.

66 Kincaid, *Postcolonial Dublin*, p.14.

67 Ibid., p.31.

68 R.M. Butler, 'The Reconstruction of O'Connell Street', *Studies* (November 1916), p.570.

69 Kincaid, *Postcolonial Dublin*, p.6.

70 Ibid., p.42.

71 *The Irish Builder and Engineer*, 'The Results of Revolution', vol.58, 13 May 1916, p.202–212.

72 *The Times*, 30 May 1916.

73 *The Times*, 8 August 1916.

74 *The Irish Times*, 31 May 1916.

75 'The Rebuilding of Central Dublin' letter from the Council of the Royal Institute of the Architects of Ireland, *R.I.B.A. Journal,* vol.23, 10 June 1916, p.262.

76 Maura Shaffrey, 'Sackville Street/O'Connell Street' in *Irish Arts Review Yearbook* (Belfast, 1988), p.151.

77 Kincaid, p.13.

78 Maura Shaffrey, p.154.

79 Ibid., p.155.

CHAPTER 3

1 Bannon, 'Irish Planning from 1921–1945 'in Bannon, *Planning: The Irish Experience 1920–1988*, p.39.

2 *Dáil Debates*, vol.33, col.1010.

3 *Irish Builder and Engineer*, 1930, vol.LXXII, p.180.

4 Manning Robertson, 'Town Planning and Slums', *Irish Builder and Engineer*, vol.LXXIII, p.245.

5 Bannon, 'Irish Planning from 1921–1945' in Bannon, *Planning: The Irish Experience 1920–1988,* p.43.

6 Attorney General (McGarry) v. Sligo County Council [1991] 1 IR 99; [1989] ILRM 768

7 *The Irish Times*, 6 November 1934.

8 K.I. Nowlan, 'The Evolution of Irish Planning 1934–1963' in Bannon, *Planning: The Irish Experience 1920–1988*, p.71.

9 *Dáil Debates,* vol.73, col.48.

10 Gough in Bannon, *The Emergence of Irish Planning 1880–1920*, p.331.

11 *The Irish Times*, 19 February 1936.

12 S.T. O'Kelly as reported in Bannon, *Planning: The Irish Experience 1920–1988,* p.48.

13 Bannon, *Planning: The Irish Experience 19201988,* p.48

14 The counties which did not pass a resolution were named as Carlow, Cavan and Offaly by the Minister in *Dáil Debate,* vol.189, col.830.

15 Berna Grist, *Introduction to Irish Planning Law* (Dublin, Institute of Public Administration, 2013), p.2.

16 Mary E. Daly, *The Buffer State: The Historical Roots of the Department of the Environment* (Institute of Public Administration, Dublin, 1997), p.289.

17 *The Irish Times*, 19 February 1936.

18 Daly, *The Buffer State*, p.286.

19 Ibid., p.289.

20 *The Irish Times*, 13 June 1942.

21 *The Irish Times*, 24 April 1944.

22 *The Irish Times*, 30 April 1942.

23 National Archives DTS 134 69, 26 August 1942.

24 *The Irish Press*, 10 April 1943.

25 *Sunday Independent*, 30 April 1944.

26 *The Irish Times*, 24 April 1944.

27 *The Irish Times*, 3 April 1944.

28 *Ulster Journal of Archaeology*, Third Series, vol.7 (1944), pp.123–124.

29 *Dáil Debates*, vol.94, col.125.

30 *Irish Independent*, 27 February 1945.

31 *The Irish Times*, 10 May 1944.

32 *The Irish Times*, 31 October 1944.

33 *Irish Independent*, 23 October 1943.

34 Erika Hanna, 'Dublin's North Inner City, Preservationism, and Irish Modernity in the 1960s', *The Historical Journal*, vol.53, no.4 (December 2010), p.1020.

35 Bannon, 'Forty Years of Irish Planning – An Overview', p.2.

36 *Cork Town Planning Report and Sketch Development Plan 1941*, p.5.

37 Ibid., p.7.

38 Ibid., p.8.

39 F.H.A. Aalen, 'The Working Class Housing Movement in Dublin 1850–1920', in Bannon, *The Emergence of Irish Planning 1880–1920*, p.175.

40 *Spark*, Vol.III, No.2, 9 April 1916.

41 Quoted in Kincaid, *Postcolonial Dublin*, p.6.

42 R.M. Douglas, *Architects of the Resurrection: Ailtirí na hAiséirghe and the Fascist 'New Order' in Ireland* (Manchester University Press, Manchester, 2009), p.103.

43 Ibid.

44 Dáithí Hanly subsequently designed Dublin's Garden of Remembrance and Knock basilica. In 1952 as town planning officer for Dún Laoghaire, he painted a positive picture of progress under the Act to the International Congress for Housing and Town Planning in Lisbon. A year later Hanly addressed the Irish Roadside Tree Association on the theme of 'Town Planning – Tree Planting'.

45 R.M. Douglas, 'Ailtiri na hAiséirghe: Ireland's fascist New Order', *History Ireland*, vol.17, no.5 (September/October 2009), pp.40–44.

46 MacCabe, 'Spatial Planning in Ireland', p.138.

47 Ibid.

48 Fergal MacCabe, 'Urbanity and rurality – the Bord na Móna villages of Frank Gibney', *Scéal na Móna* (December 2006), p.52.

49 Nowlan in Bannon, *Planning: The Irish Experience 1920–1988*, p.74

50 RIAI, *Cautionary Guide to Dublin* (1933), p.5.

51 *The Irish Times*, 26 February 1952.

52 Nowlan in Bannon, *Planning: The Irish Experience 1920–1988*, p.85.

53 Ibid., p.72.

CHAPTER 4

1 Bannon, *Planning: The Irish Experience 1922–1988*, p.130.

2 Bannon, *The Emergence of Irish Planning 1880–1920*, p.15.

3 Michael Bannon, 'The Changing Context of Developmental Planning', *Administration*, vol.31, no.2 (1983), p.117.

4   Address by An Taoiseach, Mr Lynch, at the opening of the
    Dublin Congress of The International Federation of Housing
    and Planning, 19 May 1969.
5   *Dáil Debates*, vol.197, col.1763.
6   Ibid.
7   Charles Abrams, *Urban Renewal Project in Ireland (Dublin), UN
    report TAO/IRE/2 (April 1961)*, p.v.
8   Ibid.
9   Scott Henderson, *Housing and Democratic Ideal: The Life and
    Thought of Charles Abrams* (Colombia University Press,
    New York, 2000), p.175.
10 Abrams, *Urban Renewal Project in Ireland*, p.vi.
11 Ibid., *p.1*.
12 Bannon, 'The Changing Context of Developmental Planning',
    p.119.
13 Abrams, *Urban Renewal Project in Ireland*, p.22.
14 Ibid., p.3.
15 Ibid., p.68.
16 Bannon, 'Development Planning' in Bannon, *Planning: The Irish
    Experience 1920–1988*, p.136.
17 Daly, *The Buffer State*, p.461.
18 *Dáil Debates*, vol.197, col.1761.
19 Ibid.
20 Ibid.
21 *The Irish Times*, 14 December 1962.
22 *Dáil Debates*, vol.197, col.1768.
23 Ibid.
24 Bannon, *Planning: The Irish Experience 1920–1988*, p.130
25 *Dáil Debates*, vol.197, col.1762.
26 *The Irish Times*, 28 July 1962.
27 *The Irish Times*, 10 May 1963.
28 Mary E. Daly, *The Buffer State*, p.462
29 Ibid., p.463.
30 Ibid., p.464.
31 *Seanad Debates*, vol.56, col.1690.
32 Fraser, *John Bull's Other Homes*, p.137.
33 *Dáil Debates*, vol.197, col.1761.
34 *Seanad Debates*, vol.56, col.1690.
35 *Dáil Debates*, vol.199. col.853.

36   *Seanad Debates*, vol.56, col.1690.

37   *Dáil Debates*, vol.199, col.853.

38   Ibid.

39   Select Committee on the Environment, Heritage and Local Government Debate, 22 June 2010.

40   *Dáil Debates*, vol.199, col.123.

41   Ibid.

42   Ibid.

43   *The Irish Times*, 19 November 1962.

44   *Irish Press*, 29 October 1962.

45   *The Irish Times*, 4 August 1962.

46   *The Irish Times*, 30 October 1962.

47   *Dáil Debates*, vol.197, col.1761.

48   *The Irish Times*, 24 October 1962.

49   *Dáil Debates*, vol.199, col.123.

50   *The Irish Times*, 12 November 1962.

51   Brendan Allen, address to Irish Planning Institute National Planning Conference (2012).

52   'Can Ireland avoid England's planning mistakes?' *Architect's Journal*, 7 September 1966, p.595.

53   S.B. Waddington and B. Bartley, 'The Emergence and Evolution of Urban Planning in Ireland', *Geographical Viewpoint*, no.29 (2001).

54   Grist, *Introduction to Irish Planning Law*, p.97.

55   *Dáil Debates*, vol.197, col.1779

56   Berna Grist, 'The Irish National Spatial Strategy' paper presented at 'Planning for States and Nation/States: A TransAtlantic Exploration' 15–16 October 2012, UCD.

57   Basil Chubb, *A Source Book of Irish Government* (Institute of Public Administration, Dublin, 1983), p.150.

58   Yvonne Scannell, 'The Catastrophic Failure of the Planning System', *Dublin University Law Journal* (2011), p.16.

59   *The Irish Times*, 12 November 1962.

60   Frank McDonald, *The Destruction of Dublin* (Gill and Macmillan, Dublin, 1985), p.27.

61   *Dáil Debates*, vol.199, col.876.

62   John O'Loughlin Kennedy, 'Introduction' in Valerie Bond, *An Taisce: The First Fifty Years* (An Taisce, Dublin, 2005).

63   Erika Hanna, 'Dublin's North Inner City, Preservationism, and Irish Modernity in the 1960s', p.1023.

64 McDonald and Nix, *Chaos at the Crossroads,* p.219.

65 E. O'Rourke, E., 'Landscape Planning and Community
    Participation: Local Lessons from Mullaghmore, the Burren
    National Park, Ireland', *Landscape Research*, vol.30, no.4 (2005).

66 Grist, *Introduction to Irish Planning Law*, p.82.

67 Ibid., p.83.

68 *Irish Times* supplement, 12 October 1965.

69 Michael Bannon, 'The Changing Context of Developmental
    Planning', p.122.

70 Ibid., p.123.

71 *Irish Times* supplement, 12 October 1965.

72 Bannon, 'The Changing Context of Developmental Planning',
    p.125.

73 R. Stringer, 'The Importance of Survey for Development
    Plans', in M.J. Bannon (ed.), *The application of geographical
    techniques to physical planning* (An Foras Forbartha, Dublin,
    1971), pp.34–35.

74 Bannon, 'The Changing Context of Developmental Planning',
    p.126.

75 Bannon, 'Irish Planning from 1921–1945' in *Planning: The Irish
    Experience 1920–1988,* p.58.

76 Charles Abrams, *Urban Renewal Project in Ireland (Dublin)*, UN
    Report, (April 1961), p.25.

77 *The Irish Times* Annual Review, 3 January 1966, p.60.

78 Neil Blaney, opening address to planning conference (1965).

79 Gay McCarron, 'Planning Dublin: Goals Achieved and
    Opportunities Lost', *Journal of Irish Urban Studies*, vol.3, no.1
    (2004).

80 Andrew MacLaran, Michael Punch, 'Tallaght: the Planning
    and Development of an Irish new town', *Journal of Irish Urban
    Studies*, vol.3, no.1 (2004), p.19.

81 Ibid., p.20.

82 Erika Hanna, *Modern Dublin: Urban Change and the Irish Past,
    1957–1973*, p.40.

83 Arnold Horner, 'The Dublin Region 1880–1982. An overview
    on its development and planning', in Bannon, *The Emergence of
    Irish Planning 1880–1920.*

84 Myles Wright, The Dublin Region: Advisory Regional Plan
    and Final Report (1967), p.18.

85 Ibid., p.134.

86 Ibid., p.9.

87 McDonald, *The Destruction of Dublin*, p.303.

88 J.P. Haughton, 'The Urban Rural Fringe of Dublin' in
    N. Stephens and R.E. Glassock (eds), *Irish Geographical Studies*
    (1970).

89 Patrick Shaffrey, 'Dublin: A Fading Princess?', *Studies*, vol.77,
    no.306 (Summer, 1988), p.144.

90 Hanna, *Modern Dublin*, p.41.

91 MacLaran and Punch, 'Tallaght: The Planning and
    Development of an Irish New Town', p.22.

92 Ruairi Quinn, address to Irish Planning Institute National
    Planning Conference (1991).

93 Brendan McGrath, 'Eastern Region Settlement Strategy 2011,
    ERDO, 1985', Pleanáil: Journal of the Irish Planning Institute,
    vol.1, no.5 (1985).

94 Leo O'Reilly, 'A Response to Mr. B McGrath's Review of
    the ERDO Settlement Strategy', *Pleanáil: Journal of the Irish
    Planning Institute*, vol.1, no.5 (1985).

95 Seán Ó Riordáin 'Time for a Renewed Focus on Area
    Based Public Service Delivery?', 31 October 2011, www.
    seanoriordain.ie.

96 Bannon, 'The Changing Context of Developmental Planning',
    p.126.

97 C. Buchanan and Partners, *Regional Studies in Ireland Dublin*
    (An Foras Forbartha, Dublin, 1969), p.1.

98 Bannon, 'The Changing Context of Developmental Planning',
    p.129.

99 Ibid., p.130.

100 David Meredith and Chris van Egeraat, 'Revisiting the
    National Spatial Strategy Ten Years On', *Administration*, vol.60,
    no.3 (2013), p.3.

101 Bannon, 'Development Planning', in *Planning: The Irish
    Experience 1920–1988*, p.145.

102 Bannon, 'The Changing Context of Developmental Planning',
    p.131.

103 Desmond Roche, 'Local Government' in *Unequal
    Achievement: The Irish Experience 1957–1982* (Institute of Public
    Administration, Dublin, 1982).

104 Michael Murray and Brendan Murtagh, 'Strategic Spatial Planning in Northern Ireland', in *Understanding Contemporary Ireland,* p.115.
105 James Walsh, 'Regional Development', in *Understanding Contemporary Ireland*, p.44
106 Grist, *Introduction to Irish Planning Law*, p.25.
107 Ibid., p.29.
108 Ciarán Cuffe, 'Radical Reform or Groundhog Day?', presentation to the Irish Planning Institute North East Branch seminar on local government reform and the planning system, 16th January 2014.
109 Andrew MacLaran, Michael Punch, 'Tallaght: The Planning and Development of an Irish New Town', p.18.
110 McDonald, *The Destruction of Dublin*, p.4.
111 *The Irish Times*, 14 February 1963.
112 *The Irish Times*, 12 November 1962.
113 Andrew MacLaran, Michael Punch, 'Tallaght: The Planning and Development of an Irish New Town', p.25.
114 McDonald, *The Destruction of Dublin*, p.161.
115 Ibid.
116 Michael Bannon, 'The Changing Context of Developmental Planning', p.136.
117 McGuirk and MacClaran, 'Changing Approaches to Urban Planning in an Entrepreneurial City: The Case of Dublin, *European Planning Studies*, Vol.9, No.4. (2001).
118 Andrew MacLaran, Michael Punch, 'Tallaght: The Planning and Development of an Irish New Town'.
119 Brendan Bartley, 'Planning In Ireland' in *Understanding Contemporary Ireland*, p.36.
120 *The Irish Times*, 30 October 1962.
121 *Seanad Debates*, vol.56, col.1698.
122 Ibid.
123 *Dáil Debates*, vol.197 col.1780.
124 Ibid.
125 Manning Robertson, 'The Town and Regional Planning Act, 1934', *Irish Builder and Engineer*, vol.LXXVIII, 1936, p.33.
126 Joan Caffrey, Enda Conway, Philip Jones, 'The Development of the Planning Profession in Ireland' in *A Centenary of Spatial Planning in Europe.*

127 Michael Bannon, 'The Changing Context of Developmental Planning', p.136.

128 McDonald, *The Destruction of Dublin*, p.62–63.

129 Patrick Shaffrey, 'The Origins of the Institute' *Pleanáil: Journal of the Irish Planning Institute*, Vol.1, No.5, (Winter 1985)

130 Feargall Kenny, 'A Message From the President of the Institute'. *Pleanáil: Journal of the Irish Planning Institute* (Winter 1985).

131 Berna Grist, *Introduction to Irish Planning Law*, 2013, p.6.

132 *Seanad Debates*, vol.56, col.1761.

133 *Dáil Debates*, vol.197, col.1764.

134 Mary E. Daly, *The Buffer State*, p.466.

135 Ibid., p.467.

136 Ibid.

137 McDonald and Nix, *Chaos at the Crossroads*, p.144.

138 Bannon, 'Forty Years of Irish Planning – An Overview', p.7.

139 Irish Planning Institute press statement, September 1987.

140 Bannon, 'Forty Years of Irish Planning – An Overview', p.7.

141 McDonald, *The Destruction of Dublin*, p.4.

142 Berna Grist, *Twenty Years of Planning: a Review of the System Since 1963*, p.25.

143 Michael Bannon, 'The Changing Context of Developmental Planning', *Administration*, Vol.31, No.2, p.137.

144 *The Irish Times* supplement, 12 October 1965.

145 M.J. Bannon, (ed.), *The Emergence of Irish Planning, 1880–1920*, p.15.

146 T.J. Barrington, 'Whatever happened to Irish Government?' in *Unequal Achievement: the Irish experience 1957–1982* (Institute of Public Administration, Dublin, 1982).

147 Berna Grist, *Twenty Years of Planning*, p.9.

CHAPTER 5

1 Conor McCabe, *Sins of the Father Tracing the Decisions that Shaped the Irish Economy* (Dublin, The History Press, 2011).

2 Ibid.

3 *Wicklow People*, 22 June 1889.

4 Frank McDonald and James Nix, *Chaos at the Crossroads* (Gandon Books, Kinsale, 2005).

5 Lambert McKenna, 'The Housing Problem in Dublin', *Studies*, vol.8 (1919), p.279–295.

6 Bannon, 'Irish Planning from 1921–1945' in Bannon, *Planning: The Irish Experience 1920–1988*, p.33.

7 *The Irish Times*, 3 May 1923.

8 Civics Institute of Ireland, *Dublin Civic Survey* (1925), p.25.

9 Report of the Departmental Committee Appointed by the Local Government Board for Ireland to Inquire into the Housing Conditions of the Working Classes in the City of Dublin, (Dublin, 1914), pp.212–22.

10 Bannon, 'Irish Planning from 1921–1945' in Bannon, *Planning: The Irish Experience 1920–1988*, p.67.

11 Ruth McManus, 'Blue Collars, "Red Forts", and Green Fields: Working-Class Housing in Ireland in the Twentieth Century', *International Labour and Working Class History* (2003), p.45.

12 Kincaid, *Postcolonial Dublin*, p.10.

13 Murray Fraser, *John Bull's Other Homes*, p.136.

14 Bannon, 'Irish Planning from 19211945' in Bannon, *Planning: The Irish Experience 1920–1988*, p.31.

15 Murray Fraser, *John Bull's Other Homes*, p.136.

16 Daly, in Bannon, *The Emergence of Irish Planning 1880–1920*, p.107.

17 Continuing McDonald writes 'Apart from being indecisive, O'Brien had no real concept of planning, so the 1957 Planning Scheme was drawn up by his deputy, Kevin I. Nowlan, who went on to become professor of Town Planning at UCD' (*The Destruction of Dublin*, p.11).

18 McDonald, *The Destruction of Dublin*, p.11.

19 *Irish Builder and Engineer*, no.63 (1922).

20 Most Revd John A. F. Gregg in the *Irish Builder and Engineer*, no.75 (1934).

21 '"To Hell or to Kimmage": Planning outcomes of the 1913 Church Street Disaster', *History Ireland Hedge School*, Tuesday 21 January 2014.

22 Ruth McManus, 'Blue Collars, "Red Forts", and Green Fields', p.48.

23 Fraser, *John Bull's Other Homes*, p.135.

24 McManus, *Dublin, 1910–1940: Shaping the City & Suburbs*, p.182.

25 *Irish Builder and Engineer*, vol.LII (1910), p.728.

26 Anthony O'Brien, 'The Soldiers Houses in Limerick', *The Old Limerick Journal* (1998).

27 Ruth McManus, 'Public Utility Societies, Dublin Corporation and the Development of Dublin, 1920–1940', *Irish Geography*, 1996.

28 Ellen Rowley, 'To hell or to Kimmage': planning outcomes of the 1913 Church Street disaster, History Ireland Hedge School, Tuesday 21st January 2014.

29 *Irish Independent*, 6 March 1934.

30 Quoted in Sinéad Power, 'The Development of the Ballymun Housing Scheme, Dublin 1965–1969', *Irish Geography*, vol.33, no.2 (January 2000), p.211 .

31 *Irish Press*, 31 July 1969.

32 Robert Somerville-Woodward, *Ballymun a History* (Ballymun Regeneration, Dublin, 2002), p.38.

33 *Dáil Debates*, vol.237, col.1518.

34 Gough in Bannon, *The Emergence of Irish Planning 1880–1920*, p.330.

35 Frank McDonald, *The Construction of Dublin* (Gandon Editions, Kinsale, 2000,), p.251.

36 Sinéad Power, 'The Development of the Ballymun Housing Scheme, Dublin 1965–1969'.

37 '"To Hell or to Kimmage": Planning Outcomes of the 1913 Church Street Disaster', *History Ireland Hedge School*, Tuesday 21st January 2014.

38 Andrew MacLaran, Michael Punch, 'Tallaght: The Planning and Development of an Irish New Town', *Journal of Irish Urban Studies*, vol.3, issue 1 (2004), p.23.

39 Andrew MacLaran, *Dublin: The Shaping of a Capital* (Belhaven, London, 1993).

40 Andrew MacLaran, Michael Punch.

41 Andrew MacLaran, Michael Punch, p.24.

42 *Irish Independent*, 1 January 1969.

43 *Irish Independent*, 24 February 1967.

44 *Irish Press*, 24 February 1967.

45 *Irish Independent*, 1 January 1969.

46 *Southern Star*, 28 October 1967.

47 Irish Planning Institute, National Planning Awards 2013–2014 Jury Commendation.

48 National Economic and Social Council, *Housing in Ireland: Performance and Policy* (NESC, Dublin, 2004), p.10.

49 Menelaos Gkartzios and Mark Scott, 'Planning for Rural Housing in the Republic of Ireland: From National Spatial

Strategies to Development Plans', *European Planning Studies*, vol.17, issue 12 (2009), p.1761.

50 Paddy Shaffrey. 'Settlement Patterns: Rural Housing, Villages, Small Towns' in F.H.A. Aalen, *The Future of the Irish Rural Landscape*.

51 F.H.A. Aalen, 'Houses', in F.H.A Aalen, K. Whelan, and M. Stout (eds), *Atlas of the Irish Rural Landscape* (Cork University Press, Cork, 2011).

52 Ruth McManus, 'Celtic Tiger Housing', in F.H.A Aalen, K. Whelan, and M. Stout (eds), *Atlas of the Irish Rural Landscape* (Cork University Press, Cork, 2011), p.157.

53 G. Deegan, 'Planners vie with Taliban for Notoriety', *Clare Champion*, 20 December 2002.

54 R.F. Foster, *Modern Ireland*, p.26.

55 *Irish Builder and Engineer*, 'The Spoiling of the Dublin Suburbs', Vol.LXIX (1927), p.469

56 *Southern Star*, 16 July 2013.

57 Mary Cawley, 'The Problems of Rural Ireland' in *Ireland: A Contemporary Geography Perspective*, R.W.G. Carter and A.J. Parker (eds), (Routledge, London, 1989), p.157.

58 Fergal MacCabe, 'How We Wrecked Rural Ireland in the Latter Part of the Twentieth Century', *Pleanail: Journal of the Irish Planning Institute*, no.16 (2003), p.65.

59 Olivia O'Leary in Sweeney, *Ireland's Economic Success: Reasons and Lessons*, p.105.

60 Ruth McManus, *Urban Dreams – Urban Nightmares in Engaging Spaces: People, Place and Space from an Irish Perspective* (Dublin: Lilliput Press, 2003), p.31.

61 Ibid. p.33.

62 Address to the Irish Planning Institute National Planning Conference, 1986

63 McDonald and Nix, *Chaos at the Crossroads*, p.137.

64 *The Irish Times*, 26 June 1997

65 Government of Ireland, *White Paper on Rural Development* (1999), p.114

66 *White Paper on Rural Development*, p.78.

67 Gkartzios and Scott, p.1762.

68 Gkartzios and Scott, p.1763.

69 *Sustainable Rural Housing Guidelines*, p.1.

70 *The Irish Times*, 13 March 2004.

71 McDonald and Nix, *Chaos at the Crossroads*, p.138.

72 Ibid., p.136.

73 Gkartzios and Scott.

74 Brendan McGrath, *Landscape and Society in Contemporary Ireland*, p.177.

75 Ibid., p.178.

76 MacCabe, 'How We Wrecked Rural Ireland in the Latter Part of the Twentieth Century'.

77 Mary Cawley, 'The Problems of Rural Ireland' in R.W.G. Carter and A.J. Parker (eds), *Ireland: A Contemporary Geography Perspective* (Routledge, London, 1989) p.155.

78 *Northern Ireland Regional Development Strategy: Shaping Our Future*, p.106.

79 *Seanad Debates*, vol.189, col.717.

80 An Taisce press release, 20 March 2002.

81 *Dáil Debates*, vol.199, col.122.

82 Jim Connolly, 2005.

83 Address to Clare County Council, 8 March 2010.

84 *The Irish Times*, 13 September 2002.

85 *Irish Examiner*, 22 February 2014.

86 Fergal MacCabe, 'How We Wrecked Rural Ireland in the Latter Part of the Twentieth Century', p.65.

87 Mark Lynas, 'The concrete isle', *Guardian*, 4 December 2004

88 *The Irish Times*, 20 February 2001.

89 Brendan McGrath, *Landscape and Society in Contemporary Ireland*, p.4.

90 Mark Scott, 'Managing Rural Change and Competing Rationalities: Insights from Conflicting Rural Storylines and Local Policy Making in Ireland', *Planning Theory & Practice*, vol.9, no.1 (March 2008).

91 Ibid.

92 *The Irish Times*, 13 September 2002.

93 Brendan McGrath, *Landscape and Society in Contemporary Ireland*, p.115.

94 Irish Citizens Party Manifesto 2011, p.57.

95 Ibid.

96 An Taisce, *State of The Nation A Review of Ireland's Planning System 2001–2011* (2012), p.34

97 McDonald and Nix, *Chaos at the Crossroads*, p.139.

98 An Foras Forbartha, *Urban Generated Housing in Rural Areas*, p.1.

99   McDonald and Nix, *Chaos at the Crossroads*, p.139.

100 Gavin Daly, 'Back to the Future: Planning in County
     Mayo – An Obituary to Reason', Ireland After NAMA blog
     7 March 2014.

101 *Kerryman*, 30 November 2012.

102 Diarmuid Ó Gráda, 'Mistakes of the Past Allowing Bungalow
     Blitz Must Not Determine Energy Policy', *The Irish Times*,
     18 January 2014.

103 Tom Keenan 'Planning for Groundwater Protection' paper
     presented to Irish Planning institute National Planning
     Conference (1986).

104 Mark Scott, 'Managing Rural Change and Competing
     Rationalities: Insights from Conflicting Rural Storylines and
     Local Policy Making in Ireland'.

105 Katie Hannon, *The Naked Politician* (Gill and Macmillan,
     Dublin, 2004), p.57.

106 McDonald and Nix, *Chaos at the Crossroads*, p.137.

107 Ibid.

108 *Kerryman*, 3 December 2012.

109 Clinch, Convery, Walsh, p.105.

110 Kerry IRDA, IFA and GAA, *The Rural Challenge* (2012), p.17.

111 Brendan McGrath, *Landscape and Society in Contemporary Ireland*,
     p.122.

112 An Taisce, *State of The Nation*, p.34.

113 Paddy Shaffrey, 'Settlement Patterns: Rural Housing, Villages,
     Small Towns', in F.H.A. Aalen (ed.) *The Future of the Irish Rural
     Landscape* (Department of Geography, Trinity College Dublin,
     1978), p.61

114 Ferriter, p.547.

115 Irish Planning Institute submission to the Department of the
     Environment (March 1985).

116 Michael Gough, address to Irish Planning Institute National
     Planning Conference, (1983).

117 Berna Grist, 'Planning', in M. Callanan, and J.F Keogan (eds),
     Local Government in Ireland Inside Out (Institute of Public
     Administration, Dublin, 2003), p.234.

118 *Drogheda Independent*, 25 November 2012.

119 'Planners No Longer Want to Work in Kerry County Council',
     Radio Kerry, 15 April 2004.

120 *The Irish Times*, 19 April 2004.

121 *Kerryman*, 1 December 2012.

122 MacCabe, 'How We Wrecked Rural Ireland in the Latter Part
of the Twentieth Century', p.65.

CHAPTER 6

1 Brendan Bartley, 'Planning in Ireland' in *Understanding
Contemporary Ireland*, p.36.

2 Gordon Cherry, 'A Changing Profession in a Changing World',
Australian Planner, vol.24, no.4 (1986), p.16.

3 McDonald, *The Destruction of Dublin*, p.339.

4 Ibid., p.116.

5 Ibid., p.85.

6 Ibid., p.51.

7 Ibid., p.95.

8 Ibid., p.166.

9 Ibid., p.173.

10 Ibid., p.171.

11 Ibid., p.173.

12 Ibid., p.174.

13 Ibid., p.174.

14 Ibid., p.175.

15 McDonald and Nix, *Chaos at the Crossroads*, p.225.

16 McDonald, *The Destruction of Dublin*, p.198.

17 P.J. Duffy, 'Housing History, Kilcone, County Meath' in
F.H.A. Aalen, K. Whelan and M. Stout, M. (eds), *Atlas of the
Irish Rural Landscape* (Cork University Press, Cork, 2011), p.234.

18 McDonald, *The Destruction of Dublin,* p.198.

19 Ibid., p.199.

20 Ibid., p.198.

21 Ibid., p.205.

22 Ibid., p.207.

23 Ibid., p.239.

24 Ibid., p.244.

25 Ibid., p.231.

26 Ibid., p.227.

27 Ibid., p.164.

28 *Dáil Debates*, vol.199, col.829.

29 *Dáil Debates*, vol.191, col.1886.

30 *Dáil Debates*, vol.204, col.185.

31 S. Crow, 'Third Party Appeals: Will they Work? Do We Need Them?', *Journal of Planning and Environmental Law* (May, 1995).

32 *Dáil Debates*, vol.203 col.1769.

33 Ibid.

34 *Dáil Debates*, vol.73, col.53.

35 *Seanad Debates*, vol.56, col.1748.

36 *Dáil Debates*, vol.199, col.123.

37 *Dáil Debates*, vol.199, col.150.

38 *Dáil Debates*, vol.199, col. 800.

39 Daly, *The Buffer State*, p.464.

40 *The Irish Times*, 8 December 1971.

41 T. Reynolds, 'The Local Authority and Development – The View of the Developer' paper presented to the Irish Planning Institute's 'Role of the Local Authority as a Development Agency' conference (1978).

42 *The Irish Times,* 7 February 1968.

43 *Dáil Debates*, vol.232, col.2007.

44 Brendan O'Donoghue, 'The First Board' in *An Bord Pleanála 1977–2002: Celebrating the first twenty five years* (An Bord Pleanála, Dublin, 2002), p.9.

45 Ibid.

46 *The Irish Times*, 19 March 2002.

47 Fergal MacCabe 'The View of the Planning Profession' in *An Bord Pleanála 1977–2002: Celebrating the First Twenty Five Years* (An Bord Pleanála, Dublin, 2002), p.19.

48 McDonald, *The Destruction of Dublin*, p.236.

49 Michael Bannon, 'The Changing Context of Developmental Planning', p.132.

50 Stephen Collins, *The Power Game*, Ireland under Fianna Fáil (The O'Brien Press, Dublin, 2001), p.158.

51 Ibid. p.159.

52 Ibid.

53 Foster, *Modern Ireland*, p.87.

54 Irish Rural Dwellers Association report on planning need, 2009, p.4.

55 Irish Citizens Party Manifesto, 2011, p.56.

56 Vincent Browne, Review of 'The Origins of the Irish Constitution, 1928–1941', *History Ireland*, (January– February, 2013).

57 All Party Oireachtas Committee on the Constitution, *Ninth Progress Report: Private Property* (2004), p.18.

58 Daly in Bannon, *The Emergence of Irish Planning 1880–1920*, p.96.

59 Grist, *Introduction to Irish Planning Law*, p.116.

60 Ibid.

61 Ibid., p.119.

62 McDonald, *The Destruction of Dublin*, p.95.

63 Grist, *Introduction to Irish Planning Law*, p.119.

64 Ibid., p.120.

65 O'Toole, F., *Ship of Fools: How Stupidity and Corruption Sank the Celtic Tiger* (Faber and Faber, 2009), p.108.

66 Ibid., pp.106–109.

67 Ibid. p.107.

68 *The Irish Times*, 13 October 1981.

69 Dennis Pringle, 'Partition, Politics and Social Conflict' in R.W.G. Carter and A.J. Parker (eds), *Ireland: A Contemporary Geography Perspective* (Routledge, London, 1989), p.46.

70 Ibid. p.45.

71 *Plan*, (July–August, 1972), p.32.

72 Niamh Moore, 'Rejuvenating Docklands: The Irish Context', *Irish Geography*, vol.32, no.2 (1999).

73 P.Howley and B. Clifford, 'The Transformation of Inner Dublin: Exploring New Residential Populations Within the inner city', *Irish Geography*, vol.42, no.2 (2009), pp.225–243.

74 Niamh Moore, *Dublin Docklands Reinvented: The Post–Industrial Regeneration of a European City Quarter* (Four Courts Press, Dublin, 2008), p.148.

75 Ibid., p.289.

76 *Irish Independent*, 28 March 2013.

77 Paddy Shaffrey, 'Dublin – Urban Design Influences', *Urban Design (October 1996)*.

78 Dermot Kelly, 'Dublin Metropolitan Streets Commission – Summary of draft Proposals at Time of Dissolution', *Pleanail: Journal of the Irish Planning Institute*, No.7 (1987).

79 John Montgomery, 'The Story of Temple Bar: Creating Dublin's Cultural Quarter', *Planning Practice and Research*, vol.10, no.2 (1995), p.147.

CHAPTER 7

1   Grist, *Local Government Inside Out*, p.22.

2   *Seanad Debates*, vol.513 col.1005.

3   *Dáil Debates*, vol.514, col.1150.

4   Grist, *Introduction to Irish Planning Law*, p.8.

5   *Seanad Debates*, vol.513, col.1006.

6   Ibid.

7   Grist, *Introduction to Irish Planning Law*, p.vii.

8   Berna Grist, *The Preparation of Development Plans* (An Foras Forbartha, 1984).

9   Grist, *Introduction to Irish Planning Law*, p.15.

10 McDonald and Nix, *Chaos at the Crossroads*, p.37.

11 Grist, *Introduction to Irish Planning Law*, p.41.

12 Ibid., p.124.

13 NIRSA, *A Haunted Landscape: Housing and Ghost Estates in Post–Celtic Tiger Ireland,* Working Paper Series (2010).

14 Ibid., p.37.

15 Grist, *Introduction to Irish Planning Law*, p.76.

16 C.T. Ruthen, 'Housing and Planning – A National Policy', *The Irish Builder and Engineer* vol.61 (1919), p.262.

17 The hubs are Cavan, Ennis, Kilkenny, Mallow, Monaghan, Tuam, Wexford, Ballina/Castlebar and Tralee/Killarney.

18 McDonald and Nix, *Chaos at the Crossroads*, p.74.

19 *Dáil Debates*, vol.620, col.2006.

20 Berna Grist, *The Irish National Spatial Strategy.*

21 Ibid.

22 Dr Edgar Morgenroth, presentation to the Irish Planning Institute North East Branch seminar on local government reform and the planning system, 16th January 2014

23 Ibid.

24 *Dáil Debates*, vol.620, col.450.

25 McDonald and Nix, *Chaos at the Crossroads*, p.32.

26 Department of the Taoiseach, *Framework for Action of Infrastructural Development and PPPs* (1999).

27 N.Reilly 'Planning in the Fast Lane', *Council Review* (July 2005), p.41.

28 *Dáil Debates*, vol.621, col.1361.

29 *Dáil Debates*, vol.620, col.2006.

30 Ibid.

31 Grist, *Introduction to Irish Planning Law*, p.75.

32 Lynas, 'The Concrete Isle'.

33 Iain Douglas, 'Telling it like it is', *Construct Ireland*, Issue 7 (2005).

34 Andrew Hind, President's Address to the Irish Planning Institute National Planning Conference (2008).

35 Mark Clinton, 'Castle Retention, Motorway are Still Possible', *The Irish Times*, 19 January 2004.

36 Lynas, 'The Concrete Isle'.

37 Department of the Environment, Heritage and Local Government, *Draft Development Management Guidelines for Planning Authorities* (The Stationery Office, Dublin, 2005).

38 Irish Home Builders Association submission on Development Management Consultation Draft Guidelines for Planning Authorities (2006).

39 Colm McCarthy, 'Dublin's Sprawl Threatens to Choke the Nation', *Irish Independent*, 27 July 2004.

40 Frank McDonald, 'European Environment Agency Cites Dublin as a Worst Case Scenario of Urban Planning' *The Irish Times*, 4 October 2006.

41 Lynas, 'The Concrete Isle'.

42 McDonald and Nix, *Chaos at the Crossroads*, p.41.

43 Sunnhild Bertz, 'The Peripheralisation of Office Development in the Dublin Metropolitan Area– the Interrelationship Between Planning and Development Interests', *Irish Geography*, vol.35, no.2 (January 2002).

44 Ciarán Cuffe, 'Radical Reform or Groundhog Day?' presentation to the Irish Planning Institute North East Branch seminar on local government reform and the planning system, 16 January 2014.

45 Olivia O'Leary in Sweeney, *Ireland's Economic Success: Reasons and Lessons*, p.106.

46 Simon Carswell, *Anglo Republic: Inside the Bank that Broke Ireland* (Dublin, Penguin Ireland, 2011).

47 McDonald, *The Destruction of Dublin*, p.105.

48 McDonald and Nix, *Chaos at the Crossroads*, p.29.

49 McDonald and Nix, *Chaos at the Crossroads*, p.13.

50 Nicholas Mansergh, 'Specialised building booms and the future of planning', *Pleanáil: Journal of the Irish Planning Institute*, no.12 (1995).

51 'Social Justice Ireland', *Socio–Economic Review 2013*, p.37.

52 Ibid., p.38.

53 Karl Whelan, 'Ireland's Sovereign Debt Crisis', *UCD Centre for Economic Research Working Paper Series* (May 2011).

54 Patrick Honohan, 'Resolving Ireland's Banking Crisis', *The Economic and Social Review*, Vol.40, No.2 (Summer, 2009).

55 Frank Daly, 'Address to Association of European Journalists', 21 February 2013.

56 Jane Jacobs, *The Death and Life of Great American Cities* (Random House, New York, 1961), p.293.

CHAPTER 8

1 An Taisce, *State of the Nation: A Review of Ireland's Planning System 2000–2011* (2012) p.16.

2 *Dáil Debates*, vol.197, col.1632.

3 Frances Ruane in Sweeney, *Ireland's Economic Success: Reasons and Lessons*, p.59.

4 Frank McDonald, 'One way or another, unfinished housing schemes appear to be resolved', *The Irish Times*, 29 November 2013.

5 Ibid.

6 Grist, *Introduction to Irish Planning Law*, p.156.

7 Ibid., p.186.

8 Berna Grist, 'The Irish National Spatial Strategy' paper presented at 'Planning for States and Nation/States: A TransAtlantic Exploration symposium', UCD, 15–16 October 2012.

9 NIRSA, *A Haunted Landscape*, p.41.

10 *Village Magazine,* 'How Ireland Screwed up on Planning', 1 May 2012.

11 Scannell, 'The Catastrophic Failure of the Planning System', p.6.

12 Brendan Williams, Brian Hughes, Declan Redmond, 'Managing an Unstable Housing Market', *UCD Urban Institute working paper* (2010), p.15.

13 Department of the Environment press release, 4 April 2012.

14 *The Irish Times*, 22 May 2009.

15 Irish Planning Institute press release, 'IPI Response To Knee Jerk Media Reaction on Housing Starts', 5 July 2006.

16 Irish Planning Institute press release, 'Planners Warn on Rezonings', 16 October 2006.

17 Grist, *Introduction to Irish Planning Law*, p.34.

18 Joint Committee on the Environment, Heritage and Local Government Debate, 4 November 2008.

19 Fiach Kelly, 'Zoning Frenzy Forces Minister to Rein in Several Councils', *Irish Independent*, 10 October 2009.

20 Joint Committee on the Environment, Heritage and Local Government Debate, 4 November 2008.

21 Grist, *Introduction to Irish Planning Law*, p.21.

22 Scannell, 'The Catastrophic Failure of the Planning System', p.9.

23 Grist, *Introduction to Irish Planning Law*.

24 Erika Hanna, 'Dublin's North Inner City, Preservationism, and Irish Modernity in the 1960s', *The Historical Journal*, Vol.53, No.4, December 2010, p.1029.

25 Ibid.

26 R.F. Foster, *Luck and the Irish: A Brief History of Change from 1970* (Oxford University Press, Oxford, 2008), p.87.

27 Ibid., p.89.

28 Grist, *Twenty years of planning*, p.6.

29 Michael Gough, address to the Irish Planning Institute National Planning Conference, 1983.

30 Irish Planning Institute press statement, 6 October 1981.

31 Liam Lawlor, correspondence with the Irish Planning Institute, 2 November 1981.

32 Liam Lawlor, speech to Irish Planning Institute National Planning Conference (1983).

33 Grist, *Twenty Years of Planning*, p.6.

34 Ronan Keane, *The Law of Local Government in the Republic of Ireland* (Incorporated Law Society of Ireland, Dublin, 1982), p.x.

35 Lee Komito, 'Politics and Clientelism in Urban Ireland: Information, Reputation, and Brokerage', University Microfilms International 8603660 (1985).

36 Ibid.

37 Grist, *Introduction to Irish Planning Law*, p.180.

38 *The Irish Times*, 4 April 2003.

39 Final Report of the Tribunal of Inquiry into Certain Planning Matters and Payments (2012), p.5.

40 Pat Leahy, *The Price of Power: Inside Ireland's Crisis Coalition* (Dublin, Penguin Ireland, 2013).
41 *RIAI Dispatch*, March 1997 and clarification April 1997.
42 Grist, *Introduction to Irish Planning Law*, p.183.
43 An Taisce, *Proposals for Changes in Irish Planning Law and Practice* (September 1990)
44 Grist, 'The Irish National Spatial Strategy'.
45 Ciarán Cuffe, 'Radical Reform or Groundhog Day?', presentation to the Irish Planning Institute North East Branch seminar on local government reform and the planning system, 16 January 2014.
46 Ciaran Cuffe, 'A Player Mayor', *Village Magazine*, (February/ March 2014).

CONCLUSION

1 *Irish Examiner*, 11 July 2013.
2 Taken from the Intelligent Energy Europe funded SPECIAL (Spatial Planning and Energy for Communities in All Landscapes) project, www.special-eu.org.
3 Grist, *Twenty years of planning*, p.3.
4 Bannon, *The Emergence of Irish Planning 1880–1920*, pp.15–16.
5 Ken Mawhiney, 'The future of the planning profession', proceedings of Irish Planning Institute and Irish Branch of the Royal Town Planning Institute workshop (November 1987).
6 Bannon, *The Emergence of Irish Planning 1880–1920*, p.15.
7 *Dáil Debates*, vol.73, col.63.
8 Scannell, 'The Catastrophic Failure of the Planning System'.
9 Ibid., p.4.
10 Bannon, *The Emergence of Irish Planning 1880–1920*, p.13.
11 Frank Daly, 'Address to association of European journalists', 21 February 2013.
12 Gerry Walker, paper to the 1982 Regional Studies Association conference.
13 Bannon, *The Emergence of Irish Planning 1880–1920*, pp.14–15.
14 Irish Planning Institute submission to the Department of the Environment on planning policy issues (March 2014).
15 *Dublin of the Future*, p.48.

16 Andrew MacLaran, Vanda Clayton, Paula Brudell, 'Empowering Communities in Disadvantaged Urban Areas: towards greater community participation in Irish Urban Planning' *Combat Poverty Agency Working Paper Series* 07/04 (2007), p.2.

17 McDonald, *The Destruction of Dublin*, p.4.

Selected
Bibliography

Aalen, F.H.A., (ed.), *The Future of the Irish Rural Landscape* (Department of Geography, Trinity College, 1978).

Aberdeen, Marquess and Marchioness, *'We twa' Reminiscences of Lord and Lady Aberdeen* (W. Collins Sons & Co. Ltd., London, 1925).

Abrams, C., *Urban Renewal Project in Ireland (Dublin), UN Report* (April 1961).

Bannon, M. (ed.), The *Emergence of Irish Planning 1880–1920* (Turoe Press, Dublin, 1985).

Bannon, M. (ed.), *Planning: The Irish Experience 1920–1988* (Wolfhound Press, Dublin, 1989).

Bartley, B., 'Planning in Ireland' in B. Bartley and R. Kitchin (eds), *Understanding Contemporary Ireland* (Pluto Bartley, London; Ann Arbor, 2007).

Bond, V., *An Taisce: The First Fifty Years* (An Taisce, Dublin, 2005).

Camblin, G., *The Town in Ulster* (Wm Mullan & Son Publishers Ltd, Belfast, 1951).

Craig, M., *Dublin 1660–1860: The Shaping of a City* (Liberties Press, Dublin, 2006).

Crowley, C., *The Origin of the Curvilinear Plan-Form in Irish Ecclesiastical Sites: A Comparative Analysis of Sites in Ireland, Wales and France* (PhD Thesis, DIT, 2008).

Daly, M., *Dublin: The Deposed Capital. A Social and Economic History, 1860–1914* (Cork University Press, Cork, 1984).

Daly, M., *The Buffer State: The Historical Roots of the Department of the Environment* (Institute of Public Administration, Dublin, 1997).

Douglas, R.M., *Architects of the Resurrection: Ailtirí na hAiséirghe and the fascist 'New Order' in Ireland* (Manchester University Press, Manchester, 2009).

Ferriter, D., *The Transformation of Ireland 1900–2000* (Profile Books, London, 2004).

Foster, R.F., *Modern Ireland 1600–1972* (Penguin, London, 1989).

Fraser, M., *John Bull's Other Homes: State Housing and British Policy in Ireland, 1883–1922* (Liverpool University Press, Liverpool, 1995).

Geddes, P., 'Two Steps in Civics: Cities and Town Planning Exhibition and the International Congress of Cities', *Town Planning Review*, vol. 4. no. 2 (1917).

Gibney, F., 'Dublin "Castles in the Air"', *Dublin Historical Record*, vol. 17, no. 3 (June, 1962).

Gough, M., 'The Dublin Wide Streets Commissioners (1758–1851): An Early Modern Planning Authority', *Pleanáil: Journal of the Irish Planning Institute*, no. 11 (1992–93).

Grist, B., *Introduction to Irish Planning Law* (Dublin, Institute of Public Administration, 2013).

Grist, B., *Twenty Years of Planning: A Review of the System Since 1963* (An Foras Forbartha, Dublin, 1983).

Hall, T., *Planning Europe's Capital Cities: Aspects of Nineteenth-Century Urban Development* (Alexandrine Press, Oxford, 1997).

Hanna, E., *Modern Dublin: Urban Change and the Irish Past, 1957–1973* (Oxford University Press, Oxford, 2013.)

Hourihan, K., 'The Evolution and Influence of Town Planning in Cork' in P. O'Flanagan and C. G. Buttimer (eds), *Cork History and Society: Interdisciplinary Essays on the History of an Irish County* (Geography Publications, Dublin, 1993).

Keeble, L., *Principles and Practice of Town and Country Planning* (Estates Gazette, London, 1952).

Kenny Report, *Report of the Committee on the Price of Building Land* (Stationery Office, Dublin, 1973).

Kincaid, A., *Postcolonial Dublin: Imperial Legacies and the Built Environment* (University of Minnesota Press, Minneapolis, 2006).

Komito, L., 'Politics and Clientelism in Urban Ireland: Information, Reputation, and Brokerage', University Microfilms International 8603660 (1985).

MacCabe, F., 'Urbanity and Rurality – The Bord na Móna Villages of Frank Gibney', *Scéal na Móna* (December 2006).

MacLaran, A., Clayton, V., Brudell, P., *Empowering Communities in Disadvantaged Urban Areas: Towards Greater Community Participation in Irish Urban Planning, Combat Poverty Agency Working Paper Series 07/04* (2007).

Mansergh, N., 'Specialised Building Booms and the Future of Planning', *Pleanáil: Journal of the Irish Planning Institute*, no. 12 (1995).

McDonald, F., *The Destruction of Dublin* (Gill and Macmillan, Dublin, 1985).

McGrath, B., *Landscape and Society in Contemporary Ireland* (Cork University Press, Cork, 2013).

McManus, R., 'Housing in Post-Colonial Dublin', *Irish Geography*, vol. 39, no. 2 (2007).

Scannell, Y., 'The Catastrophic Failure of the Planning System', *Dublin University Law Journal* (2011).

Taylor, N., *Urban Planning Theory Since 1945* (Sage, London, 1998).

Wallace, P.F., 'Town Layout and its possible regulation in Viking age Dublin', *Pleanáil: Journal of the Irish Planning Institute*, no. 6, (1986).

Whelan, K., 'Town and Village in Ireland: A Socio-Cultural Perspective', *The Irish Review*, no. 5 (Autumn, 1988).

Index

Aalen, FHA 40
Aarhus Convention 182-183
Abercrombie, Patrick 47-48, 51-57, 60, 67, 117
Aberdeen, Lady 41-46, 60
Aberdeen, Marquess of 41-46, 48
Abrams, Charles 80-81, 95, 111, 129, 155
Act of Union 31, 34, 37
Adamstown 138, 172-173
Ahern, Bertie 15, 175, 197-200
Aiken, Frank 111
Ailtirí na hAiséirghe 73-74
Allen, Brendan 87
An Bord Pleanála 17, 18, 134, 137, 143, 147-148, 155-158, 170-177
An Foras Forbartha 94, 102, 112-113, 134-135, 150, 162, 169, 187, 196, 206
An Taisce 91-92, 107, 132-134, 138, 141, 163, 170, 179, 180, 182, 186, 194, 197, 203
Architectural Association of Ireland 12, 46, 151
Artisans' Dwelling Company 40, 115

Bacon Reports (1998-2000) 170
Ballymun 120-123
Bannon, Michael 12, 14, 16, 45, 47-48, 51, 72, 83, 109, 113, 208-209
Barrington Report 100-101
Belfast 40, 69, 126
Blaney, Neil T 19, 78-91, 96, 103, 107-111, 120, 144, 153, 226
Boland, Kevin 84, 92-94, 145, 155
Bolton Street see Dublin Institute of Technology
Browne, Vincent 158
Buchanan Report (Regional Studies in Ireland) 1968 96, 102-103
Bunreacht na hÉireann 13, 85, 99, 123, 143, 155, 158-162, 170-171, 210
Burke, Ray 112, 150, 157, 195-199

Cavan 102, 137
Celtic Tiger 12, 15, 19, 126, 146, 181-190, 194, 210-211

Central Bank, Dublin 144-146
Centre for Public Inquiry 181-182
Christianity 21, 73, 93, 99, 118, 158
Childers, Erskine 77, 125
Civic Exhibition (1914) 9, 45-46
Civics Institute 41-48, 53-56, 59, 63,
 67, 77, 210
Civil War 14, 48, 58-60
Clare 75, 101, 124, 126-127, 133
Clarke, Harry 50-51
Clientelism 141, 189, 194
Climate change 13, 207
Construction Industry Federation
 154
Conway, Enda 108, 129
Coakley, DJ 54
Coffey, Paudie 193
Consultation see Public
 participation
Cork 19-22, 26-28, 40, 53-55,
 65-66, 72-73, 81, 88, 102,
 107-109, 112, 116, 119-121,
 126-128, 132, 172, 175, 206
Cork Town Planning Association
 53-54
Corruption 12, 146, 157, 189,
 194-202
Cosgrave, WT 60, 117, 153
Councillors 17, 86, 89, 128, 140-142,
 191, 196, 208
Cowan, Peter 44, 116
Craigavon 111, 121, 126
Crowley, Mary 212
Cuffe, Ciarán 74, 104, 162, 174-177,
 180, 190, 193, 203, 204
Cullen, Martin 130, 171, 182
Cussen, Niall 72

de Valera, Eamon 68
Decentralisation 112, 174
Dempsey, Noel 168-169, 173

Department of Local Government
 see Department of the
 Environment
Department of the Environment
 66-67, 76, 81, 93-94, 103-104,
 107, 111-112, 128-130, 154, 157,
 164, 170, 179, 192
Donegal 28, 133, 150, 174
Dublin 18, 21-41, 43-63, 66-76,
 80-81, 87-101, 104, 109-119,
 162-166, 172, 177-181, 191, 195,
 197-198, 201, 204-212
Dublin City Council 32, 39-40, 43,
 47, 52, 56-60, 71, 76, 80-81, 91,
 94-96, 100, 104-105, 116-120,
 123, 144-145, 148, 152, 162-164,
 180, 205-207
Dublin Corporation see Dublin
 City Council
Dublin County Council 94-96, 105,
 107, 123, 161, 195, 201, 204
Dublin Docklands 163-165, 172
Dublin Institute of Technology
 108-109
Dublin of the Future Plan (1922)
 46-55, 58, 71, 210, 212
Dublin Reconstruction
 (Emergency Provisions) Act,
 1916 58-60
Dublin region 62, 95-101, 104
Dublin Sketch Development Plan
 (1941) 71-72

Easter Rising 1916 43, 48-49, 58-60,
 73, 121
Enforcement 25, 32, 143, 146, 182
Environmental protection 11, 107,
 113, 138, 181, 193
Electricity Supply Board (ESB) 61,
 86, 90-92, 152

Fianna Fáil 151, 155-157, 161-163,
    168, 175-176, 194, 197
Flood Tribunal see Mahon
    Tribunal
Flynn, Pádraig 198-199
Foster, RF 35, 127, 157, 195
Frescati House 149-150
Friends of the Irish Environment
    133

Galway 21, 70, 75, 94, 102
Gandon, James 28-29
Garden cities 5, 43-45, 57, 74,
    114-121, 126
Garden suburbs see Garden cities
Geddes, Patrick 41-48, 52, 56-57,
    95, 100, 116, 119
Ghost estates 186-188
Gibney, Frank 19, 71, 74-75
Gilmore, Eamon 175
Gormley, John 191-192
Gough, Michael 25, 27, 31, 34, 64
Greater Dublin Reconstruction
    Movement 60, 180
Greystones 114-115
Grist, Berna 16, 104, 110, 159,
    168-170, 174, 188-189, 193, 203,
    208

Hanna, Erika 14, 71, 99, 194
Haughey, Charles 157, 162
Hogan, Phil 86, 175
Housing and Town Planning
    Association of Ireland
    (HTPAI) 44-46, 53, 116-117

Industrial Development Authority
    (IDA) 103, 105
Industrial Tenements Company 40

Industrial Towns see Model Towns
Irish Citizens Party 57, 134, 158
Irish Home Builders Association
    179
Irish Planning Institute (IPI) 87,
    108-109, 112, 129-130, 141, 160,
    164, 178, 183, 191, 195, 201,
    203, 211
Irish Rural Dwellers Association
    14, 130-134, 138, 158
Irish Sailors and Soldiers Land
    Trust 119
Irish Town Planning and Country
    Development Association 86
Iveagh Trust 39

Jacobs, Jane 185

Kelly, Thomas 44, 52, 117
Kenny Report (1974) 135, 138,
    161-162, 187, 210
Kerry 95, 102, 119, 133, 136-139,
    141
Kildare 23, 36, 39, 74, 96, 101, 104,
    169

Larkin, James 46, 58
Lawlor, Liam 195, 199-200
Lemass, Seán 62, 66, 77, 101, 111,
    144
Lichfield, Nathaniel 96, 101, 105
Limerick 19-21, 27, 71, 81, 96,
    101-102, 116, 124-126, 132
Local Government Board 41, 44,
    60, 116
Local Government (Planning and
    Development) Act 1963 16,
    19-20, 35, 55, 56, 64-66, 76-113,
    129-132, 144, 147, 152-155,

158-159, 168, 170, 182, 192-193, 210, 212

Louth 28, 62, 96, 141

Lynch, Jack 79, 151

MacEntee, Seán 66, 68, 69, 154

Mac Eochaidh, Colm 197

MacCabe, Fergal 14, 25, 74, 128-129, 142, 149-150

Mahon Tribunal 142, 181, 189, 194-203

Mansergh, Martin 112, 130, 183

Marino 119-120

Mayo 75, 132-135, 146, 173, 192-193

Mears, Frank 60, 119

Metropolitan Streets Commission 165

McCarthy, Charles J 44, 47

McDonald, Frank 89, 98, 104, 109, 113, 118, 129, 143, 147, 160, 181, 188, 212

McDowell, Michael 176, 182

Meath 21, 39, 62, 75, 93, 96, 101, 104, 147, 169-170, 174, 182

Model Towns 19, 28, 35-36, 212

Molloy, Bobby 198

Monaghan 139, 205

Monahan, Philip 54

Mulcahy, Richard 62, 209

na gCopaleen, Myles 70

National Asset Management Agency (NAMA) 162, 184, 210

National Institute for Regional and Spatial Analysis (NIRSA) 171, 186-189

National Planning Conference 1942-1944 45, 67-70

National Spatial Strategy 75, 104, 130-131, 173-175, 190, 202

New Birmingham 35

New Geneva 28-29

Newman, Jeremiah Rev 101

Northern Ireland 14, 22, 40, 63, 68-69, 75, 103, 111,121, 126, 131, 174, 180

O'Brien, Michael 87, 118

O'Connor, John 15, 137, 189-190

Ó Cuív, Éamon 131-132

Office of Public Works 92, 174

Ó Gráda, Diarmuid 136

Ó hUigínn, Pádraig 111-112

O'Kelly, Seán T 64, 153

O'Leary, Olivia 129, 181

One off housing see Rural housing

O'Rourke, Horace T. 53, 56, 67, 71, 119

O'Sullivan, Jan 190

O'Toole, Fintan 161, 166-167

Part V see Planning and Development Act 2000

Paxman, Jeremy 128

Pearse, Patrick 73

Planning and Development Bill 1999 168, 171

Planning and Development Act 2000 65, 104, 155, 159-160, 169-172, 179, 182, 192-194

Planning and Development (Strategic Infrastructure) Act 2006 85, 175-177

Planning and Development (Amendment) Act 2010 189-194, 202, 210

Planning regulator 202-203

Plantations 12, 22-23
Portlaw 36
Postcolonialism 13-14, 18, 56, 73-74, 80
Progressive Democrats 168, 175
Property rights *see* Bunreacht na hÉireann
Public participation 89, 94, 113, 116, 139, 144, 164, 168, 182, 195, 212

Quinn, Ruairi 100

Radburn principles 120-121, 124
Reconstruction (Emergency Powers) Act 1924 60
Regional Authorities 103-104, 202-203
Regional Planning 16, 19, 51, 67, 95-106, 169, 173, 190, 202, 209
Rezoning *see* zoning
Ring, Michael 85, 176
Robertson, Manning 10, 12, 16, 63, 65-67, 71-73, 76, 108, 120
Roche, Dick 15, 176, 179
Roscommon 136
Royal Institute of the Architects of Ireland 46, 59, 63, 76, 130, 154, 201
Royal Town Planning Institute 12, 67, 87, 107, 108, 110, 166
Rural housing 13, 39, 127-142, 147, 174, 176, 192, 203, 210

Sackville Street *see* O'Connell Street
Schaechterle, Karl-Heinz 71, 99
Section 140 128, 140-142, 189, 195, 202

Section 4 *see* Section 140
Shaffrey, Patrick 108, 109
Shannon town 101-102, 124-126
Smith, Michael 169-170, 197
Sprawl 13, 75, 97-100, 123, 178, 180
Spring, Dick 157
Strategic Development Zones 171-173
Sweetman, Peter 15

Tallaght 97-98, 123-124
Temple Bar 166
Tenements 38-41, 51, 56, 69, 116, 122-123, 159
Third party appeals 17-18, 32, 134, 151-154, 172, 177, 182, 191
Tipperary 35, 101
Tribunal of Inquiry Into Certain Planning Matters and Payments *see* Mahon Tribunal
Town and Country Planning Act 1947 (UK) 88, 113
Town and Regional Planning Act 1934 18, 62-66, 70-77, 81-82, 92, 95-96, 110, 152-153, 158, 210
Town and Regional Planning (Amendment) Act 1939 65, 76-77, 81-82, 152
Town Planning Institute *see* Royal Town Planning Institute
Tralee 95, 102
Tully, James (Jimmy) 135, 147-149, 153, 156

United Nations 79, 111, 182
University College Cork 108, 206
University College Dublin 12, 13, 58, 108, 120, 164, 174, 190

Unwin, Raymond 43, 48, 59-60,
    63, 100, 116-117, 119

Viking Ireland 21-22

Waterford 18, 21, 26, 28, 71, 74, 102,
    132
Wicklow 39, 62, 92, 96, 101, 104,
    114-115, 148

Wide Streets Commissioners 18-19,
    23-37, 58-59, 208, 211, 212
Wilde, Oscar 29-30
Women's National Health
    Association 41, 45-46
Wright Plan 1967 *see* Dublin
    region

Zoning 49, 71-72, 88, 109, 141, 146,
    158-162, 166, 180, 186-203

If you enjoyed this book, you may also be interested in...

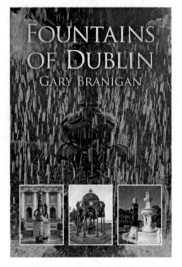

Fountains of Dublin
GARY BRANIGAN

The fountains of Dublin are many and varied, from elaborate Victorian masterpieces and modern sculptures to more modest, practical installations. Unfortunately, many of the older fountains have fallen into disuse and lie, long forgotten and derelict, in overlooked corners of the city. This book, beautifully illustrated with modern and archive photographs, documents the remaining fountains of Dublin, with each entry accompanied by a brief, and often colourful, history together with the precise locations and directions, allowing people to start enjoying these forgotten places once more.

978 1 84588 802 2

Ghost Signs of Dublin
ANTONIA HART

Have you ever noticed an old shop name painted on a gable wall, crossed a threshold made of a faded mosaic name, or passed your fingers over a pair of twined initials you can hardly make out? The signs tell the story of the city. These signs, these casual monuments, are the prizes in a visual treasure hunt, and once you start hunting you will never see Dublin, or any city, without their ghostly lights again.

978 1 84588 841 1

Visit our website and discover thousands of other History Press books.

www.thehistorypress.ie

The History Press Ireland

Lightning Source UK Ltd.
Milton Keynes UK
UKOW04f1251290914

239358UK00001B/1/P